TWENTIETH CENTURY VIEWS

The aim of this series is to present the best in
contemporary critical opinion on major authors,
providing a twentieth century perspective on
their changing status in an era of profound
revaluation.

Maynard Mack, *Series Editor*
Yale University

BYRON

B Y R O N

A COLLECTION OF CRITICAL ESSAYS

Edited by

Paul West

A SPECTRUM BOOK

Prentice-Hall, Inc., *Englewood Cliffs, N.J.*

68–03965

Current printing (last digit):

12 11 10 9 8 7 6 5 4

© 1963 BY PRENTICE-HALL, INC.

ENGLEWOOD CLIFFS, N.J.

LIBRARY OF CONGRESS CATALOG CARD NO.: 63-15412

*Printed in the United States of America—*C

Table of Contents

BYRON

Introduction

by Paul West

Three useful kinds of literary, or quasi-literary, study may be performed on Byron. There is the unabashed study of his psychology, of which Arthur Symons' intriguing 1909 essay and M. Robert Escarpit's two-volume study of *"un tempérament littéraire"* are examples. There is the related study of him as an avatar, as a figure important in the history of ideas and intellectual or social fashions (Bertrand Russell and Mario Praz have composed studies of this kind). And there is the study which, conceding the perpetual presence of the man, looks primarily at the poems. Biographers are still chewing on the remnant of his contorted and intense life; and no matter. What does matter is that they should not antagonize literary critics into an undue and futile purism. There is no excluding the biography, and it is vain to rebuke critics who invoke it: Byron is not one of those poets who can be used as a specimen for discussions of verbal chiaroscuro. It may be possible to sustain such discussions for a while on the basis of a passage here and there; but he is not a poet of clever shades any more than he is impersonal. To try excluding the man is eventually to discover that little of the poetry can stand alone and, if it is made to, seems like fragments from the hands of various pasticheurs.

No doubt this proves Byron not a great poet. If he is great, he is so for reasons not primarily poetic. But we do not always want to be reading "great" poets; and our main pleasure in reading Byron is the contact with a singular personality. It is not a silly pleasure either: it reminds us that all poems, sooner or later, return us to persons and, in Byron's case, return us to ourselves with illumination and no little shock after we have seen our own weaknesses, poses, aspirations, and manias writ large in his essentially human yet effectually exaggerative temperament. In his own time he seemed one possessed: a composite of stalking-horse and devil's advocate; and if anyone thinks these are meretricious reasons for reading a poet, he has only to think carefully about his response to Shakespeare's sonnets or Donne's. We read in order to become articulate through voluntary involvement. The fact is that, with Byron, the standard of literary craftsmanship is irregular and that, quite often, the temperament disrupts even his lax literary method, turning it into a significant absence of method: a rebuke to the terrible cosmos which Byron cannot feel he understands.

It is Byron and Byron's idea of himself which hold his work together, just as that idea enthralled Europe and summed up under the heading of Byronism a variety of European obsessions. In other words, only Byron's peculiar gifts of spectatorship, cliché-combining, and chameleonic impersonation could have produced this poetry. Whatever ventriloquism he adopts, he is always in the first person: a far cry from impersonal Keats. And the poetry, that considered overflow self-consciously proffered as unconsidered, amounts to a microcosm of Regency England and traditional European neuroses, morbidities, scandals, upsets, and dreams. It is both mythological and up-to-date; and it is the man's close presence behind (often in front of) the words—opining and attitudinizing, carping and shrugging—which makes the duality vital. The poems, whatever their quality, are the main items in a shrewdly personal performance; and to try shutting Byron out is only to admit him by the back door and to fabricate a work of pseudo-criticism on the basis of a deliberate misunderstanding.

We have to admit, then (although we may not like to), that the poems lack the autonomy of literature's great invocations, tropes, and apophthegms. Whereas such a statement as "Ripeness is all" is so much in the public domain as to leave its author behind, Byron's poems are barographic in function: they record the emotional pressure of the moment and rarely float little fragments up into the anthologies. We cannot often savor a Byron phrase, as we can one of Shakespeare's, without wondering what prompted him to utter it. His poems are advertisements for himself, as Norman Mailer would say, and even the capsule wisdom which abounds in them is so idiosyncratic that *we* have to say: This not only is in Byron's style, as the verse of *The Tempest* is distinctly in Shakespeare's style; it is nothing else—it lacks impersonality to a remarkable degree. We have always to reckon with the man's almost herculean devotion to his own mannerisms and to his conceit of himself as raw material to be satanized. He obtrudes, and he sabotages the "text-only" kind of study. He also, if we are not careful, overwhelms the study that lets him in from the outset. The poems are a biography and the biography is a loose conspectus of how it felt to be—not the essential Scotsman proposed by T. S. Eliot or the starving "viscerotonic" of Gilbert Highet or the utter Englishman proposed by Arthur Symons—but the erratic and dynamic cosmopolitan who saw Europe as all of a piece abutting on the Near East. Being so cosmopolitan did not make him a better poet, but it did (and still does) mitigate his self-concern. It tempted him into grandiosity thick with Faustian and Wertherish formulae, but it also related him to something bigger than himself and timeless. He is closer to, say,

Goethe, Baudelaire, and Thomas Mann than to his contemporaries, Scott, Wordsworth, and Southey. He was one of the first to practice comparative literature in order to secure for himself the maximum degree not only of publicity but of serious impact.

The ideal study, then, which none of us will ever write, would balance his egoism with his internationalism, his careless ease with his careful assumptions of impersonality. The difficulty is that if we respond to him at all, we respond to his temperament: not to his philosophy, for he has none; nor to his plots, which are vapid; nor to his wisdom, which is facetious; nor to his knowledge, which is disorganized. We have to accept the act of reading him for what it is: an act of inquisitiveness with a chance of felicities along the way. In *Don Juan* he has a style so perfectly suited to his ends that he seems to let it run itself, as if it were some clever little engine which needs only to be wound up: it runs, making the Byronic gestures and noises while he sits back to comment or to snigger.

If we are embarrassed we must leave him alone. This is not Keats or Shelley but the aristocratic lame voyeur who, in the words of Arthur Symons, wanted fame so much because "Fame is a personal, active thing, concerned with one's self while one lives, bringing one into the sight of other people so vividly." It takes one to know one: the key is the word "vivid," and the Byronic performance is a means of endowing himself with preternatural color. It was rage that first made a poet of him: his first lines were written at nine against an old woman he detested; and it was the need for emphasis—the need to be vivid and spectacular in his own eyes—which kept him going. He will forego all inner peace for the sake of an unceasing external show. And the show cannot be maintained unless he has the whole pageant of European life to go at and a style whose only principle is unpredictability—so that whatever comes up next, or into mind, can be thrown in without evoking even the faintest complaint. If, as he said, the poetry of Pope was "the Christianity of English poetry," his own is an apostasy in which he achieves Elizabethan profuseness without Elizabethan fecundity of concept, Augustan attitudes without Augustan decorum, and Romantic magniloquence without Romantic consistency of tone.

At the bottom of it all is the gentleman-poet's disrespect for his hobby: it is upthrown lava, whim, doodling, a second-best activity which does not require him to behave professionally. "No-one," he wrote of himself to Murray in 1820, "has done more through negligence to corrupt the language." Hence the restive, boisterous manner and that supreme quip after visiting the opera: "How I do delight in observing life as it really is!" Whatever else people claimed it was, life was an antic, a sincere fraud. No theories, Byron says:

> We live and die,
> But which is best, you know no more than I.

But he will say this at least:

> Our life is a false nature—'t is not in
> The harmony of things. . . .

His "unriddled wonder," "glorious blunder," and "awful chaos" differ
from the complaints of Arnold and Pater because he is ironic and fights
back. *Don Juan* beats the world at its own muddled game, and these
words from *Manfred* tell us how:

> It is an awful chaos—light and darkness—
> And mind and dust—and passions and pure thoughts,
> Mixed, and contending without end or order,
> All dormant and destructive.

He deals in mixture and is one of the first poets after Donne and Dryden
to write colloquially while refusing to limit poetry to supposedly "poetic"
subjects. He tries to get it all in: no cherishing of the pastoral for him.
And if he fails to produce a precise vision in the manner of Blake or
Yeats it is because only half of him wants to. The other half reports, and
his visionary spells take place in a claustral hell of the mind: they are not
integrated with his review of everyday paraphernalia. He saw, as Herzen
the exile noted in *My Past and Thoughts* (1850), that "there is *no escape,*
and proudly said so." And another exile, Mazzini, stressing "the European role given by him (Byron) to English literature" anticipated Herzen
and supplied a lead properly taken only in our own times: "The empti-
ness of the life and death of solitary individuality has never," he said in
Byron and Goethe (1839), "been so powerfully and efficaciously summed
up as in the pages of Byron." The self is the prison Byron hates; yet he
has to use the self even to protest his imprisonment. No wonder the
poems are acutely or bluntly personal.

   Northrop Frye, therefore, creates an atmosphere of instant justice
when he says that "The main appeal of Byron's poetry is in the fact that
it is Byron's." [1] *In* the fact, notice; not *is* the fact: somehow the fact is
larger than the sum of its parts. This writer of poems, Frye contends, is
an interesting man: furthermore, Byron "proves what many critics de-

---

[1] "George Gordon, Lord Byron," in *Major British Writers, II* (New York: Harcourt,
Brace, & World, 1959), pp. 152-160. Unfortunately, I was unable to obtain permission to
reprint this essay in the present anthology.

clare to be impossible, that a poem can make its primary impact as a historical and biographical document." There may of course be some fascination with poems that are mostly quilts of carefully contrived effects, even to regarding as such poems which are much more than that. But the savoring of effects has to be done with human equipment—with equipment we use for purposes remote from the reading of poems. We have not yet arrived at the stage of reading poems without involving ourselves; and if we, as readers, are present, then so is the poet himself: even if he is not parading himself overtly, he is implicated in his choice of images and sounds. There is no clinical way of dealing with a poem: it will always infiltrate us and often elude even the self-denying ordinances of the most disciplined reading mind. Byron insists on being attended to in his own right. In fact our anxious interest in his emotions or poses is just what he demands in order to feel that he is squeezing the maximum out of "every available instant." The importunate Byron is antithetical to the Byron who holds aloof. And he gets close to us—just as he got close to his contemporaries—by working his extroverted self against his inner self. His gloomy outcast appealed to tastes already thrilled by M. G. Lewis's *The Monk* and the lollipop horrors of Mrs. Ann Radcliffe; and, as Frye points out, such fiction was aimed at an English Protestant middle class and therefore entailed surroundings "Continental, Catholic, and upper class, though Oriental settings also had a vogue," as well as a tint of incest.

It was largely Byron's own fault that his contemporaries dichotomized him into "satanist" and "satirist" and chose the former, just as the English-speaking world of our own time chooses the satirist (so-called) and the continent of Europe the satanic-romantic. I remember my first taste of *Don Juan* and discussing the poem enthusiastically with a fellow-student, a Polish woman older and of more literary sophistication than myself. She would nod tolerantly: fizzing youth required such things; but the real meat of Byron was in the romances and the "mysteries," of which she made the closest exegetical study for "philosophy" and "beliefs." For her, Don Juan (not the folk-hero but Byron's impositions on him) was too far from Hugo, Rousseau, Pushkin, and Mickiewicz. As Frye notes, Byron refuses to "grow metaphysical," which is just another form of self-protection. *Don Juan,* we have to admit, is a poem of mature unconviction in which Byron feels free to condemn and deride but not to sketch cosmic patterns. It is one of the most empirical works in the language: it educates us but does not answer us, whereas the romances and plays philosophize without educating us at all (in spite of such efforts as those of E. W. Marjarum, in *Byron as Skeptic and Believer,* to extract the lessons).

G. Wilson Knight attributes this philosophizing habit to Byron's "objective human interest and lonely individualism": a passionately interpreting care for mankind combined with analysis of his own guilt and

isolation. The two come into conflict and finally break apart; Byron re-
duces "others" to "the Other" and keeps himself aloof. His candor, we
might say, is like that of Camus' Meursault, who will not say or feel what
is expected of him. It is post-Renaissance man, acutely conscious of his
power but also afraid of its significance; and Byron finally resolves the
problem by a dramatic act that consumes him. This, I think, is why Byron the man has to be attended to: he writes with all the impatient ease,
and some of the arrogant complacency, of the man of action. Knight
rightly observes that Byron "lives that eternity which is art. . . . He is
poetry incarnate. The others are dreamers: he is the thing itself." And
our effort in reading the romances is double: we have to take the poems
as they are meant—as Byron giving further specimens of himself in action—and we have to read what of ourselves we can into those faint com-
pound ghosts, the Childe and Conrad. We are helped because Byron himself is at the center of these poems—more than any of his heroes—and
because, by the time we have read one romance, we know that the center
of the romances is less a person or a plot than a current of Byronic notions. The snag is that the texture of all the romances save *Childe
Harold* is thin and feeble: the notions drift about; there is a noise of
scenery being wheeled up; an impatient rattle of the word-hoard. None
of the protagonists is as securely, as subtly, enmeshed in the written texture as, say, Heathcliff or Captain Ahab. Only Harold is, and he is really
no more than a throb in the texture; but at least a throb inseparable
from it. He is never the occasion for anything as strident as this, from
The Corsair:

> Oh! o'er the eye Death most exerts his might,
> And hurls the spirit from her throne of light.
>
> (III. 20)

Knight finds "tragic force" in that. I myself find in it only a considerable
falling-short of the meticulous, Pope-like balance of these two lines, from
the same poem:

> The solemn aspect, and the high-born eye,
> That checks low mirth, but lacks not courtesy. . . .
>
> (I. 16)

Byron reminds us of people who "hate scenes" yet make them daily, who
find hysteria and dynamic indignation conducive to their special brand
of spiritual ease. Knight presents this Dionysian side of Byron with accuracy and sympathy: we *have* to notice the swanking Lord with the
spilling heart. But when Knight appeals to the text, it sometimes lets
him down. That "especially impersonal, yet warm, sympathy with hu-

man instincts" is there all right, but the "verbal excellences" are often missing. The line, "The spouseless Adriatic mourns her lord," is lame and thin, surely; but Knight says "The utterance is weighty yet carried easily." His essay, in fact, demonstrates something important to us if we wish to define what Byron does for us moderns and what we have been doing to him. It is always tempting to enthuse under the spell of the man's brio and moody vitality, and to overpraise his animation.

Both Knight and Bernard Blackstone discuss Byron's sea: it is both eternity and an augury of imagination's power. Early on, the sea is almost taut, certainly unfemale; and then it relaxes and softens, thus becoming ambiguous. It can be all things: it is Eve, and it is the realm of Lambro who, as Blackstone remarks, is a St. Peter, a Ulysses and a pirate, God the Father and also Satan. This is the cue for Mario Praz. He puts teeth (European ones) into Blackstone's observation of "a taint at the heart of nature, and of man's heart, which turns simple instinct and spontaneous passion into a guilt which must be and is visited with retribution." Byron was familiar with all the metamorphoses of Satan: through his own experience, and through such literary versions as Mrs. Radcliffe's Schedoni and Milton's Satan. As Praz shows, Byron is directly related to all the traditions of diabolism we can find, and his legend stands on more than a deformed foot.

We might—we should—go on to wonder what Byron got out of his troubles. As Praz says, "He required the feeling of guilt to arouse in him the phenomena of the moral sense, and the feeling of fatality in order to appreciate the flow of life." This amounts to self-awakening through self-damage and—if I may extend Praz's version of Charles du Bos—increasing one's vitality by concentrating on death: like a condemned man. Many writers have observed that Byron had to intensify life in order to know he was living at all. He could live at only the highest frequencies; all the rest, which we ourselves might find strenuous, was torpor to him. He made his blood boil and turned the overflow into poetry. No wonder the brain sutures were gone and the heart ossified: the Fatal Man had to make them so. And the Fatal Man is also the trapped man of the plays: if you like, the man who feels bound to trap himself or the man who traps himself in order to cheat fate (as he thinks). The irony of the plays is that, whatever the heroes do, fate anticipates them. Like the heroes of the romances, they seek to assert their identities and to control their destinies, but end up being inevitably destroyed. For Byron, only erethism can counter the half-pagan eschatology announced in *Heaven and Earth* and *Cain*. It is not enough to say that he associates self-assertion with guilt; he reverses the matter and seeks out guilt, as Praz says, because it gives him a sense of flourishing identity. And then, because he has identity but doesn't want to be trapped through being typed, he repudiates it by turning all into farce: taking no position, shedding allegiances, ignoring obligations and etiquette. *Don Juan* is a poem of noncommitment, a protracted and interminable metaphor for casuistical freedom. It is not a poem for vague appreciation, or elegant gentlemanly relish. It is one of the most ingeniously forlorn poems in existence.

Its point is this: No matter how you wriggle, you can shed one attitude only by assuming another. Certainly Byron can be found embracing good causes in this poem, saying wise or genially gentle things. What makes the poem vastly superior in intellectual interest to the overpraised *Vision of Judgment* is the fact that we can't catch him *without* an attitude. He repudiates what he can, nonstop; but the uncommitted showman sees the irony of his own effort. We are trapped anyway, even when we choose our own trap. So, belonging to everything, we belong to nothing except the cosmic principle which binds us: yearning for identity, we lose it in pursuing freedom. Byron's escape into irresponsibility—evading commitment or even refusing to strive for harmony in the texture of the writing —is a delusion. All the same, he does not condemn man, for the poem is one of disabused compassion amid life's incongruities. What Swinburne called its "exquisite balance of alternate tones" does not really exist. More accurate is Byron's own confession that "My similes are gathered in a heap"; and Patricia Ball, writing in *The Twentieth Century,*[2] seems to have apprehended these with just the right amount of ingenuity, neither crediting Byron with too much subtlety nor denying his main intention: "When the couplet of a stanza, or the rhymes, or his other devices detonate laughter, this does not blow to pieces the mood with which it collides: each needs the other to be realized exactly as it is, for life is relative, though we live lazily and don't notice. Tears without the possibility of laughter mean little; humor postulates seriousness." Byron compels no choice upon us but constantly evokes a mood's complementary opposite. Hazlitt saw *Don Juan* as a *Tristram Shandy* in verse and others have aligned it with *Candide.* Call it what we will (and we concoct such hybrid descriptions only because it *is* unique) it serves no absolute generalizations. Going beyond summary categories, it defies attempts to extract a "philosophy" from it; it conveys life to us unmanipulated, or at least manipulated only in such a way as to suggest, through tight stanzas and preposterous rhymes, life's nature the more vividly.

As F. R. Leavis points out, Byron composes not Augustan satire but a Regency self-release in which the Augustan element is balanced by "the positive to which he appeals . . . a generous common humanity, something that is indifferent to forms, conventions and classes." W. W. Robson discerns something similar: a throwback to the Restoration, with Byron indulging in "the isolated, anarchic flouting of society we often find in Rochester, and never in Dryden." And T. S. Eliot mentions Dunbar.[3] Obviously, with such remarks in the air, our time is beginning to get the true measure of Byron's complexity. We are no longer simplifying him under headings of satyr, brute, and snob or, poetically, of satirist and idealist. Leavis and Eliot narrow him down: they show he has more affinity with Burns and Dunbar than with Pope; but Robson, deferring to bustling Rochester, strikes fresh truth when he attributes Byron's aplomb as an improviser not to any poet or code of aesthetics but to "the use of resources in Byron himself which he had not previously exploited in poetry." The letter-writer is the same man as the comic poet: masterly at "the temporary stabilization of conflicting emotions." As we have already observed, Byron cannot forget he has a reader: the fact both intoxicates him and disturbs him, so he "hastens to a superficial kind of self-revelation, for fear of a deeper self-betrayal." The improviser, essentially his own man, can always draw back, can come forward without warning. Time and again in trying to understand Byron we return to the restlessness, to the quicksands of that temperament.

Robson praises *Don Juan* as "a triumph of personality." It is exactly that; it is too, as Guy Steffan and George Ridenour demonstrate with exemplary pains, a triumph of deliberate writing: very little of its effect is accidental. The same is true of *Beppo* and *The Vision of Judgment*. The first, as Steffan notes in a brilliantly articulate essay, combines the rhetoric and formal balances of the early satires with "the pleasant trivia, the jocose frivolity, the colloquial zest, the double rhymes and the lighter and more rapid rhythms of such *jeux d'esprit* as 'Egotism.' " "Byron," he continues, "had never before got himself into, and found his way with poise and neat direction through, such a whimsical and involved labyrinth of digressions on everything from fish sauce to Shakespeare." This Byron has come a long road from Augustan decorum; his comic tone is unruly, raucous, and impolite. He is too involved to manage a cool, squinting disdain. He *talks* to us, in fact, and the simultaneous notice given in recent years to both his colloquial tone—the sheer *sound* of his verse—and the tremendous litter of rejections to be found in his manuscripts, has revealed the care he took to achieve exactness of tone and of connotation. He wrote orgiastically, it is true, but with a distinct required sound in his head, and he often calculated his effects from a profusion of *trouvailles* and afterthoughts. Because his appeal is to the world of both chatter and serious conversation—to men on the move and cocked ears—he does not write up to a high ideal of rhetoric. He doesn't want to be admired, as Pope does, for excelling in spite of self-imposed restrictions. As Steffan says in his statistical essay on *Beppo*, "He contrived in his ottava rima stanzas a conversational medium, as casual as it

---

[3] In his essay, "Byron," in *On Poetry and Poets* (London: Faber & Faber; New York: Farrar, Straus & Company, 1957). We regret being unable to include this essay in the present anthology.

was elastic, with abundant license for discursive commentary and with a serpentine movement that was flippantly varied, playfully inflated, humorously haphazard, and lightly extemporaneous. . . ." Nor did he, in spite of what he resumed from Richardson and Laclos, and in spite of his reverence for Pope, owe anything to the eighteenth century tradition of Sensibility: flaunting one's finer feelings in self-homage. He was more concerned with the condition of England and the terrors of being human.

He was a serious writer grappling with himself and his times. Helen Gardner is right to insist on this. But he is also one of those writers whom it is easy to overestimate. Ask more of him than he can give, and he suddenly becomes trivial. To read him at all we have to teach ourselves how to balance and how to bend. If we do not, we find ourselves in the position of Ridenour who, in *The Style of Don Juan,* studying Byron's rhymes and rhythms and tropes with a care as usefully mathematical as care can be, discovers three unifying devices: a metaphor of "styles," a metaphor of the Fall, and a gradually narrowing gap between speaker and protagonist. I think the poem is more relativistic than that; much less organized. Byron does harp on the Fall but he harps on a great deal else. Milton's harping is thematic and disquisitional; Byron's is decorative and incidental. Byron is now being read in times which cannot see a writer repeat an image or a phrase without attributing to him some portentous pattern of symbolism. I don't think there is any more overt Fall "symbolism" in *Don Juan* than there is in a typical issue of a Sunday newspaper. The poem can be read on the analogical level only if we suppress a great deal of what we enjoy on other levels. But Ridenour's alertness to the almost Proustian development of the poem is heartening; whether or not Byron intended it, it happens: "If Juan falls from innocence, in the course of the poem he rises to the level of the speaker." That is the sort of development Byron—the Byron of the restless, vivid letters and the alternately cockahoop and solemn notes to the poems— would naturally achieve. His "thousand colors" were cunningly arranged to appear cavalier, but I do not think this technician of texture was cunning in structures.

The dangers are patent now. It is fair and rewarding to look at the man for the sake of the writings and to look at the writings for the sake of the man; but not to study the man in his own right or (because virtually impossible) the poems in theirs. John Bayley's suggestion that "All Byron's poems demand to be reunited to their context" is just.[4] It is no use pretending. The Satanic man who satisfies the myth-hunters is not enough; neither is the text which satisfies the enumerator and the scholiast. It is no use reorganizing and tabulating the works of this scintillating and uncomfortable man. Byron is not now the celebrity or

[4] *The Spectator,* July 14, 1961, 63, Vol. 207, No. 6942.

the hot issue he used to be: so, unfortunately, the academic feels safer in trying to systematize and factorize the restless quality of the poems.

The major virtue of mid-twentieth century views of Byron is their increasing complexity; it is, of course, one of the major dangers. The cosmopolitan, the Romantic libertine, and the comedian appear by no means as simple as they once did. (Edmund Wilson, writing even in the early 1920's, rebuked Maurice Hewlett for using such words as "cad" and "blackguard.") I do not think advances in psychological science have helped us to fathom Byron better; but those advances—the fact of them —have made us more cautious. We are more willing to tolerate complexity, to acknowledge complexities of our own, and even to enjoy complicating ourselves. We now know that Childe Harold and Don Juan —even Manfred and the Prisoner of Chillon—belong to a fund of folk-figures which includes Odysseus, Hamlet, and Faust. We know too that Byron's alleged aberrations are not as unspeakable as the righteous supposed: his homosexuality, at any rate, now staggers no educated mind. What may stagger us now are the very ordinary elements Wilson spots in Byron; in fact, that 1922 essay is corrective reading for a generation proudly blasé about perversion. On the one hand is the Byronic "blaze of divine white light"; on the other the reasonable, ordinary view: "One is chilled to find the price these poets paid—and that other people paid —not only in pain and grief, but in sordidness and raw distress." To this price, as Wilson maintains, the Strachey-like ironies of some biographers are inappropriate. And yet, if we have to choose between the ponderous censures of Kingsley and Lamb, we must surely prefer the writer who, whether undertaking biography or literary appraisal, allows himself the indirect tribute of slipping now and then into Byron's own vein of mockery. Harold Nicolson, Peter Quennell, and André Maurois have all slipped into it at one time or another, and one's final impression is not of cheap scoring against Byron but of a canny understanding on their part of how Byron wanted his life and works apprehended and presented.

Wilson points to Byron's awareness of an audience and his phenomenal capacity for experience. Helen Gardner goes more deeply and draws attention to "the rapidity and vehemence of Byron's intelligence," to the fundamental brainwork done at high speed during composition, to his "intellectual vitality and vivacity." If we do not like Byron anyway it will not warm us to him to read that "There are many and obvious affinities between his age and ours, both exhausted by a great revolution and its aftermath of war; and no writer has been more heartily and consistently 'against the Establishment.'" But Byron on the power of illusion, and emerging from his discussions of that theme with wisdom though not of the highest or profoundest kind, must surely impress as a candid man, as no system's fool: in short, as one of the better liberal intelligences. Hence the sheer bulk of his writings: these *are* his mental processes, the detritus and the ore of restless self-excavation. To study it we have to put up with Byron the touring tragedian: "I think I had naturally not a bad heart," he wrote to Augusta Leigh, "but it has been so bent, twisted, and trampled on, that it has now become as hard as a Highlander's heelpiece"—a Scottish metaphor which fits nicely with the idea of Byron as an heir of Dunbar. As even that little spurt of complacent self-pity reveals, this accomplished foreigner writing English did at least create—could hardly help creating—a new kind of cultivated comic language. And it is vastly funny because, as Bertrand Russell says, there are two elements at work in Byron the rebel: "Titanic cosmic self-assertion" and "Satanism." There is a thoroughness in Byron's comedy that is rare in English literature: Chaucer derides wryly; Jonson inflates grotesquely, often coldly; Shakespeare gleams or riots, twitters or rants; Pope sneers; and Swift hates. But Byron's farce or comedy implies a metaphysical dimension, whether Calvinist or Promethean. Byron admired his ancestors who fought in the Crusades, at Crecy and Marston Moor. He eventually died as the Crusaders did, fighting the Moslem; but, unlike Nietzsche, he did not presume to play God. It was enough to be a great man at war with himself, reminiscent of Genseric, King of the Vandals, Ezzelino the Ghibelline tyrant, and one Louisiana pirate. We cannot be surprised that Thomas Carlyle was awed. Yet, as Lord Russell reminds us, "The world insisted on simplifying him and omitting the element of pose in his cosmic despair."

We must not miss out, as his admirers on the continent of Europe have missed out, his view of humor as power. His main problem was to integrate his two sides—Diogenes and Romantic—and this could be managed only through the glorification of some power not religious or corporate. It could only be leadership or humor, and he settled for both. Humor, after all, is one form of violence. Take the "hearty pistol-shooting, all-boys-together" friendships mentioned by John Wain in his essay, "Byron: the Search for Identity." These friendships, like the writing of poems, amounted to hectic self-assertion, the opposite of Rousseau's meekness. I agree with Wain when he says flatly that Byron "did not, in the deeper sense, have a self." That is why he has two quite different reputations, why his favorite mode is discordance—like the person who spills "a dish of tea over his testicles in handing a cup of tea to his charmer, to the great shame of his nankeen breeches." As pathic as his own Juan, he allowed circumstances to lead him and this, naturally enough, developed his obsession with power. Unable to integrate himself, he let circumstances decide the role he would play, but always preferred power-roles. And the humor of *Don Juan,* directed as it almost invariably is against role-taking, has persuaded people he is writing satire. On the contrary, he is almost entirely nonreformist. The inveterate man not of parts, but of fragments, he is a true schizophrenic. The romantic and the humorist are not his alternatives at all; and what we might think humor entails—a fundamental charity or a surface amiability—he detaches: humor is the one socially acknowledged role behind which he can retain absolute power. (The administrative chaos at Missolonghi proves him powerless there.) This is why he plays to what Wain calls "easily aroused responses"; the people in the gallery are his troops. I think he despised those responses and those troops. Having played the Childe until he could neither escape the role nor quite *be* it, he let the humorist take over—but take over erratically. The humorist is no role; Byron, I suspect, thought he had found a way of writing which landed him in no role at all. That "biggest one-man debunking spree the world has ever seen," to which Wain engagingly refers, extended beyond cant and ludicrous juxtapositions of words as far as politics: "Sober historians," Wain reminds us, "have gone on record as saying that Byron, single-handed, had a demonstrable influence in neutralizing the influence of the Congress of Vienna."

Sooner or later we infer an inferiority complex. Wilson attributes one; so does Wain. The more feeble one feels, the more one's fantasies of being powerful increase. "Byron," says Wain, "lies in the mud, like a crocodile, and pulls his victim down from below." How true. He is no Augustan, demolishing from on high. And although I cannot agree with Wain's two-sided Byron—although I believe that the humorist is really an attempt to dodge being a split man—I share Wain's feeling of being cheated: "I want to know," as he does, "what Byron would have *done* . . . when time finally drove him into a corner and brought him face to face with the riddle of his own character." I venture to think that be-cause, as Wain suggests, "Self-knowledge is the most decisive form of action," Byron would have seen the power in such knowledge. My guess would be more and more public life, in England, with poetry-writing as the safety valve; more of the consolidated Scottish front to match the Scottish interior; and probably a discreet conversion to Rome: the Christian faith had always haunted him and he had written approvingly of the Catholic way. Be that as it may, the paranoia noticed by Leslie Marchand would have had to bloom fully or vanish. Wain sees him as summing up "the crossroads at which European and English culture then stood." We should see him at his own crossroads too, realizing that power—even personal, privately wielded power—even the power of self-succour, indebts us if we are honest; indebts us to some godhead, in-heritance, or social group. It is of Byron on the edge of this discovery that we must think finally: as unable to settle for a law as to end *Don Juan* and, because of what happened at Missolonghi before he could execute his noble gesture, an example after his own heart of the view that life is a travesty. Robinson Jeffers has said,

It seems to me that every personal story ends more
or less in tragedy; comedy is an unfinished story.

The tragedy is there in Byron's ironic death; the comedy in his own
poems' glosses on such situations. The life is what we make of it. Byron
was neither merry nor sad because he knew he was merely part of a
cosmic process both humiliating and exhilarating. What one attitude to
take up? He never knew, but in groping for power he transcended art's
conventions as well as conventional morality. That is why it has taken
us so long to see him plain, in all his complication, and why biographers
are still skirmishing, to the neglect of his poems.

The Two Eternities

by G. Wilson Knight

I

A poet's work may often appear to contradict his life. With **Lord** Byron this is not so. He is, as a man, a vital embodiment of post-Renaissance poetry: a proud individualist, asserting the primacy of instinct through an agonized self-conflict. His social sympathies are violently given to causes of liberty. He incurs charges of immorality. He lives what others so often write, leaving his native land somewhat as Timon leaves Athens. That insistent aspiration, that aristocracy of spirit, met with variously in fiction after fiction, is here incarnate: more, it is given, as in Shakespeare's plays, an outward formulation in aristocracy of birth. Such aristocracy may be used in poetry to materialize an inner, spiritual, royalty, as in *Tess of the D'Urbervilles*: and Byron is so much the more effective, as a dramatic figure, by reason of his title. In close alliance he shows an ingrained Shakespearian respect for tradition, for history, increasing the agony and tension of revolt. He has weakness, and is tortured by a sense of sexual sin. The vice, weakness, and nobility behind all high literary adventures are his, as a man. How slight some famous poets might appear should we choose to scrutinize their apparent littleness, their failure to match in life the spectacular essences of their work. A slight shift of perspective and Wordsworth looks like an old maid; Coleridge becomes a not very pleasant blend of talkative don and dope fiend; Keats an adolescent; Shelley a seraphic blur. But Byron has warm flesh and color. His life itself falls into poetic and tragic form. Mediterranean coasts are perennially fertilizing forces to northern poetry. Italy floods the Renaissance and particularly the Shakespearian consciousness; poets from Chaucer and Milton to Browning and Lawrence have traveled there; and many have managed to die there, or thereabouts. But Byron does it all more superbly than any. Greece—to put a subtle matter crudely—seems for some time to have been challenging our traditional

"The Two Eternities." [Original title: "The Two Eternities: an Essay on Byron."] From *The Burning Oracle* (New York: Oxford University Press, 1939) by G. Wilson Knight, pp. 197-215. Copyright 1939 by G. Wilson Knight. Reprinted and excerpted by permission of the author and Oxford University Press.

Christian culture, many poets offering an Olympian or Dionysian theology as copartners with the Christian. Moreover, liberty—of spirit,
mind, body, and community—has been for centuries a widening and
pressing imaginative demand. Our dominant personal and communal
poetic directions from Marlowe and Milton through Pope to Shelley,
Browning, and Lawrence are, I should suppose, (i) something closely
related to erotic instincts, and (ii) the cause of liberty. Byron suffers social
ostracism and banishment for the one and death for the other. Incest,
says Shelley, is a very poetical thing: presumably since every act of artistic
creation involves a kind of incestuous union within the personality.
Byron is suspected of it in actual fact. Next, he dies fighting for the perfect sacrificial cause: the liberty of Greece. He lives that eternity which
is art. He is more than a writer: his virtues and vices alike are precisely
those entwined at the roots of poetry. He is poetry incarnate. The others
are dreamers: he is the thing itself.

His literary work (our only present concern) is continuous with these
impressions. He did not at first see himself as a poet, as an early preface
shows; and when he did start writing in earnest, went after stories of
color and action. His human understanding is glamorous, his incidents
well costumed. Piratical adventure mixes with passionate love; there is
the flash of steel and smell of powder. His is a cruel, yet romantic, world
where blood flows hot. It is objectively conceived. Byron can lose himself
in creation of emotional shapes outside his direct experience. He will
use a reverential Christianity for his purpose; but can equally well salute
a dying Moslem in *The Giaour* with the consummate technical ease of:

> But him the maids of Paradise
>   Impatient to their halls invite,
> And the dark heaven of Houris' eyes
>   On him shall glance for ever bright.

This is a truly Shakespearian power, one with the impersonal historical
interest of *Childe Harold* and his love of peoples and places generally.
A strong sense of a particular and honorable past lingers round each
person or place he touches. He is poetically sensitive to variations in
human tradition and culture. He is cosmopolitan and extraverted. And
yet his tales also express a certain violent and recurring psychological
experience with mysterious depths of passion and guilt variously hinted
or revealed. To this I give my primary attention.

The Giaour is a powerful example. The inside of mental agony is
revealed, Byron's poetry piercing and twisting into its center:

> The mind, that broods o'er guilty woes,
>   Is like the Scorpion girt by fire;

In circle narrowing as it glows,
The flames around their captive close,
Till inly search'd by thousand throes,
    And maddening in her ire,
One sad and sole relief she knows,
The sting she nourish'd for her foes,
Whose venom never yet was vain,
Gives but one pang and cures all pain,
And darts into her desperate brain. . . .

The rhetorical tension is maintained with a never-failing grip. Each word is charged, each sentence tight. What universes are here housed in the tiny yet deadly form of the scorpion: its own venomous nature makes its agony the more terrifying. The little drama symbolizes the horror, which is one with the energies, of biological existence: it gets at the very nerve behind ecstasy and anguish alike. Byron's in-feeling into animal life and energy is from the start distinctive. *The Giaour* is rich with it:

Go when the hunter's hand hath wrung
From forest-cave her shrieking young,
And calm the lonely lioness:
But soothe not—mock not, my distress!

He continually attributes sensitive nerves and minds to the animal creation; or may delight in its more lyric vitalities, as when he sees a butterfly

. . . rising on its purple wing
The insect queen of eastern spring

being chased by a boy, and makes subtle comparison between this and love. Either the fleeting loveliness rises far above the "panting heart," or, if caught

With wounded wing, or bleeding breast,
Ah! where shall either victim rest?
Can this with faded pinion soar
From rose to tulip as before?

See the choice placing of a well-considered diction; also the peculiarly soft use of consonants. Stern as are his tales, Byron's poetry masters with equal ease a lyric grace and wrenching guilt: and through all burns deep sympathy for animals, often small ones (as in Pope); which is again one with his penetration to the central energies, the springs of action, in beast or man. The two are continuous. The hero of *The Giaour* is typical of Byron's tales, a man in hell, yet unbowed, and with a certain obscurity as to the dark cause of his suffering:

> Wet with thine own best blood shall drip
> Thy gnashing tooth and haggard lip;
> Then stalking to thy sullen grave,
> Go—and with Ghouls and Afrits rave;
> Till these in horror shrink away
> From spectre more accursed than they!

This ends a passage of towering satanic virulence; and its compressed explosiveness must surely win respect even from those whose direct response will be most impeded by the traditionally modeled—though pulsing—phraseology. Though the hero retires to a monastery where it "soothes him to abide," for "some dark deed without a name," he nevertheless "looks not to priesthood for relief." The balance of some irreligious passion against orthodox Christianity approaches in tone that of *Eloisa to Abelard;* while the rejection of religious assistance as powerless to ease the dark anguish and alter an inevitable course recalls *Faustus, Wuthering Heights,* and Byron's own *Manfred.* The close is subdued:

> I would not, if I might, be blest;
> I want no paradise, but rest.

He would be buried with no record but a simple cross. The Moslem's hatred for the infidel is here burningly proud and fierce; but Christianity is also at the last reverenced. Such opposites of pagan fire and Christian gentleness are characteristically Byronic; and they are to be in poem after poem subdued, as here, to an eternal peace.

Perhaps Conrad in *The Corsair* is the finest of his early human studies:

> Lone, wild, and strange, he stood alike exempt
> From all affection and from all contempt.
>
> (I. 11)

The narratives revolve generally on an inward psychic, or spiritual, conflict. Though Conrad is a pirate chief of stern and ruthless action, his is a deeply spiritual bitterness. His anguish is almost brutally revealed:

> There is a war, a chaos of the mind,
> When all its elements convulsed, combined,

> Lie dark and jarring with perturbed force,
> And gnashing with impenitent remorse.
>
> (II. 10)

The lines suit Macbeth: and though we may be reminded of Crabbe the Byronic hero has a tragic direction not found in *Peter Grimes*. He is noble and Miltonic:

> His was the lofty port, the distant mien,
> That seems to shun the sight—and awes if seen:
> The solemn aspect, and the high-born eye,
> That checks low mirth, but lacks not courtesy. . . .
>
> (I. 16)

No captive girls ever seduce his attention from Medora. "None are all evil" (I. 12), we are told, and at the core of his personality is a love, a "softness"; this word, or "soft," recurring throughout Byron's work with the deepest central significance. In this very poem Antony is the "soft triumvir" (II. 15). Conrad is, however, a grim figure; and his endurance whilst awaiting torture is given terrible poetic disclosure. Yet he refuses to save himself by a cowardly murder and is nauseated by a woman, Gulnare, doing it for him. Indeed, all horrors of his wide piratical experience or natural imagination are shown as nothing to that arising from this desecration of feminine gentleness. From none

> So thrill'd, so shudder'd every creeping vein,
> As now they froze before that purple stain.
>
> (III. 10)

The passage is most powerful, tracing territories explored in the conception of Lady Macbeth. The hero suffers originally through determination to save women from his own piratical massacre: which, though perhaps irrational, is intensely Byronic. Frequently we come across such ruthless evil and cynical callousness enshrining a strangely soft, almost feminine, devotion. Conrad's heart "was form'd for softness, warp'd to wrong" (III. 23). The poem's conclusion holds a reserved depth of feeling reminiscent of Pope. He finds Medora dead:

> He ask'd no question—all were answered now
> By the first glance on that still, marble brow.
>
> (III. 21)

Notice how strongest emotion is uttered through a simple statement: "all were answer'd now"; and how that makes of one human death a vast eternity, almost an assurance. So

> his mother's softness crept
> To those wild eyes, which like an infant's wept. . . .
>
> (III. 22)

Yet he is not sentimentalized. As in *Macbeth,* the poet dares to end with a condemnation, leaving the human delineation to plead its own cause:

> He left a Corsair's name to other times,
> Link'd with one virtue, and a thousand crimes.
>
> (III. 24)

From the start, the central complex of loneliness and cruelty is undefined. The same figure recurs in *Lara.* Though cold, ruthless, and with a smile "waned in its mirth and wither'd to a sneer" (I. 17) the hero is yet one "with more capacity for love than earth bestows" (I. 18) on most men. The dark mystery shrouding his past is never lifted. They are all, like Heathcliff and Captain Ahab, personalities tugged by some strange evil between time and eternity.

The poetic vigor of each narrative, depending on choice and exact statement rather than abstruse analogy or magic sound, never fails. Subtle rhythmic variation may finely realize description, as this of a floating corpse, from *The Bride of Abydos*:

> As shaken on his restless pillow
> His head heaves with the heaving billow.
>
> (II. 26)

Continually a fine thing is said as a way to realize some great feeling. Especially strong are the darkest moments, as "I want no paradise, but rest" and "This brow that then will burn no more" from *The Giaour.* The decasyllabic couplets of *The Corsair* hold an equal tragic force:

> Oh! o'er the eye Death most exerts his might,
> And hurls the spirit from her throne of light.
>
> (III. 20)

Verbs play a major, often a dominating part, as in the remorseless beat of the line "Eternity forbids thee to forget" (I. 23) from *Lara.* The diction accepts personifications of a vast yet simple and unornate kind, and traditionally "poetic" words of various sorts. These, as in Pope, are chosen to express a ready-made fusion of the particular and general. The influence of Pope may be at times very obvious, too, in couplet modulation, as—to take random examples from a wide field—in *The Corsair*, I. 11, and the lines beginning "No danger daunts . . ." from *The Bride of Abydos*, II. 20. As in Pope, each word is exactly used but loaded with more than its natural maximum of force. The lines cry to be uttered and can be understood, if not fully appreciated, at once. The emotional precision is unerring, defined yet never metallic: like the twang of a taut string.

However perfect the control, the energies—spiritual or physical—set in action are striking. Many fine animal creations are symptomatic of the Byronic mastery of the vital and organic, as in the wild Tartar horse of the later story *Mazeppa* with the "speed of thought" in his limbs, and the other thousand with

> Wide nostrils never stretch'd by pain,
> Mouths bloodless to the bit or rein. . . .
>
> (xvii)

Byron feels in and with the animal. There is the "stately buffalo" with his "fiery eyes" and stamping hoofs attacked by wolves in *The Siege of Corinth* (xxiii); the insect stinging to save its property (compare the wren in *Macbeth*) and the adder seeking vengeance when trodden on, in *The Corsair* (I. 13-14). The end of *The Prisoner of Chillon* provides perhaps the best; where the hero, after an eternity of dark imprisonment, has actually made such friends with the spiders of his dungeon and so long loved the mice at their "moonlit play" that he is reluctant to leave; and I doubt if the whole range of Byron's work provides a sweeter instance of his uncanny penetration into the most secret chambers of a mind in agony and loneliness. The moon in Byron has elsewhere such tragic associations. Continuous with these animal intuitions is the Shakespearian feeling for human personality, characterized by ability and desire to give vital action and project figures of innate dignity—quite apart from their ethical standing—and blazing courage; and women, including Gulnare in *The Corsair*, of an utterly instinctive, yet magnificent, devotion.

The tales are characterized by (i) vivid and colorful action, and (ii) a recurring psychological conflict normally related to some feminine romance-interest. You may get mainly action, as in *The Bride of Abydos* and the nightmare frenzy of the ride in *Mazeppa*; or mainly a psychological study, as in *Lara*. *The Corsair* I think the finest in its balance of both. The atmosphere of *The Giaour* is powerfully realized, but the hero's remorse seems disproportionate to the occasion. The central guilt complex is, of course, always best left without premature definition, as in

Hamlet and *Macbeth*. We can feel the poet aiming at a story-action tha
fits his intuition. However, in the tightly woven and sustained power o
Parisina a short plot is cleverly devised to condition logically the mind
state of the Byronic hero, the story stopping where he begins. The perfec
fusion of inward experience and active plot is never perhaps quite mas
tered. There is no deeply significant outer conflict, no clash of universa
forces, unless the balance of religions in *The Giaour* might so qualify
Profundities are found in most searching human comment continually
but the action is not by itself profound. A bridge of some sort is needed
a conduit to flood the whole setting with something of the hero's tragi
power. The narratives are to this extent slightly inorganic in compariso
with Shakespeare: they have a hero, but no heart. A field of dramati
meaning has not been generated—an individual psychological and spir
itual study, however deep, cannot quite do this—and the incidents and
persons accordingly lose generalized significance and stature: though th
tragic direction generally works to create a sense of some mysteriou
eternity at the close. Only a judgment most insensitive to the deadl
marksmanship of Byron's peculiar excellences would stigmatize them a
"melodramatic."

II

These tales of action and geographic color are strung together by a
central, expressly personal, experience. The human penetration, th
revelation of mental suffering, is always primary. But *Childe Harold* i
more consistently extraverted, though it has a similar twofold appea
with, again, a separateness: nature-descriptions, however, doing some
thing towards a fusion, as I shall show. A series of meditations on place
and events is given unity by the shadowy conception of Harold, that is
Byron. Yet, this once forgiven, we are struck by the amazing vitality o
creation. Byron is the only poet since Shakespeare to possess one o
Shakespeare's rarest gifts: that of pure artistic joy in the annals—afte
searching I can find no better word—of human action; in close associ
ation, moreover, with places. He feels the tingling nearness of any heroi
past. Gray had something of this; so had Scott; and Hardy gets it in hi
Dynasts as a whole, perhaps, if not in the parts. This is something quit
beyond our contemporary sophistication. It is an ability to love no
mankind, as did Shelley, but men; and men—or women—of variou
sorts, places, and times:

> Is it for this the Spanish maid, aroused,
> Hangs on the willow her unstrung guitar. . . .
>
> (I. 54)

Or, of Waterloo:

> And wild and high the "Cameron's gathering" rose!
> The war-note of Lochiel, which Albyn's hills
> Have heard, and heard too have her Saxon foes—
> How in the noon of night that pibroch thrills. . . .
>
> (III. 26)

And this of the dying gladiator:

> He reck'd not of the life he lost nor prize,
> But where his rude hut by the Danube lay. . . .
>
> (IV. 141)

He is fascinated with the persons of one scene or event after another. The scattered incidents are given a sincere unity by the autobiographical thread; this extraverted interest, almost love, being integral to the Byronic imagination.

But the suffering behind every glamorous association is not forgotten. Historic excitement is often one with a condemnation of history: since a fundamental love of men is involved and history often cruel. For example:

> Ah, monarchs! Could ye taste the mirth ye mar,
> Not in the toils of glory would ye fret;
> The hoarse dull drum would sleep, and Man be happy yet!
>
> (I. 47)

There is no facile militarism: but rather an opposition to the clang and fury of world affairs of simple—and often, as here, sensuous—joys. On the eve of Waterloo a "heavy sound" of cannon breaks short the pleasures of the dance. Then are there

> cheeks all pale, which but an hour ago
> Blushed at the praise of their own loveliness;
> And there were sudden partings, such as press
> The life from out young hearts, and choking sighs. . . .
>
> (III. 24)

I point not merely to verbal excellences but to the especially impersonal, yet warm, sympathy with human instincts. So from "Beauty's circle" they are shown next in "battle's magnificently proud array"; and finally hurled, horse and rider, friend and foe, "in one red burial." The fervor which so admires courage and battle finery is one with that which pities

the transition from dance to slaughter. It is a total awareness of the
Shakespearian sort. Byron can start to describe a bullfight in a glamorous
stanza (I. 73) of steeds and spurs and ladies' eyes; only to give a poignant
sympathy to the suffering of bull and horse in a "brutal" sport. The same
sympathy is accorded the dying gladiator in Book IV butchered for
Rome's enjoyment: yet this does not preclude a feeling for Rome's imperial greatness. The poet is aware of emotional opposites involving each
other, or rather of a single emotion taking opposite forms of assertion
and pathos: just as the agonized conflicts and evil passions of his heroes
are somehow one with their instincts of chivalry and tenderness. So he
lets himself be, as it were, annihilated continually before each splendor
and pathos in turn.

His feeling for human nobility past and present is also one with his
acceptance of a traditional poetic diction. This repays our close attention.
Few poets have accomplished so much effortless force in single lines, as,
for example:

> Stop!—for thy tread is on an Empire's dust!
> (III. 17)

Or

> The spouseless Adriatic mourns her lord. . . .
> (IV. 11)

Or

> Oh Time! the beautifier of the dead. . . .
> (IV. 130)

The utterance is weighty yet carried easily: the thing said seems to be all
in all, with no attempt at original expression. There is a play of metaphor
and often what Ruskin—in a confused and misleading essay—named the
"pathetic fallacy": but such call no attention to themselves and are
accompanied by no especial excitement. The style here, as in the tales, is
peculiarly assured, involving a use of words where the fusion of general
and particular, philosophic meditation and objective description, has
already been performed; though in *Childe Harold* both the general
scheme and stanza form alike demand a more fluid and less packed and
explosive language. No effort is expended on abstruse comparison or the
jerking of word or image from its habitual use or associative value.
Personifications and abstractions are frequent but never cloudy, denoting
concepts generally accepted. They are always words of an adequate
syllabic weight; words, as it were, tested in the past and found to ring
true; words of poetic lineage. In the first two lines just quoted "tread,"

"dust," "spouse," "mourns" all strike me as examples of what might be called a middle diction, a workmanlike poetic, but not too poetic, manner. This may rise even to

> Their praise is hymn'd by loftier harps than mine
>
> (III. 29)

without loss of sincerity. So we have strong nouns, plain, usually active, verbs, sentences cleanly turned out, well drilled, and marching to their purpose. No verbal magic is allowed at the expense of clarity. Similarly, Byron's religious intuitions are based on a preliminary acceptance of the conventional, seen in the robust Johnsonian phraseology—as well as thought—of

> I speak not of men's creeds: they rest between
> Man and his Maker.
>
> (IV. 95)

As a rule every accent is poetically distinguished with none superlative: nor meant to be. But the thing said, or the object seen, may be of superlative grandeur, as in this, of Rome:

> The Niobe of nations! There she stands,
> Childless and crownless, in her voiceless woe.
>
> (IV. 79)

The sympathy with the present pathos of ruins cannot be detached from that acceptance of the one-time historic splendor which also chooses well-worn associations such as the splendor of "nations," the awe of crowns, the traditional poetic appeal of a word such as "woe." Byron likes, as a poet, what is already warm with human contact. He injects into it his own vitality, whether in admiration or rebellion. He likes human society and its history: which is but a surface effect of that deeper in-feeling into animal or human vitality that enables him to display both convincing action and a moving pathos.

And yet again he stands outside the world he writes of, balancing human purpose against human futility. *Childe Harold* is a lamentation in noble phrases over the widespread ruins of a dead chivalry and a dead tyranny. Byron is superbly conscious of the whole of Europe. But he also sees it as one vast theater of tombstones: though at his touch the dead are temporarily raised, and in the poetry there is no futility. He ranges across the centuries accepting and cherishing a past—or recent present—which he simultaneously repudiates and regrets. So he hymns

empires whilst hating the wrongs of tyranny; recognizes the "lion" in
Napoleon whilst decrying servility to "wolves" (III. 19); glories in patriot
battlefields though attacking the iniquities of wars by which monarchs
"pave their way with human hearts" (I. 42); at the limit, he praises life
whilst entranced by death. He is a militant pacifist, exposing the fallacies
of ambition (I. 42-4). The tragic notes are his surest, the richer for the
human excellences apprehended. The whole poem is written from a vast
eternity-consciousness to which historic events, as events, are the negative
symbols of its expression. There is thus a very "life" in "despair," a
mysterious "vitality of poison" (III. 34). Particulars are vivid chiefly by
reason of their felt transience. Somehow their transience *is* their eternity:

> Far other scene is Thrasimene now. . . .
>   (IV. 65)

Or, when we come to Rome, the mystery of time itself takes ghostly form,
entwined with infinite space and natural magic:

> But when the rising moon begins to climb
> Its topmost arch, and gently pauses there;
> When the stars twinkle through the loops of time,
> And the low night-breeze waves along the air
> The garland-forest, which the gray walls wear,
> Like laurels on the bald first Caesar's head;
> When the light shines serene but doth not glare,
> Then in this magic circle raise the dead:
> Heroes have trod this spot—'tis on their dust ye tread.
>   (IV. 144)

The grandeur of Rome lives most in its ruins. After visiting the Coliseum
and wandering through memories of a dead empire we come to St. Peter's,
which strikes from the poet both a magnificent religious fervor and subtle
architectural appreciation in living terms, characteristically, of the
human mind unable to take in the whole splendor with a single glance,
yet at last distended to eternal comprehension; and end with the great
invocation to the sea, imperial beyond all empires—

> Roll on, thou deep and dark blue Ocean—roll!
> Ten thousand fleets sweep over thee in vain. . . .
>   (IV. 179)

ith what sureness are handled, as in Gray's *Elegy*, the noble platitudes
often composing the greatest poetry. "Assyria, Greece, Rome, Carthage,
hat are they?" he asks. Their life was conditioned by that spirit (he
lls it "freedom" but perhaps we should give it a wider name) that alone
n preserve, without which they are dust. That spirit is reflected by both
) the poet's ranging consciousness—the "eternal spirit of the chainless
ind" of his Chillon sonnet—autobiographical soliloquy significantly
lternating with the scenic progress and reaching its culmination in the
reat personal apologetic and satiric outburst near the close; and (ii) the
a, unfettered by temporal law.

> Time writes no wrinkle on thine azure brow:
> Such as creation's dawn beheld, thou rollest now.
>
> (IV. 182)

his vast unfathomable interlocks itself with that humanism, that social
nd historic sympathy, so dearly deep in Byron; something other, draw-
ıg him near the awe-struck naturalism of Wordsworth.

Childe Harold has, continually, passages of more elemental sort, show-
ıg a continual swerve in comment from particular to general. My
:marks on diction do not say the whole truth. Often a metaphor may
art up with at once surface flash and revealing psychological depth, the
ıore vivid for the generally level style:

> And how and why we know not, nor can trace
> Home to its cloud this lightning of the mind. . . .
>
> (IV. 24)

[atural immensities fill out wide areas of the later Cantos III and IV,
cting as a bridge between the hero and his world: his own consciousness
shown as, personally, more akin to them than to the human drama
ıat was his first story. The process reflects that dissociation found first
ı *Timon of Athens* and urgent since: but no other poet of Byron's
eriod shows a range of sympathy sufficient to include both sides of the
pposition. So the sea is felt as a bounding freedom (as in *The Corsair*),
specially freedom from stifling human contacts (III. 2, 3). He now invokes
maternal Nature" (III. 46). That other vastness of mountains so weightily
ısistent in the imagination of Byron's day is duly honored:

> Not vainly did the early Persian make
> His altar the high places, and the peak
> Of earth-o'ergazing mountains. . . .
>
> (III. 91)

Such an association may be referred back to both Wordsworth an
Coleridge. And there are passages more finely detailed, more energ
striking than this: as that describing the roar and hell-caldrons of
Kubla Khan mountain waterfall, the rising mist above, the ever fertilize
green turf, the peaceful river of the plain; and, as we look back, an Ir
rainbow shot through the dreadful waters, still and brilliant abov
agonized distraction, like "Love watching Madness with unalterabl
mien" (IV. 69-72): a line whose depth and fervency of human—or other—
understanding shows the author to be, potentially, a tragic artist c
Shakespearian stature.

Often such a swift transition transfixes its mark with quivering ir
tensity: Byron's nature-images are, normally, made to serve, or at leas
blend into, some human purpose. But they are also great in their ow
right: so we have "shaggy summits" (IV. 73) where, when storm an
darkness riot, there are flashes lovely as—typically—a woman's "dar
eye," as

> From peak to peak, the rattling crags among
> Leaps the live thunder!
>
> (III. 92)

"Live": a living ecstasy continually energizes Byron's work. But he ca
also treat of mighty glaciers or the placid Rhone with immediate descrip
tive force. All such vast natural symbols objectify that in himself tha
demarks him from men's society. Any man "who surpasses or subdue
mankind" is as a mountain looking on the hate of those below (III. 45
Himself he is a "portion" of that nature "around" him, rejecting th
agonies of human society, finding life in natural kinship with the "mour
tains, waves, and skies," as "part" of his soul, and looking to death fo
cosmic freedom (III. 71-5). He knows the secrets of "pathless woods" an
"lonely shore" (IV. 178). They and their eternity are the watchtowei
from which he looks down on the rise and fall of empires. Yet he neve
for long forgets man. "I love not man the less but nature more" (IV. 178
is really an overstatement. All his finest nature-impressions up-pile t
blend with the supreme human grandeur of Rome. His mind outdistance
his companions, that is all: if he could put all of himself into one wore
that word were "lightning" (III. 97). The choice is exact: and the imag
can be reversed. His brow, like that of his own Azo ploughed by th
"burning share" of sorrow (*Parisina*, 20), may be, metaphorically, fe
kin also to that of Milton's Satan which "deep scars of thunder ha
intrench'd"; or the She-wolf of his own description, the "thunder-stricke
nurse of Rome" whose limbs lightning has blackened (IV. 88); or, be

f all, the bust of Ariosto "doubly sacred" by the thunder-flame that
tripped it of its crown (IV. 41).

Few poets show so instinctive a human insight: yet he is being forced
against his will into the individualism of Wordsworth and Shelley. Yet
here is a difference. He assimilates, but is not subdued by, the splendors
of nature. He has been blamed for lightly and theatrically making poetic
gestures not deeply felt; and it is true that certain lines in *Childe Harold*
appear to merit the charge. Sometimes the transition from the more
Augustan diction of the tales (mostly written before the later cantos of
Childe Harold) to a newly vital nature-imagery is not perfect. Byron
seems to gather in his new material with something of too sweeping a
gesture, too aristocratic a superiority: he takes it for his own, more
human, purpose. He is not, any more than Shakespeare, subdued to
nature-mysticism. Yet he can, when he cares to, turn it to a far finer,
because more human, account, as in the image of love and madness
recently noticed, than any poet of his day. He is always above, not below,
his contemporaries. The others rave over cataracts and mountains: and
he too goes to mountains for inspiration. As it happens, they serve him
magnificently: probably as a man, certainly as a poet. But they do not
rank so importantly with him as that other more Shakespearian vastness,
the sea. That from *The Corsair* (which contains some fine sea-poetry) to
The Island and *Don Juan* is a permanent possession, whereas mountains
affect him deeply only now, in mid-career. No English poet has written
more finely of the sea, as in the rolling volumes—got by "o"-sounds—of

> Thou glorious mirror, where the Almighty's form
> Glasses itself in tempests; in all time,—
> Calm or convulsed, in breeze or gale or storm,
> Icing the pole, or in the torrid clime
> Dark-heaving—boundless, endless, and sublime,
> The image of eternity, the throne
> Of the Invisible; even from out thy slime
> The monsters of the deep are made; each zone
> Obeys thee; thou goest forth, dread, fathomless, alone.
>
> (IV. 183)

"The image of eternity": the concept pulses throughout Byron's work.
Contrast this with his great denunciatory and prophetic passage (IV.
133-7) where he piles on the heads of mankind his curse of "forgiveness";
next strikes the exact note and manner of Pope's satiric epistles ("petty
perfidy," "the small whisper of the as paltry few," "venom," "reptile");
and finally asserts the undying powers ("something unearthly") of his

poetry to reassert his rights. You can see how the two elements—objective human interest and lonely individualism—of the early narratives are rending apart. He is torn between history and tragic insight, mankind and lonely self-conflict, time and eternity. The disparity is bridged by sea and mountains, infinite expanse and lifting mass, each at once symbols of both the natural and the eternal.

Guilt and Retribution in Byron's Sea Poems

by Bernard Blackstone

Nothing links Byron more decisively with the earlier generation of
poets—Blake, Wordsworth, Coleridge—than the emphasis he gives to the
theme of sin and its punishment. The Fall motif is almost an obsession
with him. We can trace it in the dramas, in *Childe Harold* and many of
the minor poems from *Mazeppa* to *The Vision of Judgment*. In the
present paper I confine myself to notes on the sea poems, in particular
The Island and the Haidée episode in *Don Juan*.

There is no need to establish the sea's fascination for Byron nor the
fact that his verse takes on an added complexity and depth under the
sway of its rhythms and images. His early reading in books of travel
rivals that of Coleridge; whole passages of *Don Juan* are versified from
contemporary accounts of shipwrecks, and of *The Island* he writes: "The
foundation of the following story will be found partly in Lieutenant
Bligh's 'Narrative of the Mutiny and Seizure of the Bounty, in the South
Seas, in 1789'; and partly in 'Mariner's account of the Tonga Islands'
. ." The sea washes through the early "Eastern Tales," with the exception of *Lara* (a main reason, perhaps, why *Lara* is the least successful, the
least resonant, of the four). And as his powers mature, we watch his
vision of the sea widening and deepening. In the early poems the ocean
is uncompromisingly masculine:

> boundless, endless, and sublime,
> The image of eternity, the throne
> Of the Invisible . . .

Power is stressed, and sincerity: feminine weakness and guile are set
against the sea's robust freedom in the first lyric of *Childe Harold,* I; and
the theme is already there in the very early *Stanzas Written in Passing
the Ambracian Gulf*. But with the Eastern Tales the sea begins to take
on its role as a complex symbol. We are here in a world of stern mascu-

"Guilt and Retribution in Byron's Sea Poems," by Bernard Blackstone. From *A Review of English Literature*, II.1 (January 1961), 58-69. Copyright © 1961 by Longmans,
Green & Co. Reprinted by permission of the author and Longmans, Green & Co.

linity counterpointed with a melting femininity. The setting is classical
the tone Hebraic. All these poems revolve round Biblical axes: Eden
sin, expulsion, murder, exile. In all of them a Miltonic struggle between
reason and passion is presented.

Zuleika, in *The Bride of Abydos,* makes her entrance as the prima
Eve:

> Fair, as the first that fell of womankind,
>   When on that dread yet lovely serpent smiling,
>   Whose image then was stamped upon her mind—
>   But once beguiled—and evermore beguiling . . .

All Byron's antinomies meet in this description (too long to quote i
full); though, confessedly, in somewhat raw and theatrical guise. W
might suspect that the consistent Fall imagery, here and in the rest of th
Tales, is no more than a handy vehicle for his passionate paradoxes, ha
we not his later poems before us. Yet in the *Bride* itself we find significan
strokes. The Wanderer—a key figure for Byron—is guided by love's star

> Aye! let me like the ocean-Patriarch roam,
>   Or only know on land the Tartar's home . . .
>   Bound where thou wilt, my barb! or glide, my prow!
>   But be the star that guides the wanderer, Thou!
>   Thou, my Zuleika, share and bless my bark;
>   The Dove of peace and promise to my ark . . .

That is not great poetry. The title of "ocean-Patriarch" is fine: but th
later star, dove, ark and rainbow belong to the category of simple stereo
types. What is interesting is to see the feminine principle, from which
the Childe had fled, welcomed on board the vessel of salvation. Byron ha
come to a more complex appreciation of woman, the seducer and de
vourer, as also the savior: Coleridge's Life-in-Death and Mary-Queen
Conrad, in *The Corsair,* chooses impalement rather than treachery, bu
Gulnare saves him, by deceit and murder, despite himself. In *The Island*
a much more important work than any of the early Tales, and Byron'
last considerable poem, Neuha is Torquil's rescuer through the medium
of a beneficent sea.

We shall find the paradox stated more forcibly in *Don Juan*: mor
forcibly, but not more winningly than here; and if I consider *The Island*
first, it is because it forges a link between *The Ancient Mariner* and *Do*
Juan and makes certain comparisons possible. Coleridge's main theme
are very closely paralleled, though disposed in quite a different pattern
We are still in the context of solitude, of guilt and retribution, of tor

mented souls adrift on a wide wide sea; but now the Fall leads to and not from Eden: "Their sea-green isle, their guilt-won paradise." In Coleridge's poem the central episode is played out on the "earth's central line" under the domination of the feminine principle, in her double aspect. The centrality is there too in *The Island,* and so is the principle —in Byron's poem, naturally, much more sensuous, more "tropical." "Neuha, the South Sea girl," is the prize of Torquil's rebellion; in their union the wildness of the Orkneys and of Tooboonai meet: north and south are reconciled.

> Here, in this grotto of the wave-worn shore,
> They pass'd the tropic's red meridian o'er;
> Nor long the hours—they never paused o'er time,
> Unbroken by the clock's funereal chime . . .
> What deem'd they of the future or the past?
> The present, like a tyrant, held them fast:
> Their hour-glass was the sea-sand, and the tide
> Like her smooth billow, saw their moments glide;
> Their clock the sun, in his unbounded tow'r,
> They reckon'd not, whose day was but an hour . . .

Certain items of Coleridge's situation are closely followed: the earth's central line, the sun "in his unbounded tow'r," the stasis of time, and, later, the absence of twilight. The cave is a focus, or an axis: here the vertical shaft of the sun bisects the meridian. There is an escape from mechanical time into a living now—which, however, Byron is careful to stigmatize as a "tyrant" because it is lived purely on the natural level and holds no possibility of redemption. His pitying sense of the fragility of human life and happiness emerges, and may perhaps be called "Christian" in its mature apprehension of strength made perfect in weakness. This reveals itself again, on the nonhuman plane this time, in his sketch of the nautilus:

> The tender nautilus, who steers his prow,
> The sea-borne sailor of his shell canoe,
> The ocean Mab, the fairy of the sea,
> Seems far less fragile, and, alas! more free.
> He, when the lightning-wing'd tornados sweep
> The surge, is safe—his port is in the deep—
> And triumphs o'er the armadas of mankind,
> Which shake the world, yet crumble to the wind.

Set this against Shelley's evocation of the nautilus in *The Revolt of Islam* (VII, 26): both are beautifully done, and Shelley's is the more exquisite, but Byron brings in a third dimension in the power-weakness paradox incarnate in the small creature.

The cave is indeed focal in *The Island.* "Womb" and "refuge" meanings run together, for the poem's theme is precisely that of an escape to the womb. Torquil is consistently spoken of as a "boy," and the maternal aspect of Neuha's love as consistently stressed. While still on the *Bounty,* the crew look *back* to the island paradises they have left:

> Young hearts, which languish'd for some sunny isle,
> Where summer years and summer women smile.

They prefer "the cave / Of some soft savage to the uncertain wave." And round this focus imagination weaves a lotus-eating Eden:

> The gushing fruits that nature gave untill'd;
> The wood without a path but where they will'd . . .
> The freedom which can call each grot a home;
> The general garden, where all steps may roam . . .

It is Byron's own imagination, and longing, and anticipation; he was aging, more rapidly than his years suggest, and the island dream—which should it be? Ithaca? one of the Cyclades?—had long been with him. *The Island* focuses a crisis in Byron's inner life, and is all the richer and more immediate for that. Neuha represents his own ideal. She is compact of sun and sea; and if "dusky like night," it is:

> night with all her stars;
> Or cavern sparkling with its native spars;
> With eyes that were a language and a spell,
> A form like Aphrodite's in her shell . . .
> Such was this daughter of the southern seas,
> Herself a billow in her energies . . .

"The sun-born blood" suffuses her skin:

> Like coral reddening through the darken'd wave,
> Which draws the diver to the crimson cave.

She is the incarnation of pure instinct, of spontaneity, beyond the mode even of Zuleika, Leila, or Gulnare, for she is quite untouched by civilization. Yet she is the representative of a tradition, a culture. When she sings to Torquil at the entrance to her cave, she draws on the poetry and music of her race. Byron is careful to stress this:

> Such was this ditty of Tradition's days,
> Which to the dead a lingering fame conveys . . .
> For one long-cherish'd ballad's simple stave,
> Rung from the rock, or mingled with the wave,
> Or from the bubbling streamlet's grassy side,
> Or gathering mountain echoes as they glide,
> Hath greater power o'er each true heart and ear,
> Than all the columns Conquest's minions rear . . .

It is characteristic of Byron to connect the traditional "ditty" with elemental forces: and Neuha's song has its point in the total structure of the poem, it is not a simple decoration. Similarly, in the short comic episode of Ben Bunting (II, xx) the ceremony of "crossing the line" is praised as a relic of tradition:

> Still the old god delights, from out the main,
> To snatch some glimpses of his ancient reign.

We are here in the presence of a direct and powerful perception.

The idyllic moment is followed by disaster. Retribution overtakes the mutineers in the shape of a British man-of-war; only four survivors, Christian, Torquil, Ben Bunting and Jack Skyscrape, manage to get away, in canoes piloted by friendly savages. Neuha takes her lover to a rocky islet:

> The haunt of birds, a desert to mankind,
> Where the rough seal reposes from the wind . . .
> Here the young turtle, crawling from its shell,
> Steals to the deep wherein its parents dwell . . .

Urging Torquil to follow, she dives. The pursuing sailors wait for them to resurface, but in vain, and after some search they withdraw. The lovers are safe in a submarine cave which Neuha has had the foresight to provision against just such an emergency. In the elaborate description given by Byron (of which I quote only a part) the rounded, pristine forms we have already seen adorning the rock are reasserted as a group of fertility emblems:

> For food the cocoa-nut, the yam, the bread
> Borne of the fruit; for board the plantain spread
> With its broad leaf, or turtle-shell which bore

> A banquet in the flesh it cover'd o'er;
> The gourd with water recent from the rill,
> The ripe banana from the mellow hill . . .

And here Neuha and Torquil live until the danger has passed. In this sense the mutiny is successful. True, Torquil's three companions are killed or captured (Byron has to kill Christian off, for his rebellion is rooted in hatred of tyranny and not love of pleasure: he is the true Byronic hero, and such heroes never survive) but love is triumphant. Neuha and Torquil live to enjoy:

> Their sea-green isle, their guilt-won paradise.

Not so in *Don Juan*. This is of course a much more complex poem, and we cannot be sure how Byron meant to complete it (if indeed he had any idea himself). What can be traced with the greatest clarity is the ubiquitous Fall theme; and here it is a progressive Fall, to be set against the sudden Fall of *The Island*. There is a Miltonic pity too in *Don Juan*: the pity that wrings our hearts at the episodes in Eden, that wrung even Satan's heart. Throughout Byron's poem we are conscious, behind the satire and the farce, of a double tenderness, a tenderness for the hero and for his victims. And from this, in part, the poem derives its peculiar obliquity. At each descent of Juan into the sensual whirlpool there is the suggestion of virtue gone out of him, of a diminished integrity. The encounter with Haidée even, with all its idyllic freshness, is an outrage. Poor Juan weathers the horrors of storm and shipwreck to be confronted with the immediate demands of a new liaison. Superb as the picture of Haidée bending over the exhausted hero is, there is something intensely predatory about it. Juan wakes to see "A lovely female face of seventeen":

> 'Twas bending close o'er his, and the small mouth
> Seemed almost prying into his for breath . . .

The vampire touch is there. Haidée, "the lady of the cave," is Juan's protectress, but she presents some curiously ambivalent features. "The maid, or whatsoe'er she was" is very tall; her eyes are "black as Death," and:

> Forth from its raven fringe the full glance flies,
> Ne'er with such force the swiftest arrow flew;
> 'Tis as the snake late coiled, who pours his length,
> And hurls at once his venom and his strength.

We might be with Geraldine in the dark wood, or with the Belle Dame on the cold hillside. But Byron's point is this, that there is no innocence in love; he sees it, with Hardy, as "cruel as the grave." It demands, and in demanding it mutilates and kills. Here we have the link with Blake, and Byron's intuition delving deeper into the stress of the contraries than does any other of his contemporaries'.

Constantly we are astonished by his insight (masked as flippancy, farce, or bawdry), into the existential dilemma. How packed with meaning, for instance, is this description of Juan's second awakening:

> He woke, and gazed, and would have slept again,
>   But the fair face which met his eyes forbade
> Those eyes to close, though weariness and pain
>   Had further sleep a further pleasure made:
> For Woman's face was never formed in vain
>   For Juan, so that even when he prayed
> He turned from grisly saints, and martyrs hairy,
> To the sweet portraits of the Virgin Mary.

It is instinct with irony, and beneath irony, with pathos. Juan is doomed from every point of view—even his moments of devotion are permeated with a taint which it would be inadequate to call "sexual." And how closely, a little later on, memories of Byron's own childhood return in the simile:

> He ate, and he was well supplied; and she,
>   Who watched him like a mother, would have fed
> Him past all bounds, because she smiled to see
>   Such appetite in one she had deemed dead.

Every phrase is ambivalent. Not only does "like a mother" recall Mrs. Byron, but we are taken back to *Paradise Lost* and the Adam who:

> scrupl'd not to eat
> Against his better knowledge, not deceav'd
> But fondly overcome with Femal charm.

Adam too had "seemed dead" to an Eve bored with the simple felicities of Eden.

A taint at the heart of nature, and of man's heart, which turns simple instinct and spontaneous passion into a guilt which must be and is visited with retribution: here we have the center of Byron's vision to which he returns again and again. "Our life is a false nature, 'tis not in / The harmony of things" is no flourish: it expresses a profound conviction. Thus, when the idyll reaches its consummation (for Juan, a second Fall), Byron's irony draws again on the perennial obliquity of the man-and-nature nexus:

> It was the cooling hour, just when the rounded
>   Red sun sinks down behind the azure hill . .
> With the far mountain-crescent half-surrounded
>   On the one side, and the deep sea calm and chill,
> Upon the other, and the rosy sky
> With one star sparkling through it like an eye.
>
> And thus they wandered forth, and hand in hand,
>   Over the shining pebbles and the shells,
> Gliding along the smooth and hardened sand,
>   And in the worn and wild receptacles
> Worked by the storms, yet worked as it were planned—
> In hollow halls, with sparry roofs and cells,
>   They turned to rest; and, each clasped by an arm,
> Yielded to the deep Twilight's purple charm.

The pressure of thought through imagery is remarkable here; each detail goes to compose a unity, each visualization is a symbol. First the image of completeness, "circling all Nature" (in an unquoted line), within which the four elements find a unity in relationship: the rounded red sun, the mountain-crescent, the deep sea, the rosy sky. Here we have the geometry of eternity. Counterpointing this perfection, the hapless human pair, wandering forth hand in hand (the Miltonic reference is inescapable); and, ominous over it all, the divine eye.

The "umbrageous Grots and Caves" of *Paradise Lost,* the "caverns measureless to man" of *Kubla Khan,* symbols of a primeval and unconscious happiness, are dream foci such as we have already noted in *The Island.* The Haidée episode is riddled with them. There are three main cave-scenes, coming at the beginning, the middle, and the end. In the first, as we have seen, Juan lies sleeping, watched over by the virginal, maternal, and predatory Haidée, "the lady of the cave." Juan himself is Haidée's "ocean-treasure"; he is "a rich wreck," and is frequently assimilated to cave-forms by such epithets as "wave-worn." Their passion is consummated against a back-cloth of "voiceless sands and dropping caves":

> Amidst the barren sands and rocks so rude,
> She and her wave-worn love had made their bower.

The ground-note of solemn warning which underlies all the idyllic sweetness of Milton's Eden is richly reinforced in *Don Juan* by the pervasive murmur of the sea (and, it may be remarked, Byron manipulates his stanza-form in such a way as to embody the rhythms of the sea's ebb and flow). For the sea is above all the element of Haidée's "piratical papa" Lambro, the "old man who lived upon the water." This Old Man of the Sea exercises a perverted apostolate: he is a fisher of men like St. Peter, but sells his catch in the slave market. He is to prove a Ulysses too, returning unexpectedly home. With immense virtuosity Byron weaves his strands together: we witness the magic, time-annihilating bubble of young love approached, menaced, and finally punctured by the slowly moving arrow of retribution. The situation is Hardyesque, as dramatic and as moving as *The Convergence of the Twain*.

Byron introduces his final episode—the discovery of guilt and the expulsion from Paradise—with an invocation of the Virgin Mother immediately preceding a dream of death. The pattern of *The Ancient Mariner* is again inverted, but the inversion must not distract our attention from the identity. We are in the midst of complex Fall symbolism: the Old Man of the Sea is Ulysses, is God the Father, is also Satan. While the lovers sleep after a nuptial feast he has made his way into Eden; and Haidée, like Eve, dreams a dream:

> She dream'd of being alone on a sea-shore,
>   Chain'd to a rock; she knew not how, but stir
> She could not from the spot, and the loud roar
>   Grew, and each wave rose roughly, threatening her . . .

After a time she is released:

> and then she stray'd
> O'er the sharp shingles with her bleeding feet.

Something, wrapped in a sheet, rolls before her; she tries to catch up with it, but cannot. Then the dream changes: she is in a cave hung with marble icicles:

> And wet, and cold, and lifeless, at her feet,
>   Pale as the foam that froth'd on his dead brow,
> Which she essay'd in vain to clear (how sweet
>   Were once her cares, how idle seem'd they now!)
> Lay Juan . . .

As she gazes, his face alters into the semblance of Lambro's:

And starting, she awoke, and what to view?
Oh! Powers of Heaven! what dark eye meets she there?
'Tis—'tis her father's—fix'd upon the pair!

The sea has resumed its role as the enemy. In bringing Lambro back to
the island it symbolically drowns Juan. Haidée's dream is a conflation
and a reversal of all she has been through since she found her lover
unconscious at the cave's mouth. In her dream she is alone; she lives the
past in isolation; and in the lines:

she stray'd
O'er the sharp shingles with her bleeding feet . . .

we have the dream-obverse of the idyllic "And thus they wandered
forth. . . ." Finally, the "one star sparkling . . . like an eye" which
kept tender watch over their love is transmogrified into the terrible gaze
of Lambro.

There may be more brilliant episodes in *Don Juan* than this (one
might name the harem scene in Canto V) but none, I think, which bears
so closely and so deeply on the theme of my essay. In the harem episode
we are on the Bosphorus, and the peculiar ocean resonances which are
hardly less than integral to his theme are absent. The action is enclosed,
the atmosphere stifling; we miss the pity and the passion. In maturing
Juan grows more cynical; in passing from the Mediterranean warmth
towards the Pontic cold (and later to the icy Danube and Neva) he is
moving outside the sphere of sun-caressed love to the artificialities and
stuffiness of court life. It is in the Haidée episode, with its natural setting,
that Byron is able to make his profoundest statement of the theme of
guilt and retribution. The love of Haidée and Juan cannot survive in
the world of adult experience:

for they were children still,
And children still they should have ever been;
They were not made in the real world to fill
A busy character in the dull scene,
But like two beings born from out a rill,
A nymph and her beloved, all unseen
To pass their lives in fountains and on flowers,
And never feel the weight of human hours.

Haidée dies; Juan lives to "feel the weight of mortal hours" and remorse
for Haidée's death. His responsibility is indirect, but so was the Giaour's
for the murder of Leila, yet he can say:

> But look—'tis written on my brow!
> There read of Cain the curse and crime.

"The web of being blindly wove" none can escape; but for Byron, unlike
Shelley, the blindness itself is criminal.

Metamorphoses of Satan

by Mario Praz

Even if there can be no doubt of the Anglo-Germanic origin of the colors used by Byron for his portrait of the bandit-hero, it is, however, quite possible that the poet's hand was guided in his design by Chateaubriand. It is difficult to calculate exactly how much Byron owed to him. French critics, basing their judgment on the words of the *Mémoires d'outre-tombe* (repeated in the *Essai sur la littérature anglaise*), tend to exaggerate the amount of this debt. Byron's silence on the subject of Chateaubriand gives the whole question a curious similarity to that other debatable question of Chaucer's knowledge of the *Decameron*.

S'il était vrai que René entrât pour quelque chose dans le fond du personnage unique mis en scène sous des noms divers dans Childe-Harold, Conrad, Lara, Manfred, le Giaour; si par hasard lord Byron m'avait fait vivre de sa vie, il aurait donc eu la faiblesse de ne jamais me nommer? J'étais donc un de ces pères qu'on renie quand on est arrivé au pouvoir?

Thus, among other remarks, wrote the author of *René*.

The question, at any rate, is limited to this latter work, for any attempt to see in Harold's pilgrimage an imitation of the *Itinéraire* (1811)—an idea which Chateaubriand himself suggests and which Reynaud without hesitation develops—does not bear examination of the facts. Apart from the fact that the publication of the *Itinéraire* was later than Byron's own journey (which started in 1809) and the composition of the first cantos of *Childe Harold,* this journey, in spite of Byron's various plans, some more, some less ambitious, resolved itself in the end into the Grand Tour which it was the usual custom for Englishmen of rank to take for the completion of their education. Therefore the argument of the similarity between Harold's and René's journey loses a good deal of its force; the latter also had wandered and meditated among the ruins of the ancient world. Even though there are many similar characteristics—ennui, love of solitude, a secret which gnaws the heart, voluntary exile—it must on the other hand be remembered that some of these qualities had become the common inheritance of growing Romanticism. It may sometimes be more exact to speak of a relationship of ideas arising from the same sources, rather than of actual imitation. On the subject of Chateaubriand's claim that Byron had imitated him, Sainte-Beuve remarks:

> Il y a là de l'enfantillage vraiment. Ces grands poètes n'ont pas eu besoin de s'imiter l'un l'autre; ils ont trouvé en eux-mêmes et dans l'air du siècle une inspiration suffisante qu'ils ont chacun appropriée et figurée à leur manière, en y mettant le cachet de leur talent et de leur égoïsme. Tous ces types sont éclos en Allemagne, en Angleterre, en France, sous un même souffle, sous un même courant atmosphérique général qui tenait à l'état du monde à ce moment.

It would be much easier to prove had it been possible for Byron to have seen *Les Natchez*, but this was not published until his death. In this, much more than in *René*, Chateaubriand expatiates on the fatality which pursues his hero:

> Aimer et souffrir était la double fatalité qu'il imposait à quiconque s'approchait de sa personne. Jeté dans le monde comme un grand malheur, sa pernicieuse influence s'étendait aux êtres environnants. . . . Tout lui devenait fatal, même le bonheur.

After he is dead René threatens to become a vampire—quite in accordance with one of the developments of the Byronic hero, of which I shall have to speak later:

> Le génie fatal de René poursuivit encore Céluta, comme ces fantômes nocturnes qui vivent du sang des mortels.

Byron never saw these passages, and if his work contains some that are similar, it can only be due to the common background from which both drew their inspiration. There are some who even go so far as to say that Byron's incest with his half-sister was a plagiarism, because Byron committed in reality the crime of which René had conceived the horrible possibility. But the subject of incest is by no means confined to Chateaubriand. We shall see, incidentally, how important a part it played in the "tales of terror," whose influence on Byron is obvious. Besides, Chateaubriand himself was an admirer of Milton's Satan, whom he defined as "une des conceptions les plus sublimes et les plus pathétiques qui soient jamais sorties du cerveau d'un poète," though the attitude of Satanic defiance, an important quality in Byron and in the villain-heroes of the "tales of terror," is not to be found in René, who has a stronger affinity with Werther: he accepts his fatal quality as a misfortune, possesses the evil eye, and never ceases to ask pardon for the disasters which his presence brings.

The Giaour, the Corsair, and Lara, therefore, derive not so much from Zeluco and René as from Mrs. Radcliffe's Schedoni. From Schedoni we can go back to Milton's Satan, from Milton's Satan to the Satan of Marino, and finally discover the charm of the terrible, demoniac eyes of all these haunted creatures contained in a nutshell in the line

> Negli occhi, ove mestizia alberga e morte,

which Marino took, with slight alterations, from a line of Tasso. Is it all a mere game of literary decantation?

It is quite possible that Mrs. Radcliffe drew the figure of the sinister monk Schedoni mainly from her own study of the books which, as a literary bluestocking, she used to read: but Byron's case is more complex. Did he not, in any case, declare that "the *Corsair* was written *con amore,* and much from *existence*"? Given the vanity of his own nature, what is more probable than that he should have deliberately modeled himself upon the figure of the accursed angel? Who can be sure that he may not have studied every detail in front of a mirror, even to the terrible oblique look with which he frightened people, particularly his mistresses? But however artificial the methods by which Byron cultivated his character of Fatal Man, he possessed by nature not only "le physique du rôle." but also the psychological tendency handed down to him from a long chain of ancestors who conformed more or less to the type of the "noble ruffian."

Cave a signatis: in his very physical deformity Byron saw the sign of his destiny. To what point, as an actor, he was convinced by his own role it is impossible to say, but he was always sincere in feeling himself "a marked man," stamped with a sign among ordinary mortals, "an outlaw." Does the whole Byronic legend then stand on no firmer a pedestal than a club foot? A club foot, hence the *besoin de la fatalité* . . . ?

The question is more complicated than that. Yet, though not denying the importance of small matters, one would not wish to reduce Byron to the level of the man who, having received a present of a gold-topped stick, felt it his duty to put the rest of his costume in harmony with it, and so ran up debts, was ruined, and finished up with his corpse at the Morgue. Let us at any rate consider the conclusion of du Bos as being justified.

> Il semble qu'il soit né blasé, et qu'il ne puisse sentir vraiment que hors
> la loi. Aussi, lorsqu'on envisage comme factices, comme conventionnels, les

innombrables portraits que Byron a tracés de lui-même sous la figure de
l'*outlaw,* on commet à son sujet le contresens irréparable, car ces portraits
émanent, remontent tous de la couche la plus profonde de sa sincérité. Dans
la loi, il n'éprouve rien; hors la loi, il sent à fond.

It was in transgression that Byron found his own life-rhythm. Du Bos
very aptly recalls the title of one of the *Diaboliques* of Barbey d'Aurevilly
—*Le Bonheur dans le crime.* It suffices here to sum up the case again—
the subject is a very trite one, and today, since the books of Ethel Colburn Mayne, du Bos, and Maurois, there is no more room for controversy
—by saying that Byron sought in incest a spice for love ("great is their
love who love in sin and fear": *Heaven and Earth,* line 67), and that he
required the feeling of guilt to arouse in him the phenomena of the
moral sense, and the feeling of fatality in order to appreciate the flow of
life.

Le fonds byronien est bien cette mélancolie innée, due peut-être à un
cœur, si je puis ainsi m'exprimer, en soi statique qui, pour percevoir ses
battements, a besoin que ceux-ci s'accélèrent jusqu'à la folie.

I think that du Bos has here found the key to Byron's character. It
seems a paradox, and yet the most genuine thing that this monster of
energy—if ever there was one—possessed, was the force of inertia. The
function which violent exercise and a drastic régime fulfilled for him
physically, checking his tendency to grow fat, was fulfilled for his moral
nature, which was naturally idle, by tumultuous emotions. "Passion is
the element in which we live: without it we but vegetate," said Byron in
his mature years to Lady Blessington—much in the manner of Vauve-
nargues ("une vie sans passions ressemble bien à la mort"), and of Cham-
fort ("les passions font vivre l'homme, la sagesse le fait seulement durer").
He had to key up his life to such a high state of tension in order to
make it yield him anything, that when it came to the post-mortem it was
found that both brain and heart showed signs of very advanced age: the
sutures of the brain were entirely obliterated and the heart bore signs of
incipient ossification. Yet Byron was only thirty-six. His blood had to boil
like lava for him to feel it beating in his pulses: did not the Giaour say
of his own blood

> But mine was like the lava flood
> That boils in Ætna's breast of flame?

Paroxysm became his natural atmosphere; hence the jarring and
clamorous discords which strike one in so many of his productions. This
necessity of forcing the tones may account for Byron's behavior during
what he called his "treacle-moon." His conduct towards his wife seems

to have been of a moral cruelty so exceptional as to make one for a moment doubt the reliability of the historical evidence. But one quickly comes to see that no episode in Byron's life is more true to type than this. The actual story of this episode must be read in Ethel Colburn Mayne's *The Life and Letters of Anne Isabella, Lady Noel Byron,* for which Miss Colburn Mayne was enabled to consult and draw upon private records in the possession of Byron's descendants.

Byron puts forward heroic arguments in order to extract sensations from marriage. "The great object of life is sensation, to feel that we exist, even though in pain," he had written to his future wife, who, though she might have been forewarned by it, was impelled by love and protective instinct towards her ambitious and rather puerile attempt to reform the poet. The first thing Byron said to her after the wedding ceremony was that it was now too late, that Annabella could have saved him if she had accepted him the first time he had asked for her hand, but that now there was no remedy: something irreparable had happened, Annabella would realize that she had married a devil, because he could only hate her: they were a damned and accursed pair. Even this was not enough. Annabella must be made to believe that the marriage was the result of a pique, of a bet, in which the woman had been treated as a mere object. Had Annabella refused Byron's hand the first time? Byron had plotted with Lady Melbourne to punish her stubbornness. Now he held her in his power, and he would make her feel it. At the moment of going to bed, Byron asked his wife if she intended to sleep in the same bed with him: "I hate sleeping with any woman, but you may if you choose." After all, provided she were young, he went on, one woman was as good as another. . . . In the middle of the night, according to Samuel Rogers's story, Annabella heard her husband cry out: "Good God, I am surely in Hell!" [1] The fire in the grate shone through the red curtains of the marriage bed. Profiting by his youthful reading of *Zeluco,* John Moore's romance, Byron entertained his wife on the means employed by that monster to get rid of his own child. And he concluded: "I shall strangle ours." Later, when Annabella was suffering the pains of childbirth, Byron told her that he hoped she would perish together with her baby, and when the child was born, the first thing he asked on coming into the room was "The child *was* born dead, wasn't it?"

But the most subtle torture, the torture which was to wring the most exquisite cry of anguish from its victim, was this: Byron, by every kind of allusion and insinuation, sought to instil into Annabella the suspicion of his incest with Augusta, his "terrible" secret. When Augusta was living under the same roof, Annabella must be given to understand

---

[1] See however Doris Langley Moore, *The Late Lord Byron* (London, John Murray, 1961) , pp. 55-56, where Rogers's statement is considerably qualified.

that Medora was Byron's daughter, and must be convinced that Augusta was still having intercourse with him (which was not true). Byron felt a perverse joy at the simultaneous presence of the two women, with all the amusement of innuendoes and double meanings which it afforded him, and the continual sensation of hanging over the edge of an abyss. Annabella was beside herself with desperation, to the point of feeling herself driven to kill Augusta: the thought of imminent catastrophe filled Byron with exultation:

> . . . There was that in my spirit ever
> Which shaped out for itself some great reverse.

Compared with these moral tortures his ostentation of physical ferocity seems a mere childish game, but Byron used to pace through the house with ruthless steps, armed with daggers and pistols, in imitation of the fifth Lord Byron, the "Wicked Lord." Like Capaneo, like Satan, Byron wished to experience the feeling of being struck with full force by the vengeance of Heaven. He sought to measure the depth of his own guilt in Annabella's anguish, in Augusta's remorse. However, the material responded only imperfectly to the artist's intention: Augusta was amoral and therefore proof against the sense of sin, and his wife, that patient Griselda, was a practical character and, although in love with him, would never commit a folly of the kind for which Caroline Lamb, Byron's first *maîtresse en titre,* became so celebrated. Byron alternated brutality with blandishment and made his tortures more agonizing by contrast; but Annabella never rose to the pitch of despair which he desired and did not lend herself to the melodrama of fatality. She was like a sailor who persists in lowering the lifeboats instead of helping to flood the hold, as the correct playing of the part assigned to her required, and Byron strove in vain to give orders to sink the ship immediately.

There were touches of comedy in this gloomy tragedy of Byron's life, whose scene was laid in a moral torture-chamber. Byron's moral sense functioned only in the exceptional conditions of a crisis, and it was only in the painful functioning of that moral sense that he found the gratification of his particular form of pleasure—*le bonheur dans le crime.* To destroy oneself and to destroy others:

> My embrace was fatal
> .   .   .   .   .   .
> I loved her, and destroy'd her.

It may be claimed that this version of Byron's married life is based mainly on his wife's statements. But Lady Byron's truthfulness was recognized by everyone, and by no one more fully and explicitly than by Byron himself. Nor were Lady Byron's statements disfigured by hatred, since Annabella never came to hate her husband; on the other hand, she sought to educate her daughter Ada to respect whatever was noble in her father. Into her account of their married relations Annabella introduced no distortion of truth except the inevitable one of her own point of view. A rather professorial and too self-conscious character, isolated in a form of narcissism different from Byron's, Annabella ended by realizing, at the age of forty, that *"not to see things as they are* is then my great intellectual defect."* She saw only one side of Byron. But the poet's words and deeds during their married life, in whatever way they are regarded, do not admit of a favorable interpretation. Perhaps he wished to joke, but joking in such circumstances amounts to cruelty.

What Manfred said of Astarte ("I loved her, and destroy'd her"), what Byron wished to be able to say of Augusta and of Annabella (see the Incantation in *Manfred*), was to become the motto of the "fatal" heroes of Romantic literature. They diffuse all round them the curse which weighs upon their destiny, they blast, like the simoon, those who have the misfortune to meet with them (the image is from *Manfred,* iii. 1); they destroy themselves, and destroy the unlucky women who come within their orbit. Their relations with their mistresses are those of an incubus-devil with his victim. Byron realizes the extreme type of Fatal Man described by Schiller in the *Räuber* and by Chateaubriand in *René.*

The following are some of the innumerable Fatal Men who came into existence on the pattern of the Byronic hero. Jean Sbogar, the nobleman-bandit of Charles Nodier (1818), exercises upon Antonia the charm of an obsession. In a dream she feels that a lost soul is prowling round her house, and has glimpses of a cruel eye which watches her night and day. Dumas' Antony, the most popular of the "fatal" rebels, makes the following comment upon himself in the lines (written in 1829) which serve as a preface to the play:

> Que de fois tu m'as dit, aux heures du délire,
> Quand mon front tout-à-coup devenait soucieux:
> Sur ta bouche pourquoi cet effrayant sourire?
>   Pourquoi ces larmes dans tes yeux?
>
>   .   .   .   .
>
> Malheur! malheur à moi que le ciel en ce monde
> A jeté comme un hôte à ses lois étranger;
> A moi qui ne sais pas, dans ma douleur profonde,
>   Soffrir longtemps sans me venger!
>
> Malheur! . . . car une voix qui n'a rien de la terre
> M'a dit: Pour ton bonheur, c'est sa mort qu'il te faut!

Et cette voix m'a fait comprendre le mystère
Et du meurtre et de l'échafaud.

Viens donc, ange du mal, dont la voix me convie,
Car il est des instants où si je te voyais,
Je pourrais pour ton sang t'abandonner ma vie
Et mon âme . . . si j'y croyais!

But the worthy Dumas, who adopted the idea of the Fatal Man at a stage when it is difficult to distinguish between the Schilleresque and the Byronic elements, makes him stab Adèle out of jealousy (as Karl Moor stabbed Amalie in the *Räuber*): he treats as a trite subject of ordinary passion, such as any normal man can understand, that which in Byron was a subtly perverse pleasure in destruction. For, once a fashion is launched, the majority imitate its external aspects without understanding the spirit which originated it.

The Plays

by Paul West

. . . my dramatic simplicity is *studiously* Greek, and must continue
so: *no* reform ever succeeded at first. I admire the old English dram-
atists; but this is quite another field, and has nothing to do with
theirs. I want to make a *regular* English drama, no matter whether
for the Stage or not, which is not my object,—but a *mental theatre.*
(Letter to Murray, 23rd August 1821)

The Simplicity of the plot is intentional, and the avoidance of *rant*
also, as also the compression of the Speeches in the more severe
situations.   (Letter to Murray, 20th September 1821)

Ranging from the turgid "mystery" pastiche *Heaven and Earth* to
the surrealistic farrago *The Deformed Transformed,* Byron's plays present in a more animated manner than the romances the theme of the
trapped man. The action takes place very much under the aspect (and
almost beneath the dignity) of eternity; and tends to surfeit the mind's
eye, at which it is aimed. The nature of the theme itself has an effect
of depopulating the plays; and, oddly enough, the surrealism of *The
Deformed Transformed* has more flavor of everyday life than the others
have. These plays are pageants *à thèse,* at once exploring further the
theme of the romances and falling short of the philosophical interpreta-
tions they promise. Byron, as ever, is more interested in emotions than in
ideas, in attitudes rather than motives, in flourish rather than steady
observation, in similitudes rather than analysis.

The situations, on their respective levels, are similar. Marino Faliero,
Doge of Venice, has more dignity than power: Michel Steno has care-
lessly smirched the reputation of the Doge's wife; but the Forty, the
omnipotent synod of which Steno is a member, merely order a token
punishment of a month's close arrest. Feeling that he counts for nothing,

"The Plays." From *Byron and the Spoiler's Art* (New York: St. Martin's Press; London: Chatto & Windus and Macmillan and Company, Ltd.; Toronto: Clarke, Irwin &
Co., 1960) by Paul West, pp. 100-120. Copyright © 1960 by Paul West. Reprinted by
permission of the author, St. Martin's Press, and Chatto & Windus.

that he, his office, family and forbears have been insulted, the Doge joins and leads an insurrection which fails. He is tried, sentenced and beheaded within the hour.

Sardanapalus, effete and despised king of Nineveh and Assyria, is renowned for a clemency that has in it more of indolence than high principle. His life is one long, languid debauch: surrounded by concubines and wearing a crown of flowers, he preaches pacifism while the forces of treason slowly gather. He lives apart from his queen and children, and spends most of his time with Myrrha, an Ionian female slave. Only Salemenes, his brother-in-law, can see what the outcome will be. He tries to convince the king; but Sardanapalus only half-attends until, in fact, a *coup d'état* is almost complete, and the insurgents are within his palace. Then the transformation occurs: sybarite becomes warrior, inspired and indefatigable—but in vain. So, after giving away his treasure to the survivors, evacuating his wife and children with the rest, he and Myrrha set fire to the palace, and burn together. He thus preserves the line of Nimrod although the rebels prevail.

In *The Two Foscari,* the Doge's son is being tried for plotting against the state. Many think this a trumped-up charge, and that the real motive of certain members of the Council of Ten is the extermination of the Foscari line. No sooner has the son been sentenced to exile than he dies from the effect of accumulated torture. The Doge is then asked to resign, and eventually agrees. Preparing to leave the ducal palace in state, he calls for water, takes a poisoned cup from Loredano, the most vindictive of the plotters, and dies instantly.

In *Werner,* its seriousness broken by the egregious and Falstaffian Gabor, Werner seeks in his own honorable way the inheritance from which he has been barred. But his son Ulric murders Stralenheim, who stands in their way, and discloses this fact to his father only as the play ends, with Werner become Count Siegendorf. Byron's interpretation of this is in terms of the trapped man; these two trap each other: "a son pre-destined to evil by the weakness and sensuality of his father, a father punished for his want of rectitude by the passionate criminality of his son." Byron first read the original tale (in Lee's *Canterbury Tales*) when he was about fourteen. It made a deep impression on him; and in the Preface he says that it "may, indeed, be said to contain the germ of much that I have since written." It may: there is an Old Testament grimness in much of his work. But, in his view, vengeance and retribution come in *this* life; indeed, in the Preface to *Cain,* he asks the reader "to bear in mind (what few choose to recollect), that there is no allusion to a future state in any of the books of Moses, nor indeed in the Old Testament."

Of the plays that resort to the supernatural, *The Deformed Transformed* sees Arnold the hunchback magically transformed into the shape of Achilles, and joining in an attack on Rome; *Manfred* enacts the pursuit of oblivion, power and immortality; *Cain* shows the apostate becoming the criminal; and *Heaven and Earth* illustrates the folly of brooking divine decree. The themes are typical of Byron's half-pagan eschatology; and they are not always clearly presented. It almost seems as if the attempt to articulate in terms of cosmic principles clouded his view.

Yet it is possible to specify the types of predicament illustrated in these plays without having to probe the Byronic theology, or theory, of guilt. Marino Faliero has a choice: he can remain in office, an amiable and respected cipher, or try to cleanse the body politic and win real power. Provoked by the Steno insult, he still has a choice. Perhaps such things are best ignored; perhaps the Forty are right to make little of the alleged affront. The Doge is eighty: he has, personally, little to lose, but much to gain for his position. So it is that an old head, a substantial motive and the right pretext combine to lead him into precipitate action. And however debatable may be the best way of dealing with the insult, it is truth that he perceives and acts upon: the truth of his ineffectuality. One misdemeanor by a member of the Forty alerts the Doge to the pernicious nature of the whole body. But the attempt to change the nature of things is doomed from the start: even the Doge suspected as much. Just before he is led out to execution on the Giant's Staircase he says to his wife:

> . . . *there was that in my spirit ever*
> *Which shaped out for itself some great reverse;*
> *The marvel is, it came not until now—*
> *And yet it was foretold me.*
> ANGIOLINA: *How foretold you?*
> DOGE: *Long years ago—so long, they are a doubt*
> *In memory, and yet they live in annals:*
> *When I was in my youth, and served the senate*
> *And signory as podesta and captain*
> *Of the town of Treviso, on a day*
> *Of festival, the sluggish bishop who*
> *Convey'd the Host aroused my rash young anger*
> *By strange delay, and arrogant reply*
> *To my reproof: I raised my hand and smote him. . . .*

Byron always associated self-realization with guilt: to link oneself with the universe was an act of reverence; to strive towards a full sense of one's separate identity was apostasy. Cain was the archetype that brought together Sardanapalus, royal pansy turned Bellona's bridegroom; Arnold, sport of nature transformed into Achilles; Doge Foscari, broken, sacked, but calling for the water that he knows will be poisoned; Werner, down with his principles, then up with his title; Manfred, lucubrating on his aspiration to godhead; and Japhet, transgressing according to the best light he had:

> JAPHET: *Father, it cannot be a sin to seek*
> *To save an earth-born being; and behold,*
> *These are not of the sinful, since they have*
> *The fellowship of angels.*
> NOAH: *These are they, then,*
> *Who leave the throne of God, to take them wives*
> *From out the race of Cain; the sons of heaven*
> *Who seek earth's daughters for their beauty?*

Self-assertion taints and destroys. If a man repudiates what is forced upon him, he has to take the consequences, whether or not he is being treated justly. Marino Faliero rejects ineffectuality; Sardanapalus, the popular image of himself—astonishing his own troops as well as the enemy; Arnold illicitly rejects his stunted body; Doge Foscari chooses the only positive act left to him, rather than a humiliating dotage; Werner rejects an improper station; Manfred rejects corporeal being; Cain and Japhet, orthodoxy. The gesture is the same, but the motives vary a good deal. Faliero invokes the public good, as does Sardanapalus. Arnold, like Manfred, wishes to cheat for his own ends. Werner cherishes his honor every bit as much as his ambition. Doge Foscari manages a last gesture of defiant pride. The defiance of Cain and Japhet is allegedly humane. But in all these examples, motives and circumstances affect the outcome not at all.

It would not be onerous to extract from Byron's own life the ingredients of such themes. Repudiations, shifts, transformations and heady aspirations were the stock-in-trade of the man who, arriving at the Hotel d'Angleterre in the suburb of Sécheron, in his twenty-eighth year, signed his age as 100. A bit of bravado, of course, but significant bravado. This master of evasion, as lewd as Ovid and with a soul as wrinkled as Gide's was going to be, composed his own *Metamorphoses*. Not for him the truly heroic poem about a lone man surmounting all in order to fulfill an elaborate design of destiny. Not for him the epic hero as raw material for the gods' whims, proving his mettle in adversity. What Byron chose was much more chaotic, much narrower: the futility of the human will in everyday affairs. In some of his plays and romances the lesson is straightforward, given in terms of ethics; in others it is presented symbolically and with supernatural apparatus. It is even possible to argue that Byron's deep sense of the will's ineffectuality led him not only to his theme of the trapped man but also away from a deep respect for human beings. People, this argument would run, were puppets, fit for farce only. And whether they were to be used as mere properties as in *The Deformed Transformed* (unfinished and therefore inscrutable) or as unrespected *personae* in *Beppo* and *Don Juan,* they would exemplify not just a facile fatalism but the principle that self-fulfillment (essence, not existence) is possible only in terms of failure. It is this principle which explains and integrates Byron: the apathy, the disaffected air, the exotic *personae,* the social and literary fulminations, the messianic pose, the melancholy farce and the ludicrous brooding, the early recourse to landscape, the later one to interiors, the cult of magic, the urge to eliminate, the progressive apathy, and the final effort to renew, efface, or regain his identity. For Byron, a personal identity was both attractive and repulsive: something to be proud of in the teeth of fate, something to obliterate as an earnest of limitation; something at once seductive to the creative man in him, and yet balking to the pantheist.

It is the romantic who longs to be a soul of indefinite extent but wants to circumscribe the extent in order to savor it. Byron's trapped men cannot escape themselves; each one has a conscience which he is not profligate enough or irresponsible enough to ignore consistently. Each one is romantic enough to enjoy the feeling of being "self-made," yet is sufficiently aware of the workings of society, destiny and politics to discern his own transgressions. Self-indulgence wars with conscience: "All a man can betray is his conscience," says Conrad's Razumov in *Under Western Eyes.*

But surely, we are bound to ask, did the communication of such a truism entail all the lavish paraphernalia of Turkish tale, mutiny, incest, beheading, dilapidated castles, Venetian plotters, limp and brisk Assyrians, hunchbacks, swollen rivers, Biblical ventriloquism, and Faustian rant? Yes. All this was necessary to Byron both as a poet expressing his deepest feelings and as an acknowledged entertainer. What was instinctive was also good box-office. Indeed, in a sense, Byron's exotic and dramaturgical effects served to objectify vividly; to disguise a subject too familiar to himself. What he eliminated from his spiritual system had to be disclaimed but recognizable; in order to satisfy himself that he had separated it from himself, it must not look so familiar as to be overlooked—as could easily happen. After all, the exotic romance extended back to fable and legend and Byron had a strong sense of the miraculous and the primitive. His writings are exorcisms, and bear many signs— naïve and touching ones—of a yearning familiar to us in many guises: The Fresh Start; "getting out of himself"; "breaking new ground"; Adonis myths.

This is not to say that Byron ever articulated the precise nature of this yearning; but determined extrapolators would probably link his deracination with escapism, selfishness, paranoia, inconsistency, and so on. It is not part of this study to pursue such inquiries. It is more to the

oint to observe that, for Byron, identity was magical and the world was
destructive element. An obsession with self-escape led him naturally
o certain themes: escape from a trap, a rôle, a position, an affair, a wife,
reputation; metamorphosis—really transmogrification—into someone
lse or into a different order of being; contracts with the devil; immer-
ion in action, in poetry, in the exotic; imprisonment; debauchery;
right chatter and foreign travel. And of course the torrential letter-
vriting, the menagerie and the changing harem fit into this pattern.
inally he broke free into farce, in which there were no traps. "Anything
oes" is the method of *Don Juan*. The poet usually remains uncommitted,
vith nothing to escape from or transcend except the strain of his immun-
ty. Even the inveterate evader knows what he is; and to try evading such
nowledge is merely to involve oneself all over again with people and
bjects. *Don Juan* approaches an extreme ideal: an absolute in which
Byron has small faith. It is the solution to problems he explored in the
omances and plays, and the embodiment of a literary attitude which
e could not fully adapt to his life. *Don Juan* and the plays run in par-
llel. Right up to Missolonghi, the problems intrigued, the solution
empted, and the multiple personality looked for a proper combination
f the two.

As literature, the plays are far from perfect; Byron did not often test
is powers in them. They communicate a sense of futility—men of stature
eing fiercely hemmed in by a force which wrecks dignity and stunts
esponsibility. The straight lines of idealism become inevitably con-
orted; even the virtuous and the noble fall foul of their own principles.
Life cheats but death cannot. These ideas emerge clearly, but too often.
There is none of the drama's suggestion of life's movement: the plays
re statuesque. Every character is relentlessly ruminative, has no minor
emotions, no trivial ideas. If we are to be convinced and disturbed, it is
paroxysm that has to do it—paroxysm and proclamation. There is too
ittle of the subtle, irrelevant texture of life; there are too few of those
etty but revealing human tricks that keep us sane and the social his-
orians in perpetual business. Everything is made to sound important,
lmost as if each play contained Station Standing Orders for Good Men
Hard Pressed. There is too much elaboration of the crumbling temperament, the stiffening resolve. The main characters—Faliero, Sardanapalus,
Foscari, Werner and Manfred—make an inexorable destiny look flimsy.
There are long waits between rounds, and there is too little diversifica-
ion of the approach to an obvious ending. Most of the secondary characters are the merest figments. There is insufficient use of contrast. The
plays proceed like theorems, yet much of the versification is sloppy:
yllable count deposes spoken stress; there is too much recourse to speech-
pinning devices like anaphora; the language too often lacks trenchancy
nd wit; much of the verse is careless prose put in layers. There are too

few really dramatic images that leap out and epitomize. There is no
chatter and too much rant; there is too little play of monosyllable against
polysyllable, of concrete against abstract. The pageant is too insubstantial, too tame, too consciously tricked up in the style of "plays for study."
And yet for the patient searcher, there is gold—at least, good dramatic
pyrites.

To wake us up, for instance, there is verse like a clatter of pans:

> *Be not so quick! the honour of the corps*
> *Which forms the baron's household's unimpeach'd*
> *From steward to scullion, save in the fair way*
> *Of peculation; such as in accompts,*
> *Weights, measures, larder, cellar, buttery,*
> *Where all men take their prey; as also in*
> *Postage of letters, gathering of rents,*
> *Purveying feasts, and understanding with*
> *The honest trades who furnish noble masters. . . .*

This comes from *Werner*, a play not without comic relief, and shows
Byron at his cataloguing best. The mouthing bombast catches attention,
yet the words seem to impede the ideas' arrival. There is care to supply
variety of structure and of movement, but too little attention to a consistent principle of rhythm. Why, in the last four lines, push syllabic
count so far as to amputate "in" and "with" from their nouns when,
elsewhere in the passage, speech-stress lengthens two lines by an extra
syllable? If "with" needs to be exposed to distinguish it from "of," "in"
certainly does not. The passage is representative of Byron's blank verse
style: there is a half-grudging, half-rhapsodical drive at the idea; and
disregard reinforces the inconsistency. But in this play, and in *The Deformed Transformed*, Byron at least gets his characters talking in a
monstrous version of the colloquial—part Jonson, part Shakespeare, part
the Byron of the Letters—which, in appearing to refer to everyday
speech, goes much further than the idiom of his other plays. Parody is
nearer to life than is the imitation or the dramatically elevated. In the
following, Idenstein considers the suitability of a damp room for Stralenheim, who has just been rescued from the river:

> *But then he comes from a much damper place,*
> *So scarcely will catch cold in't, if he be*
> *Still liable to cold—and if not, why*
> *He'll be worse lodged tomorrow. . . .*

This vein of the callous bland is common enough in Shakespeare, and
frequent in various applications in Byron—for fun, harsh satire, and

hysterical hate. Sometimes he pointedly goes through the act of averting his gaze; at other times, he looks on, amused. But there seems to be in his attitude something of the immunity of the gods in Lucretius. Once Byron can regard the person in hand as an object, he writes vividly and secures more attention. About the deformed Arnold in *The Deformed Transformed* he is brilliantly heartless:

> *Were I to taunt a buffalo with this*
> *Cloven foot of thine, or the swift dromedary*
> *With thy sublime of humps, the animals*
> *Would revel in the compliment.*

Mr. Punch is using his thick stick on the "thinginess" of the language. There is a wooden, clumsy sound to this outrageous piece; pathos mingles with bravura, sensitivity with brutishness. We are in the presence of farce. We soar up with "sublime" and are thumped down by the grotesque, lewd sound of "hump"—a nice counterpoint of vowels preparatory to the malice of the last line. Jonson's "Down is too hard, I'll have my beds all stuff'd" belongs with this; but Byron preferred casual farce to such ingenuity, and never achieved Jonson's exquisite inflations of language. Occasionally Byron throws out phrases—"the helmless dromedary," "vassals / From their scant pallets," "the lead doth / With its greased under-stratum," "A spur in its halt movements"—which indicate a gift for startling combinations of plain elements. Sophistication goes begging, and the delight in conjunctions that sound uncouth, and look preposterous, prevails:

> *. . . Yesterday he would have given*
> *His lands (if he hath any), and, still dearer,*
> *His sixteen quarterings, for as much fresh air*
> *As would have fill'd a bladder, while he lay*
> *Gurgling and foaming halfway through the window*
> *Of his o'erset and water-logg'd conveyance. . . .*

But Byron has subtler methods. He can work the abstract into a deft mimicry of the tangible:

> *. . . coarse lusts of habitude,*
> *Prurient yet passionless, cold studied lewdness,*
> *Depraving nature's frailty to an art. . . .*
> *. . . but rather lessen,*
> *By mild reciprocal alleviation,*
> *The fatal penalties imposed on life. . . .*

He gains breathtaking advantages merely by setting something ordinary amongst the highfalutin:

> *Shelter'd by the grey parapet from some*
> *Stray bullet of our lansquenets, who might*
> *Practise in the cool twilight.*

This is at least as good as Tourneur or Shirley; and the following is as fine a *trouvaille* as you find anywhere in Byron:

> *I tell thee, be not rash; a golden bridge*
> *Is for a flying enemy.*

It persuades—captures—before its relevance becomes clear. And such, after all, is the function of the dramatic image, even in a dramatic poem. It must epitomize before it can be scrutinized: indeed, scrutiny should be unnecessary, because such an image leaps to the observer's (reader's) need:

> *Ask of the bleeding pelican why she*
> *Hath ripp'd her bosom?*
> *My lord, these are mere fantasies; there are*
> *No eyes in marble.*
> *You feel* not*—you go to this butcher-work*
> *As if these high-born men were steers for shambles. . . .*

It is well to see these images in isolation, for they necessarily isolate themselves from their context. These three preceding come from *Marino Faliero,* which is organized into prodigious leaps from one event to the next. Fortunately, at most of the moments of high intensity—as here at the climaxes of the Doge's first heart-baring to Israel Bertuccio, the conspirator; his first clandestine meeting; and his first qualms about the planned massacre—there is a pregnant image, renewing attentiveness and suffusing what follows. But *Marino Faliero* no less than *The Two Foscari* and *Sardanapalus* starts too slowly and ends too late. Of essentially three-act length, not five, the plots cannot support a viscous magniloquence. In the following passage from *Marino Faliero* the inventive faculty is countering imminent paralysis with frenzied and well-planned exercise:

> I. BER.: *You must come alone.*
> DOGE: *With but my nephew.*
> I. BER.: *Not were he your son.*
> DOGE: *Wretch! darest thou name my son? He died in arms*

> *At Sapienza for this faithless state.*
> *Oh! that he were alive, and I in ashes!*
> *Or that he were alive ere I be ashes!*
> *I should not need the dubious aid of strangers.*
> I. BER.: *Not one of all those strangers whom thou doubtest,*
> *But will regard thee with a filial feeling,*
> *So that thou keep'st a father's faith with them.*

'he play is upon the words, not upon our feelings. Byron gains a mere-
icious continuity: the use of "son" and "strangers" seems intended to
eep things moving in a false reciprocity. As it happens, the repetition
. dramatic, but the language marks time and suggests speech-spinning.
. similar inertia, prompting the poet into gesticulations, appears as
naphora in another speech from the same play:

> *From the hour they made me Doge, the Doge THEY made me—*
> *Farewell the past! I died to all that had been,*
> *Or rather they to me: no friends, no kindnesses,*
> *No privacy of life—all were cut off:*
> *They came not near me, such approach gave umbrage:*
> *They could not love me, such was not the law;*
> *They thwarted me, 'twas the state's policy;*
> *They baffled me, 'twas a patrician's duty;*
> *They wrong'd me, for such was to right the state;*
> *They could not right me, that would give suspicion;*
> *So that I was a slave to my own subjects;*
> *So that I was a foe to my own friends;*
> *Begirt with spies for guards, with robes for power,*
> *With pomp for freedom, gaolers for a council,*
> *Inquisitors for friends, and hell for life!*

Now this is a very important speech, intended to carry the maximum of
eeling. True, too, an impassioned person with some bent for rhetoric
ends to resort to anaphora. But so does the poet who wants to accumu-
ate lines; and here the speech feeds on itself. The question is not: is it
rue to life? but: is its truth to life artfully suggested? To go further:
. piece of perfect casting may well entail little or no effort from the
ctor. But our pleasure at the play is very much bound up with the
nowledge that the whole thing is artificial. And what Byron does, with-
ut the stanza form to tax him, is to under-exercise his art. He writes
blank verse as if it were an organ of the body, and not an instrument
with imposed rules and an arbitrary purpose. Byron the man becomes
amiliar with the medium and ignores the formalities. He has little
onception of art's ventriloquism and too intense a concern with art as

sheer self-expression. This is not to say that he cannot project himsel
into a character, but that he is too interested in such vicarious experienc
to retain a strong sense of his medium's artificiality. He treats art as i
it were a game of identities and not a struggle with objects. So it is tha
his best writing occurs when he is tussling with a stanza form and writin
as himself in unabashed first person. The obvious fusion of these i
Don Juan.

It is possible to go on from this to say that the sort of thing he write
varies according to fixed conditions. In the first person he derides. If h
is *en caractère*—as in the romances, *Childe Harold,* the plays—he usuall
mistakes art for the exotic, the lifelike, the obedient landscape. Second
even in the first person and tussling with form, he remains naïve abou
his art. He guards sincerity from feminine rhymes and tries too har
for stunts: the one move is narrow-minded, the other reckless. And third
he wants always to restrict his medium—to make it more and more of
personal thing. In other words, he tried to specialize without developin
his taste. He wanted his writing to be as personal as a facial tic, and jus
as uncontrollable too.

Much of *Don Juan, The Deformed Transformed, Werner* and *Man
fred* comes under the heading of stunt. A stunt travesties our ideas o
congruity, and so was dear to Byron. His mystery plays are stunts; hi
romances are; and his ducal and royal themes seem intended to provok
an exclamation—"well, of all things!" Even the exotic was a stunt fo
him: it is true that he did not reconnoiter the Near East with expres
literary intention; but he found that the exotic enabled him to get awa
with stunt-themes. *Anything* could happen in Turkey, as his friend
must have thought from the outlandish tales he invented about his lif
there. But once he had seen his way clear to farce, which made the stun
a virtue in its own right, he needed no cover and no pretext; what i
exotic in *Don Juan* is therefore either restrained or merely decorative.

But whether the plays are stunts with the time-machine, like *Th
Deformed Transformed,* or merely specimens of stunted magniloquence
like *Sardanapalus,* there are lovely or pithy passages for the finding
There is a long speech in *Marino Faliero* which perfectly represent
Byron when he is fitting himself into a lyrical occasion:

> *The high moon sails upon her beauteous way,*
> *Serenely smoothing o'er the lofty walls*
> *Of those tall piles and sea-girt palaces,*
> *Whose porphyry pillars, and whose costly fronts,*
> *Fraught with the orient spoil of many marbles,*
> *Like altars ranged along the broad canal,*
> *Seem each a trophy of some mighty deed*
> *Rear'd up from out the waters, scarce less strangely*

> *Than those more massy and mysterious giants*
> *Of architecture, those Titanian fabrics,*
> *Which point in Egypt's plains to times that have*
> *No other record. All is gentle: nought*
> *Stirs rudely; but, congenial with the night,*
> *Whatever walks is gliding like a spirit.*
> *The tinklings of some vigilant guitars. . . .*

He is determined to be magniloquent: of course the result is fustian, but is just redeemed by its smoothness and by his eye for objects. The passage could be Rogers, and is anybody; it is built according to the book, with all the right devices. Obviously Byron shared Milton's addiction to the large unit—the paragraph and the self-fed declaration; but he had little of Milton's ability to vary the constructions, to carry many qualifications without losing the pattern of the argument. The most that Byron can attain in this direction is exemplified in the following passage from *Marino Faliero:*

> *I do believe you; and I know you true:*
> *For love, romantic love, which in my youth*
> *I knew to be illusion, and ne'er saw*
> *Lasting, but often fatal, it had been*
> *No lure for me, in my most passionate days,*
> *And could not be so now, did such exist.*
> *But such respect, and mildly paid regard*
> *As a true feeling for your welfare, and*
> *A free compliance with all honest wishes,—*
> *A kindness to your virtues, watchfulness*
> *Not shown, but shadowing o'er such little failings*
> *As youth is apt in, so as not to check*
> *Rashly, but win you from them ere you knew*
> *You had been won, but thought the change your choice;*
> *A pride not in your beauty, but your conduct;*
> *A trust in you; a patriarchal love,*
> *And not a doting homage; friendship, faith,—*
> *Such estimation in your eyes as these*
> *Might claim, I hoped for*

There is a good deal of dramatic verse inferior to this. Byron achieves a peculiarly apt motion here: constant interpolations in the form of qualification and honest asides give the passage an air of self-interrupting sincerity—a steady pendulum between rehearsed admission and the impulse of the moment. Yet the main drift is never quite lost, largely because, as soon as the reader has as much as he can intelligently carry,

Byron resorts to parallelism not spread over several lines but based on the single line. The last five lines very gently assist us to earth, and yet add to the information already given. Their function is to calm the reader, to denote the speaker's regained grip on himself after an impassioned outburst. In the same way as a phrase of music repeated *diminuendo,* these last lines attain a dimissory effect which is moving and of which Byron, when he chose, was the master. ("So, we'll go no more a roving" exploits the same device.)

Sufficient to say, then, that Byron was merely too impatient to secure architectonic effects well within his power. But I suggest that the reason underlying the impatience was—in the case of *Marino Faliero, The Two Foscari,* and *Sardanapalus* especially—boredom with working out the detail of an appealing theme. That is why these three plays suffer from sameness of texture—not an unflagging excellence but the monotony of habit. At least *Werner* and *The Deformed Transformed* have novelties of texture and character blatant enough to keep our attention and sustained enough to have kept Byron reasonably imaginative while composing. *Manfred,* although more of a private pageant-poem than these two, extorts the same kind of attention—the kind we accord to Punch and Judy, *Ubu Roi, Bartholomew Fair,* and *Waiting for Godot.* All are stunts; but the ideal stunt is short. And Byron's most effective operational unit was the miscellaneous canto's discipline of stanzas. Whatever he laid under contribution could be dismissed without warning; and an argument was as well ended with a flourish in the stanza's last two lines as with a logical clincher.

But in detecting the existence, and in lamenting the failure to operate, of this architectonic gift we should not forget Byron's mastery of the concise—a mastery essential to the stanza-packer:

> *. . . I ne'er*
> *Can see a smile, unless in some broad banquet's*
> *Intoxicating glare, when the buffoons*
> *Have gorged themselves up to equality,*
> *Or I have quaff'd me down to their abasement.*

The verbs "gorged" and "quaff'd" are no idle mannerisms, and will stand up to investigation of the ideas they seem to contrast "feed up," "drink up," "drink down," and so on. This does not assume that Byron intended to be deep; but simply that the contrast is sound enough to bear extrapolation. For he could sharpen the edge of wit with small labor; in the following, he does so by the inclusion of one word, "magnetic":

> *. . . novel perils, like fresh mistresses,*
> *Wear more magnetic aspects. . . .*

There are some trenchant exchanges too. Bertuccio declares his motive:

> I. BER.: *Freedom!*
> BEN.: *You are brief, sir.*
> I. BER.: *So my life grows: I*
> *Was bred a soldier, not a senator.*

There is even the old Adam of mock self-consciousness:

> ARN.: *Prithee, peace!*
> *Softly! methinks her lips move, her eyes open!*
> CAES.: *Like stars, no doubt; for that's a metaphor*
> *For Lucifer and Venus.*

Pungency is here too. Sardanapalus, although effete, has a core of common sense, or at least an instinct for what sounds like sense:

> *But what wouldst have? the empire has been founded.*
> *I cannot go on multiplying empires.*

That first line has an almost Thurber-like quality rare in Byron. But whether we are haunted by unusual phrases ("the big rain pattering on the roof") or by Byron's frequent flirtations with aphorism, the fact remains that these plays give us enough of neither. There are flashes of workmanlike economy:

> *Some sacrifices ask'd a single victim,*
> *Great expiations had a hecatomb. . . .*

Occasionally his ear for conversation predominates over his prosy formalities, and the text springs to life briefly:

> *Oh! you wax proud, I see, of your new form:*
> *I'm glad of that. Ungrateful too! That's well;*
> *You improve apace;—two changes in an instant,*
> *And you are old in the world's ways already.*
> *But bear with me. . . .*

Further life accrues from very short and rapid consultations:

> SAL.: *Satraps!*
> BEL.: *My prince!*
> SAL.: *Well met—I sought ye both,*
> *But elsewhere than the palace.*
> ARB.: *Wherefore so?*

SAL.:   *'Tis not the hour.*
ARB.:   *The hour!—what hour?*
SAL.:   *Of midnight.*

But this is everyday device, like the stale epic formulae which Byron
appropriated. And a *sortes virgilianae* on the plays is more than unlikely
to expose a prodigy, although with their plain and repetitive language,
and properly truncated, they might make very suitable pieces for radio.

What is most lacking is a sense of particularity which might tempt the
reader to study the imagery. But so much is shallow in this magniloquence meant for casual ears; so much is unsubtle, colorless, and passionless. There is more wit than we find in Tennyson the playwright; more
energy than in the Johnson of *Irene;* less audacity than in Jonson; less
originality than in the Keats of *Otho the Great,* and in all respects less
skill than in the Shelley of *The Cenci.* Byron was simply too unimagina-
tive to compose drama: when he wants to brighten things up, he engineers
a stunt. He tends to supply factitious energy, to jerk the action along
when he himself is bored. The plays really amount to prodigious solilo-
quies set out as drama; and he seems happiest when he has a long stretch
ahead of him into which he can pour himself regardlessly. States of mind
intrigue him; events hardly at all.

None of this is surprising in a man devoted to his own moods, a man
who released them like wild animals, or pitiable invalids, among the
civilized public merely to see what effect they had. Such self-obsession
necessarily leads to technical deficiencies such as those already noted. But
the themes of the plays really are worth attention, not because they
enlighten us about his life, but because they are exhaustive dossiers on
special aspects of the human condition. They give no strikingly evident
solutions. And this is why I think we are likely to find him readable;
for this indolent, wayward, confused, and often desperate man was
enough of a showman not to try giving answers. If there is any answer,
it is in the farce of *Don Juan.* Life, in the plays, remains ineluctable for
Doge and hunchback alike; and in striking through fustian, cant, and
panache to the eternal themes, Byron is at his most serious and sincere.
He thought highly of these plays, and so did Goethe. Perhaps they were
right. Life is no mere question-and-answer game, and Byron's disdain of
packet wisdom is clear from *Don Juan.* Instead, for those who try to
think things out, life becomes very often a slowly expanding insight into
why the questions are unanswerable anyway. Byron's plays make us think,
long-winded as they are. They do not explain or recommend, but il-
luminate in an uncompromising way the flaws and yearnings of most
reflective people. There is a point, after all, at which anguished speculation is seen to be futile, and a steady look at the demons heals better
than any exorcizing homily.

The Devil a Bit of Our *Beppo*

by Guy Steffan

Byron's earlier satires (*English Bards and Scotch Reviewers, Hints from Horace, The Curse of Minerva,* and *The Waltz*—all of them done by 1812) were written in the heroic couplets, the epigrammatic balances, and the formal rhetoric of his eighteenth century predecessors, and he had in them occasionally achieved a vigorous and witty brilliance. In the five years after 1812, he gave most of his literary effort to more sober or more popular productions—*Childe Harold,* the six Eastern narratives, and *Manfred.*

Then came *Beppo,* which he intended as a surprise for his publisher Murray and his public. In the summer of 1817, in Venice, while Byron was engaged with the serious grandiloquence and the ambitious meditations of Canto IV of *Childe Harold,* he read Frere's *Whistlecraft* and was so taken by its satiric manner that he soon tried it himself. The result was his first completed masterpiece in a kind of verse that he found superlatively congenial to his talents. In *Beppo* he fused some of the rhetorical techniques of the earlier formal satires with the pleasant trivia, the jocose frivolity, the colloquial zest, the double rhymes, and the lighter and more rapid rhythms of such *jeux d'esprit* as "Egotism," "Queries to Casuists," "Lines to Mr. Hodgson, Written on Board the Lisbon Packet," and the "Farewell to Malta."

Though many of the particular devices and qualities of *Beppo* can be found in Byron's previous writing, it is, in its composite assimilation of older methods and in its several new achievements, a break away from his immediate literary past. In *Beppo* he adapted to comic purposes the technique of associational elaboration and continuity that he had used to string together his reflections in *Childe Harold.* By combining this associative technique with colloquial irreverence and incongruity, he contrived in his ottava rima stanzas a conversational medium,

"The Devil a Bit of Our *Beppo*," by Truman Guy Steffan. From *Philological Quarterly*, XXXII, 2 (April 1953), 154-171. Published 1953 by the State University of Iowa. Reprinted by permission of the author and *Philological Quarterly*. See also "Forecast," Ch. 1 of *Byron's* Don Juan, Vol. I: *The Making of a Masterpiece* (Austin, Texas: University of Texas Press, 1957). Copyright © 1957 by the University of Texas Press. This gives the same author's discussion of some matters not taken up in the above essay.

as casual as it was elastic, with abundant license for discursive commentary and with a serpentine movement that was flippantly varied, playfully inflated, humorously haphazard, and lightly extemporaneous, jerked onward at intervals by the slenderest of narratives, and invigorated by some sketches of foolish folk, by a few comic situations, and by frequent wit and self-conscious irony.

In both manner and matter, *Beppo* was something new for Byron, as he boasted in his correspondence. For the first time he tried his trick of abruptly contrasting the tone within and between related sections, as he very effectively did when he mingled his serio-comic praise of all things Italian with sharp disparagement of all things English and then swung into a series of ironic parallelisms on what he "liked" about his native institutions. No preceding work of his, moreover, had anything like those saucy, frivolous, audacious, and mocking passages in *Beppo* on Lent and the Carnival, on the gondola, the Cavalier Servente, and "the poor dear Mussulwomen." [1] Byron had never before got himself into, and found his way with poise and neat direction through, such a whimsical and involved labyrinth of digressions on everything from fish sauce to Shakespeare. Nor had he ever drawn character types like those of the Count and "Botherby," nor even in *The Waltz* offered such gleeful presentation of feminine artifice as Laura's parting from Beppo, her uneasiness during his absence, her rationalizing acceptance of the services of the Count, her versatile performance at the Ridotto, and her masterful outbreak upon the return of her husband, where the calculated and breathless incoherence of her speech races to the farcical climax of a little episode that had meandered through ninety-nine stanzas. [2]

Thus, as Byron knew, *Beppo* was an experiment in form and substance and a forerunner of *Don Juan,* which he began shortly after he was assured that *Beppo* was a financial success. Although the slighter *Beppo* has been overshadowed by the mightier *Don Juan,* Byron, within the limits of what he tried to do, achieved a triumph of comic mischief and controlled facility. Its merits have not often won much critical attention, and it is a little strange that the first draft MS of *Beppo* has been ignored, for there we can watch a skillful artist consciously at work on a novelty that was soon to become his natural and most compelling habit of expression. [3]

[1] In the order mentioned these passages occur in stanzas 41-49; 1-10; 19-20; 36-37; 40; 70-72; 77-78. To see the difference between *Beppo* and some of his previous writing, one need only place beside these passages from *Beppo* some from *Childe Harold* on Lent and a carnival, a British sabbath, the domestic confinement of Moslem women, Napoleon and the fickleness of fortune; e.g., Canto I, stanzas 52, 53, 69, Canto II, stanzas 61, 78, Canto III, stanzas 36 ff. For the "fortune" passage in *Beppo* see stanzas 61-62.

[2] In the order mentioned these passages occur in stanzas 30-34; 73-76; 28-30, 53-54; 65-67, 69; 91-93.

[3] I wish to thank the trustees of the Pierpont Morgan library for permission to study and reproduce parts of their holograph MS.

He began *Beppo* on September 6, 1817, and finished his first draft of 84 stanzas on October 10. Within two weeks (October 23) he had written five more stanzas and before he sent his publisher a fair copy in January, 1818, had increased the poem to 95 stanzas. These were published on February 28 and four more appeared in the fourth edition later in the spring.[4]

The first general problem of Byron's composition of *Beppo* that arises, as soon as one looks over his first draft, concerns the stanzas that came to him as afterthoughts. Since he numbered consecutively both the eleven leaves of his original draft and its 84 stanzas, which we may term the matrix of the poem, it is easy to identify the fifteen stanzas that were written subsequently to the matrix. Nine appear on separate sheets inserted between the matrix leaves, and one was written on the last matrix page.[5] Byron gave numbers to eight of these ten stanzas to indicate their approximate place of insertion, but he did not renumber all matrix stanzas following the new ones. Thus his last MS stanza is numbered "84," which corresponds to the ninety-ninth in all modern editions. The following table, based on an analysis of the MS and on a comparison between the MS and the first edition, reveals what were matrix stanzas and what were added stanzas. The italicized numbers in parentheses are the original ones that Byron used on his MS and show clearly the consecutive order of the matrix.

Matrix Stanzas	Added Stanzas
1-27 (*1-27*)	
	28 nms., 4th ed.
29-32 (*28-31*)	
	33-34 un. ins.
35-37 (*32-34*)	
	38-39 nms., 4th ed.

[4] Byron recorded the terminal date of the first draft (October 10, 1817) on his MS. E. H. Coleridge in his introduction to *Beppo* gave the beginning date as September 6 and cited as a source of his information Byron's letter to Murray on October 12, 1817, but this letter did not mention either the initial or the terminal date of composition (*The Works of Lord Byron. Poetry* [London, 1905], IV, 157; *Letters and Journals*, edited by R. E. Prothero [London, 1900], IV, 172-73.) Byron in later letters to Murray reported the addition of five stanzas by October 23 and the despatch of his fair copy in January, 1818, and of four more stanzas, "a fortnight" before March 25, 1818. (*Letters and Journals*, IV, 176, 193-94, 216.) These last four arrived too late to appear in the first edition. Coleridge gave February 28, 1818, as the date of the publication of the first edition and also stated that the four missing stanzas appeared in the fifth edition on May 4, 1818. A copy of the *fourth* edition in the Rare Book Collection of the University of Texas Library contains these stanzas. Coleridge cited no sources for his dates of the publication of the first and fifth editions.

[5] Five other stanzas are missing from the MS (28, 38, 39, 64, 80). Coleridge notes that only four stanzas were missing. He does not record 64 as omitted, nor does he indicate that ten stanzas were obvious insertions into the original draft.

40-44	(35-39)
47-51	(40-44)
53-63	(45-55)
65-72	(56-63)
78-79	(64-65)
81-99	(66-84)

45 ins.   (42)
46 written on last
   matrix page (44)

52 ins.   (48)

64 nms.

73-77 ins.   (64-68)

80 nms., 4th ed.

KEY:
ins.   —stanza was inserted on separate leaf into matrix leaves of Pierpont Morgan MS.
un.   —stanza was unnumbered on the Pierpont Morgan MS.
nms.   —stanza does not appear with Pierpont Morgan MS.
4th ed.—stanza was first published in the fourth edition.

The evidence assembled from the Pierpont Morgan first draft, the letters, and the first and fourth editions permits us to suggest the following chronology of composition:

1) The matrix of 84 stanzas was written by October 10, 1817.

2) Of the eleven added stanzas that appear on the first draft, all of which were printed in the first edition, five—stanzas 73-77 on Botherby —appear together on a separate leaf of the Pierpont Morgan MS with Byron's own instruction for insertion ("additions for page 9") and are numbered "64-68." The Botherby group is the only one that he numbered correctly. The original number of matrix stanza "64" was changed to "69." Such careful provisions and the fact that these five stanzas are all on one subject support the not unreasonable theory that they were the first to be added between October 10 and 23.[6]

3) Five others (33, 34, 45, 46, 52) that were also added to the matrix and one that does not appear with it (64) were presumably written after October 23 but before Byron sent his fair copy to Murray in January, 1818. Two of the five that appear with the matrix were unnumbered, and the other three were incorrectly numbered. Moreover he took the trouble to change the number of only one matrix stanza to indicate where the new stanza 52 went and even there he blundered. Such carelessness indicates that they were added after the Botherby group, when the physical arrangement of the MS was less fresh in his mind and he was uncertain about the exact place of insertion. Since all six stanzas were printed in the first edition, they must have been written before he submitted his fair copy for publication. Stanza 64 was likely the last to be added because it does not appear on the Pierpont Morgan MS.

4) The four remaining stanzas to be accounted for (28, 38, 39, 80),

[6] As we have already noted, Byron's letters to Murray recorded the addition of five stanzas between these dates, though Byron did not specify which they were.

none of which appears either on the Pierpont Morgan draft or in the first edition, must be those which he sent by letter "a fortnight" before March 25, 1818, too late to get into the first edition. They were accordingly added to the fourth edition.

The fifteen stanzas that were added at various times after Byron completed his matrix of 84 stanzas on October 10 pose some interesting questions. Why were they added? What was the material that he thought significant enough to be injected into a completed first draft? What creative force or caprice of expansion was at work? How were the new stanzas fitted into their context and what did they contribute? Their special isolation as a series of afterthoughts focuses attention on the reasons or incentives for their insertion. Some of them are important because they enrich the content of *Beppo* and all of them are conspicuous examples of several temperamental impulses and artistic methods that are typical of Byron's composition. The very fact that they were additional spurts of activity allows us to see Byron's creative mind at work.

The largest and most important accretive block was his satire of Sotheby (stanzas 73-77). Byron admitted that the origin of this passage was a personal grievance. He thought Sotheby was the anonymous author of a letter sent to him in Rome with a marked up copy of a volume of Byron's poetry containing unfavorable criticism.[7] Out of this pique came a new passage for *Beppo,* that is not just a relic of personal animosity but a derisive sketch of a character-type that has general universality, with vigorously concrete particulars. This digressive afterthought, engendered by punitive emotion, is one of two set character pieces in the poem.[8] Byron linked the new section so carefully to preceding and following matrix stanzas that it fits into the associative pattern and does not seem to interrupt the casual flow of the verse. The matrix stanzas 70-72 had used Turkish women in ironic contrast to ridicule some foibles of English women, especially the intellectual pretensions of the Bluestockings. Stanza 72 ends with a couplet about "bustling Botherbys" who show the Blues "that charming passage in the last new poem." Then follows the inserted satire of the perennial Botherby, the vain, incompetent, tenth-rate scribbler, "the sublime / Of mediocrity, the furious tame, / The echo's echo," the earnest professional aspirant to literary fame who, in spite of toil, never rises to distinction and always remains a dull, posturing hack. In the last stanza of the insertion (77) Byron returns to Turkish women in order to make a transition to matrix stanza 78 ("No chemistry for them unfolds her gases") and so he is back with his original topic.

---

[7] See several letters to Murray, *Letters and Journals,* IV, 125, 210-11, 230, etc.

[8] The passage on the Count is the other, and it too was expanded after the matrix was finished. The excellent characterization of Laura is not a single set piece like those of Botherby and the Count, but distributed over several sections.

Two other new stanzas (33-34) provided as rich an addition to the poem as did the satire of Botherby. These also deal with character by developing qualities of Laura's Count that are not present in the matrix. The first bestows on him accomplishments that make him not only the formidable critic he is in the matrix, but an active dilettante of the arts, an *improvisatore* himself, a singer, a storyteller, a seller of pictures, and a dancer. The new couplet of stanza 33 furnishes the climax of this part of the characterization by deflating the dilettante: "to his very valet [he] seem'd a hero." The other new stanza dwells upon the Count's second major merit—his perfection as a faithful lover.

Stanza 28, on the pathetic parting of Laura and Beppo, exploits a matrix situation for a new irony about human experience and makes out of this one domestic separation a satire of all sentimental and insincere farewells. Stanzas 38 and 39 are a long parenthesis in the section on the institution of "Cavalier Servente." The first of these says little, but the second is another sharp stroke at a universal character type, the shy and awkward debutante, "All Giggle, Blush; half Pertness, and half Pout," warily dependent on Mama, and still smelling of "bread and butter." A weaker new pair of stanzas, 45 and 46, was inserted into the section that praises Italy and disparages England. The first of these expands his tribute by commenting on the physical beauty and emotional transparence of Italian women. The second admires Raphael and Canova as artists who have given a superlative expression of Italian beauty. The three remaining additions are whimsical afterthoughts, the least significant of the fifteen. Two (52, 64) are inevitable autobiographical intrusions, one jesting about his *Beppo* style, the other, in serio-comic vein, explaining that he goes to the Ridotto out of boredom and finds some amusement in guessing at faces behind the masks. Both of these frivolous stanzas, however, are completely in tone with the rest of the poem and wholly representative of both its substance and its manner. Stanza 80, the only addition that is loosely attached to its context, is a good example of the curious and clever amalgam of materials that one finds in *Beppo* and that is one of its most attractive qualities. It humorously affects a nostalgia for the innocence of the golden age, seriously rebukes the degenerate present, and then laughs at the equivocal position of one who may long for "old Saturn's reign of sugar-candy!" but who meanwhile drinks to its return "in brandy."

The fifteen stanzas that Byron added at various times to his first draft are an epitome of his inveterate literary habits and of the ever-present personal and social stimuli that account for the composition of *Beppo*: (1) the autobiographical urge and preoccupation that is here expressed not soberly but either flippantly or ironically; (2) the mockery and ridicule of social and psychological folly, realized most dramatically by concrete vignettes of general character types and by particular situations;

(3) the literary use and abuse of a loosely associational coherence that is one of the special marks of the *Beppo* style and that permitted digression within digression, sometimes neatly dovetailed by verbal or suggestive transition, and sometimes just thrust in with peremptory and humorous disregard for continuity. A study of the MS additions thus affords an intimate view of the creative forces that operated in the making of the whole poem.

An examination of the Pierpont Morgan MS also reveals much about Byron's artistic principles in those small details of composition that count heavily in the overall stylistic effect that he was experimenting with in *Beppo*. Though its conversational verse today seems casual and effortless, much lighter and more graceful than most of *Don Juan* or "The Vision of Judgment," Byron expended on it a great deal of revision, most of it done at the moment of composition. The quantity of this MS revision can be quickly tabulated:

1) Number of lines completely crossed out and rewritten: 42
2) Number of fragments or "false starts" of a line deleted: 83
3) Number of verbal and phrasal substitutions: 235
4) Number of changes made at a later stage of composition, either on the fair copy or on proof sheets[9]: 57
5) Total number of major revisions[10]: 417
6) Number of lines changed at least once: 296 (about 40% of all lines on the MS)
7) Number of stanzas in which 4 or more lines were revised: 35 (about 37% of all MS stanzas)

The most notable fact about the distribution of the changes among the eight lines of his stanza is that line 7 received almost a fourth of all the revision (97 alterations out of 417). Such concentration is emphatic evidence of the care Byron gave to the important climactic value of the couplet ending of his new stanzaic form. The remaining changes were rather evenly scattered among the other lines, with line 6 receiving more than the rest (61).

[9] These were easily ascertained by comparing the text of the Pierpont Morgan MS with the first edition. A word or phrase that appears on the MS but not in the first edition must have been altered during a later period of revision. Since Byron made his own fair copy and since he explicitly forbade his publisher to make any changes, we can reasonably conclude that Byron made these 57 substitutions himself. I have not had access to the fair copy, which was advertised for sale in February, 1951. It was then the property of Lord Lovelace. My colleague, Mr. W. W. Pratt, reports that a letter of advertisement noted that there were only about fifty revisions and that four stanzas were omitted. The letter was obviously too enthusiastic in claiming that this fair copy was the only complete and original draft.

[10] I have not included in this count 88 minor changes of pronouns, tense of verbs, conjunctions, prepositions, etc.

The quality of Byron's revision is just as surprising as its quantity,[11] for one would scarcely expect that the easy-flowing verse and diction of *Beppo* was the result of much deliberate thought. The MS shows, however, that he was consciously and consistently following certain stylistic principles. The small amount of physical action in *Beppo* required a compensating energy in diction if the verse was to have the animation that he usually liked in his writing. He was therefore alert in revision that made his verbs more active and his physical detail more energetically concrete. There must be movement in the material even though there was but a tiny narrative. Hence people first [go to], then [like], and finally *flock to* see a melodrame.[12] He kept his restless eye on those verbs that denote action that can be visualized in a particular scene. Italian beauties *lean over* a balcony instead of passively [gazing out of] it, and Laura's Count was not merely [waiting ready] with her shawl but *at her elbow* with it.[13] These are small touches, but dozens of them make the difference between sluggish movement and lively activity in line after line. Consistent with such dramatic revision was his preference for more vigorous verbs. Napoleon was not just [stopped] by the Northern Thor but *crushed* by him. Byron substituted *flashing* for [sparkling], *stare* for [gaze] at the stars, *shone* for [looked], and, twice, the more emphatic *love* for [like]. Gentle liquids do not vaguely [come] but actively *glide* "all so

---

[11] Coleridge in his edition of *The Works of Byron, Poetry*, IV, 159-189 printed only six MS readings: the deleted couplet of stanza 30; three other rejected lines, stanza 45, ll. 2, 8, stanza 60, l. 4, stanza 87, l. 7, and the MS spelling of one word, "philoguny," which Byron capitalized on *PM* (stanza 70, l. 3). The several discrepancies between his readings and the *PM* lead me to believe that he saw only Byron's fair copy and not his first draft. For the differences in the couplet of stanza 30, see page 76 and note 20 of this essay. For line 4 of stanza 60, he gave the following version: "Of Imited [*sic*] Imitations, how soon—how." The *PM* MS has "Of imited Imitators, [how] soon—how." Byron first wrote "Imitations" and then wrote "ors" over "ions." The "imited" is clearly not capitalized and there is a dash, not a question mark, after "soon." Furthermore Byron on the *PM* MS in the next line went on to write "[Soon—Lamentably] soon decline alas!" for which he substituted "*Irreparably* soon decline alas!" If Coleridge had consulted the first draft, it is odd that he would record Byron's trifling misspelling of "imitated" and ignore the more significant change from "Lamentably" to "Irreparably" in the very next line. Finally, in line 8 of stanza 45 the *PM* MS has "Like her own Clime—all Sun—& [fruit] bloom—& skies." Coleridge's MS version differs both in his omission of the deleted "fruit" and in the ampersand, punctuation, and capitalization: "Like her own clime, all sun, and bloom, and skies." Since this later deleted version (with all the nouns capitalized) appeared on photographs of three pages of the fair copy that were included in the advertisement mentioned in note 9, it seems obvious that the fair copy was the only MS that Coleridge used in his edition. Recall also that Coleridge did not note the omission of stanza 64 from the *PM* MS.

[12] LXI, 6. The brackets enclose deleted or rejected words and lines; italics show the final version.

[13] XI, 7; LXXV, 5.

pat in," and no exhibition weekly [shows] but boldly *glares* "with annual pictures." [14]

Byron in a letter to Murray (April 11, 1818) demonstrated his concern for vigorous phrasing when he suggested a variant for line 6 of stanza 74 in the added Botherby passage. His MS shows the following evolution of line 6 in his second and entirely recast version of the stanza:

[And quoting compliments—each word a L] (intended to write "Law")
Gorging the little that he gets—all raw—

Later he wrote a revision: "Gorging the little fame he gets all raw." Then in the letter written after the publication of *Beppo,* he suggested "Gorging the slightest slice of Flattery raw." His reason for the last revision was that he had used *fame* as a rhyme in the preceding stanza, but he was still not sure that his latest version did not sacrifice vigor just to avoid a repetition, and he was willing to tolerate repetition to keep the phrasing strong.

Perhaps the line is now a little weakened, because "all raw" expresses the Cormorant Cameleon's avidity for air, or inflation of his vicious vanity; but—ask Mr. Gifford, and Mr. Hobhouse, and, as they think, so let it be, for, though repetition is only the "soul of Ballad singing," and best avoided in describing the Harlequin jacket of a Mountebank, yet anything is better than weakening an expression, or a thought.[15]

This letter offers one of the few occasions when Byron, by self-criticism and by detailed explication of one of his own images, showed us how carefully he calculated the force and connotation of his diction, even in "The devil a bit of / Our Beppo."

Byron's well-known scruple about factual accuracy accounted for his insistence on phrasing that was precisely appropriate for his subject. Laura, Beppo, and the Count thus [rowed] [glided] *floated* in their gondola "o'er the silent tide." Beppo, who did not like the thought of [coming] *steering* home, later [found] *hired* a vessel "come from Spain." [16] In the following line, Byron's grasp on the value of physical precision reached for the flimsy but quite tangible cloth of the thinly clad girl:

A seventh's [so thinly clad—'twill sure] be *her* bane—
A seventh's thin Muslin surely will be *her* bane. (LXVI, 6.)

[14] LXI, 1; XLVI, 6; XXIII, 7; XLI, 3; XLIV, 1; XLIV, 5; LXXVIII, 6, 7.
[15] *Letters and Journals,* IV, 218.
[16] LXXXVII, 2; XXVII, 4; XCV, 6.

Byron's habit of converging narrowly on the more specific word also brought a gain in connotation and rhythmic and harmonious fluency:

> [Laughing] *Giggling* with all the Gallants (II, 6)
> the [less light she leaves] the better
> *the more duskily the better* (II, 2)
> The name of this [fair she—I shall] not mention
>   *Aurora I'll* not mention (LXXXIV, 1)

Even where his revision worked with more general words, he strove for phrasing that is both more exact and more agreeable to the ear:

> For fear [in some false note he'd find a] flaw
>   of *some false note's detected* flaw (XXXII, 4)
> All [the arts of foolery]—and dress
> All *kinds of buffoonery* and dress (XXI, 4)
> A woman of the [soundest] principle
>   *strictest* principle (XXVI, 7)
> [snobbish] set—*vulgar* set (LIX, 4)
> [Orchards] *vineyards* copied from the south of France (XLI, 8)
> she [saw] the ship with [greater] ease
> she *could discern* the ship with ease (XXV, 6)

The few changes that are less vigorous, less specific, either in sense or expression, than his first version were made in the interests of discreet propriety and showed an uncommon restraint. A rough allusion to the cloudy windiness of Coleridge gradually became less pointed, a bold parody of the Anglican litany vanished altogether, and some slurs at women were politely softened:

> [No Coleridge metaphysically lectures]
> [No mad Metaphysician] [da] [weekly lectures] (intended to write "daily")
> [No madman metaphysically] lectures
> *No Metaphysics are let loose in* lectures (LXXVIII, 2)
> [From—Good Lord deliver us]
> But—[God preserve]—Old England
> *But Heaven preserve* Old England (XXXVII, 7)
> Why [harlots, but I will not now] discuss
>   *naughty women—but I won't* discuss (LXVIII, 2)
> Those brazen [women suit their horse-like] taste
> Those brazen *creatures always suit their* taste (LXVII, 8)

Perhaps the greatest improvement was the addition of substance to lines that were originally thin. *Beppo* is an intentionally light and play-

ful poem, but still Byron tried to give some ballast to its volatility. "That
very beautiful invention] / A charming woman," becomes "that *patent
work of God's invention.*" The [young men] who kept filing [In long
array] before Laura were refashioned into *well-drest males* who filed by
and *passing bowed.*[17] In the following lines, note how Byron both increased the content, by adding to a series already begun, and at the same
time neatly adjusted his structural and rhythmical balance. Turkish
women

> Were never [known to study for a witticism]
>   *caught in epigram or witticism*
> [Nor yet have been enlightened by] reviews
> *Have no romances—sermons—plays—*reviews (LXXII, 3-4)
> They lock them up—& veil [them—& so forth]
>   *& guard them daily* (LXXI, 1)
> [He calls] [Her coach—a gondola]
> [Her coach—a gondola] he goes to call
> *Coach—servants—Gondola—*he goes to call.[18]

New substance is most effective when the revision carries with it
derogatory connotation or satiric bite. [Men] of paper were slashed into
shreds of paper, and the almost respectful [Mister Botherby] was tagged
and scornfully diminished to [bardling Botherby] and then multiplied
into an active infestation—*bustling Botherbys.* When stiff *prudery* instead of pleasant [fun] "flings aside her fetter" in the carnival, Byron
scored one of his main ironies about the conduct of people in that uninhibited season.[19]

The most thorough revision occurred when Byron abruptly changed
the entire meaning or emphasis of a line. In the following passage he
substituted personal experience—a reminder of his self-exile in 1816—
for a simple quotation from Cowper and then, contrary to his usual
practice, gave up some specific material (the names of two definite places)
for a colloquial expression of his literary independence and for a chance
to use a word that was to become a favorite of his in *Juan* ("lucubrate"):

> "England with all thy faults I love thee still"
> [So Cowper says—and I] have not forgot it,

[17] LXXXIV, 3; LXIX, 5-6.
[18] XL, 7. A curious substitution in the concluding line of this couplet may have only
a rhythmical motive:
>   And carries fan—[& lapdog]—gloves—and shawl
>   and tippet . . .
Perhaps Byron's favorite MS imp, "Printer's devil," jogged his memory with a query:
"Do English or Venetian ladies carry such animals?"
[19] LXXV, 7; LXXII, 7; II, 4.

> *I said at Calais and* have not forgot it.
> I like [St. Paul's Churchyard—and Ludgate hill]
> *I like to speak and lucubrate my fill.* (XLVII, 1-3)

As the statistics about the quantity of revision implied, some of his most telling changes to completely new ideas occurred in the couplets of his ottava rima stanzas. A few samples will have to suffice to show how the introduction of new ideas or subtle variations in diction gave him his climaxes:

1)   A Count of wealth [unequal to his] quality
      [Which rather limited his] liberality—
      A Count of wealth *they said—as well as* quality
      And (in his pleasures) of great liberality— (XXX, 7-8)

(Byron reversed his view of the Count completely and kept the cavalier pocket full in order to characterize his life of pleasure with a witty play on "liberality.")[20]

2)   [For people like]
           [eager people]
      [When the Mind's opinions much engage her
      Most people like to back them with a wager]
      For most people till by losing rendered sager
      Will back their own opinions with a wager. (XXVII, 7-8)

(The mockery of human vanity was increased by the new idea that men become humble only after embarrassing losses.)

3)   I'd preach [a sermon on this subject weekly]
                 on this till Wilberforce and Romilly
      Should [praise the moral of my weekly homily]
                 [quote to Senates from my weekly homily] [21]
                 quote in their next speeches from my homily. (LXVIII, 7-8)

(The revision made the couplet topically vital by citing two contemporary notables who first praise and then prove their regard for Byron's

---

[20] This is the couplet for which Coleridge gave a MS reading somewhat different from that on *PM:*

> A count of wealth inferior to his quality
> Which somewhat limited his liberality.

Since it is hardly possible that he could have so misread the *PM* first draft, he must have been quoting the fair copy.

[21] There is a short intermediate stage, but the single word after "quote" I find illegible.

homily by publicly quoting from him. The couplet thus rises to high, self-conscious, dramatic farce.)

4)   [and wert thou Antony may boast]
      [This World is every winter won and lost]
           how easily "the World" is lost—
      By love—or war—[imprudence or]
           and [in one case]—*by frost.*
           now and then—by frost. (LX, 7-8)

(Antony is soon ditched without regret as Byron worked out his collapse of "the World" by mighty agencies, until he came to the bathetic understatement of that catastrophic trifle—frost.)

5)   [But I must do the best I can—Heaven knows
      How ill—but I am in for 't—so here goes.]
      And [mingled] with [modern] Sentimentalism
      [Give] samples of the "finest Orientalism."
      And [give] *you mix'd with western Sentimentalism*
        sell
      Some samples of the "finest Orientalism." (LI, 7-8)

(Byron at first ran off one of his chatting octave endings before he thought of a quip at his own (and others') prosperous exploitation of Eastern claptrap. He used part of his rejected couplet in the next stanza.)

Since one of Byron's aims in *Beppo* was colloquial and humorous facility, a few revisions clearly have that purpose in mind:

    I've half a mind to [try my hand] in prose
          tumble down in prose (LII, 7)
    Several oaths which [do not suit] the Muse
          [ill become] the Muse
          would not suit the Muse (VII, 6)
    His name Giuseppe—called [for shortness]—Beppo
          more briefly—Beppo (XXV, 8)
    [I can't think on / A] place
    I can hit on No place (V, 6-7)

One sign of the freedom with which Byron revised while writing his first draft is the number of rhyme alterations. There were fifty-six in all. Twenty-nine were complete changes to a different rhyme sound, confined to the first and last two lines of his octave, where such revision did not require that a whole stanza be recast. Twenty-seven were substitutions of different words within the original rhyme scheme, and eighteen of these were made in the middle lines (3, 4, 5, 6). Since illustration of such flexible rhyme manipulation has already been given in the discussion of other forms of revision, three instances will adequately illustrate the process. One couplet revision shows us that Byron at first wanted Laura's name to be Rosanna, but this obviously did not slip into his verse as easily as he had hoped:

> And so we'll call her [if you please Rosanna / A name]
>   *Laura if* [ye] *you please*
> Because it slips into my verse with ease. (XXI, 7)
> Sunburnt with travel, [both by land and wave]
>   *yet a portly figure* (XXVI, 2)

In spurning a rhyme that he did not want to sustain through the rest of the stanza, Byron also managed to give Beppo another physical characteristic in place of the rather pointless padding about his sunburn.

> [well—the bark did skim]
> *well—the ship was trim* (XCVI, 6)

This simple shift, that keeps the rhyme scheme already set for the stanza, is typical of his expertness in finding a phrase, within rather narrow limitations, that is less awkward in sense and sound than his initial attempt.

No survey of Byron's methods and principles of composition would be complete that did not stress the care that he took with the sound of his verse. He has never been acclaimed as a graceful writer nor as a singer of limpid and musical verse. Yet *Beppo* reads aloud with more consistent fluency and grace of expression than most of Byron's work. Many MS revisions show that he was, after all, a poet with an alert ear for the sound of his phrasing, and that he often strove for aural attractiveness, partly because he knew that alliteration, assonance, and consonance were an auxiliary of sense:

> [reign of Dandies]
> *dynasty of Dandies,* (LX, 2)
> [our smoky chimnies]—and our chilly women
> *our cloudy climate*—and our chilly women (XLIX, 5)
> [And then are songs, & tinklings of]
>   [Guitars]
> *And there are songs—and* [quavering]—*roaring—humming,*
>   *quavers* (II, 7)

for such a wife [no man here] bothers
for such a wife *no mortal* bothers (XVIII, 7)

He even gave up a substantial image about coffee in order to get a
thinner, simpler, colloquial line that runs more rapidly and smoothly:

[That sable fountain which matured by flame]
Although the way they make it's not the same (XCI, 3)

Just as common were the revisions that were controlled by his rhythmic
pulse. Unless the material or the emotion had a special need for a halting, rugged phrase, he again and again rearranged the order of words
until the metrical flow satisfied him, even in lines that are not notable
for their content and where the rhythmic difference between the two
versions was indeed slight. Generally when he altered the order of words,
his ear caught the natural rhythm of ordinary speech:

But stories [lengthen somehow] when begun
        somehow lengthen (XCIX, 8)
And bid [her faithful heart once more] rejoice
        once more her faithful heart rejoice (XXX, 4)
No [antique solemn] Gentleman of rhyme
        solemn antique (LXXIII, 1)
[And whatever may be their rank and] station
However [high or low their rank and] station
        high their rank, or low their station (I, 6)

Once in a while the clumsiness of the first version is almost unbe-
lievable, but a few simple alterations got rid of the congestion:

                                what without our youth—
[Is] [Were Love worth?] [or] [what were youth worth without love?]
Would love be? what would youth be—without love? (LV, 1-2)

A double substitution in one phrase gave it more imaginative distinction as well as more agreeable harmony with an internal rhyme:

                and [light] the fires
                        stir the fires
[Of Hell with souls of] every mother's son
Of Phelegthon with every mother's son (IV, 5-6)

Occasionally he had to try several times to fit even a parenthesis into a rhythmic pattern.

> And [grapes, instead of walls—upon their tree]
>   [not twined]
>   [transferred]
> *And vines (not nailed to walls) from tree to tree* (XLI, 4)

It would be a valuable and illuminating experience for Byron students were his MSS published in a complete edition, but because of the prohibitive cost of such an enterprise I doubt that our generation will see in print the whole first draft of *Beppo*. Within the confines of this article I have been able to select only a small number of representative readings. Taken as they are from widely separated lines, in order to illustrate certain principles of Byron's composition, they do not exhaust the resources of the MS, nor do they give a realistic view of the writing process as it went on from stanza to stanza. I should like, therefore, in closing, to reproduce from the MS three entire stanzas, unencumbered by analytical comment. In them one can observe in operation and in their natural continuity the impulses and deliberate methods that we have been methodically pacing over. These few stanzas should demonstrate the care that Byron took with the experiment of *Beppo* and make clear one reason why he was successful with a medium that belied the artistic effort and skill that went into its composition.[22]

XLII

1 a [And when on] Autumn evenings [I] ride [forth]
  b *I like on Autumn evenings to ride out—*
2 a [Pricking my steed]
  b *Without being forced to* [tell] *my Groom be sure*
  c   *bid*
3 a My [Great-coat round his middle's] strapped about;—
  b *My cloak is round his middle strapped about;—*
4 a [And when narrow Green lane's shall allure]
  b *Because the* [rain] *skies are not the most secure—*
5 a [And when some wagon stops me on my route]
  b [And] [some] [that] [if some stoppage may impede my route]
  c *I know too that if stopped upon my route*

---

[22] In these transcriptions, as before, brackets enclose actual MS deletions and also rejections (i.e., material that he allowed to stand on the first draft but for which he made a revision at a later stage). Italics indicate the final published version. In order to make it easier for a reader to follow the composition, I have lettered the steps and I have repeated some words that Byron did not write out but that he intended to carry down from one version to another.

6 a [In the narrow Green lane]
   b *Where the Green alleys windingly allure—*
7 a [Tis full & almost (?)] [choaked with purple grapes]
   b [Tis] [Tis full of gushing grapes that bar the]
   c [A waggon full of Grapes will bar my way]
   d [Waggons of red grapes cause the xxxx delay]
   e   [only stop the way]
   f   [bar the way]
   g *Reeling with grapes red waggons choke the way,—*
8 a *In England* [would a dung cart bar the way]
   b   [a Dung Cart bars your way]
   c   *twould be dung, dust or a Dray.*

XLV

1 a *I like* [tall (?)] *the women too—*[God help my frailty]
   b   *forgive my folly,*
2 a *From the* [tall peasant with her] *ruddy bronze*
         rich peasant-cheek of ruddy bronze,
3 a *And* [like] *large black eyes that* [dart] *on you a volley*
   b   *flash*
4 a *Of* [beams] *that say a thousand things at once—*
   b   *rays*
5 a *To the* [fair] *Dama's* [glance] *more melancholy*
   b   *high*   *brow*
6 a [And fair] *& with a wild & liquid glance,*
   b [Yet] *clear*
   c *But*
7 a *Heart on her lips and* [soul] *soul within her eyes*
8 a [Like her own Clime—all Sun & fruit—& skies]
   b   [bloom]
   c *Soft as her Clime, and Sunny as her skies.*

LXXIV

1 a [Dealer in sentences—and awful phrase]
   b *A stalking Oracle of awful phrase—*
2   *The approving "Good" (by no means Good in law)*
3 a [Perplexing]
   b [Excruciating with his blundered praise]
   c [Teazing with blame—Excruciating with praise]
   d *Humming like flies around the newest blaze*
4 a [And quoting Compliments]—[each] [each a Law]
   b   [all]   [each word a Law]
   c *The bluest of Bluebottles you e'er saw—*
5 a [Humming like flies around the newest blaze]

   b   *Teasing with blame,—excruciating with praise,*

6 a   [The hugest of Bluebottles you ever saw]

   b   [bluest of Bluebottles you eer saw]

   c   [And quoting compliments—each word a L] (intended to write "Law")

   d   *Gorging the little* [that] *he gets—all raw*—[23]

   e   *fame*

7 a   [Poet—Translator—Critic]

   b   *Translating tongues he knows not even by letter—*

8 a   *And* [writing] *plays—so middling—Bad were better*[24]

   b   *sweating*

---

[23] For another version of this line sent by letter see page 73.

[24] To save space I have given a composite transcription of this stanza which was completely crossed out at first. Since in the second writing Byron retained lines 1 and 2, I have not indicated that 1 b and 2 were deleted and recopied. Note that in rewriting he interchanged the positions of his first version of lines 3 and 5, 4 and 6, and then wrote a new version for line 6.

Byron's Satire

by F. R. Leavis

> Such is the force of wit! but not belong
> To me the arrows of satiric song;
>
> . . . . .
>
> Shall gentle Coleridge pass unnoticed here?
> To turgid ode and tumid stanza dear?
> Though themes of innocence amuse him best,
> Yet still obscurity's a welcome guest.
> If Inspiration should her aid refuse
> To him who takes a pixy for a muse,
> Yet none in lofty numbers can surpass
> The bard who soars to elegise an ass.
> So well the subject suits his noble mind,
> He brays the laureat of the long-ear'd kind.

Byron's incapacity for Augustan satire could be properly suggested only in much longer quotations. It is made the more apparent by his local approximations to the wit of Pope (and sometimes of Dryden). For success in an Augustan mode there would have to be an easy sureness of diction and tone, a neat precision and poise of movement and gesture, an elegant constancy of point and an even decorum: none of these things can Byron command. His triumph in *The Vision of Judgment* (and an account of that poem applies in obvious respects to *Don Juan*) depends upon his having found a way of dispensing with these virtues.

> He's dead—and upper earth with him has done;
> He's buried; save the undertaker's bill,
> Or lapidary scrawl, the world is gone
> For him, unless he left a German will:

"Byron's Satire." From *Revaluation* (New York: W. W. Norton & Company; London: Chatto & Windus, 1936) by F. R. Leavis, pp. 148-153. Copyright 1947 by George W. Stewart, Publisher; copyright 1932 by Chatto & Windus. First published in the Norton Library 1963. Reprinted by permission of the author, W. W. Norton & Company, and Chatto & Windus.

But where's the proctor who will ask his son?
    In whom his qualities are reigning still,
Except that household virtue, most uncommon,
    Of constancy to a bad, ugly woman.

"God save the king!" It is a large economy
    In God to save the like; but if he will
Be saving, all the better; for not one am I
    Of those who think damnation better still:
I hardly know too if not quite alone am I
    In this small hope of bettering future ill
By circumscribing, with some slight restriction,
The eternity of hell's hot jurisdiction.

I know this is unpopular; I know
    'Tis blasphemous; I know one may be damn'd
For hoping no one else may e'er be so;
    I know my catechism; I know we're cramm'd
With the best doctrines till we quite o'erflow;
    I know that all save England's church have shamm'd,
And that the other twice two hundred churches
And synagogues have made a *damn'd* bad purchase.

If we started by noting that Byron here might at least be said to have
in common with Pope the use of spoken idiom and the speaking voice,
it would only be to note at the same time the radical differences in the
use, the voice, and the idiom. Byron speaks as a man of the world and
a gentleman, but not only is he not polite, the very essence of his manner is a contemptuous defiance of decorum and propriety. Irreverence
about religion is something we cannot imagine in Pope, and when he is
ironical about the House of Hanover, it is with perfect decorum:

Wife, son, and daughter, Satan! are thy own,
His wealth, yet dearer, forfeit to the Crown:
The Devil and the King divide the prize,
And sad Sir Balaam curses God and dies.

Where Pope is insolent and improper, the effect depends upon a complete and formal urbanity and perfect manners:

'Tis strange, the Miser should his Cares employ
To gain those Riches he can ne'er enjoy:
Is it less strange, the Prodigal should waste
His wealth, to purchase what he ne'er can taste?

Not for himself he sees, or hears, or eats;
Artists must choose his Pictures, Music, Meats:
He buys for Topham, Drawings and Designs,
For Pembroke, Statues, dirty Gods, and Coins;
Rare monkish Manuscripts for Hearne alone,
And Books for Mead and Butterflies for Sloane.
Think we all these are for himself? no more
Than his fine Wife, alas! or finer Whore.

The impudent, high-spirited recklessness of the Byronic irreverence—

"God save the king!" It is a large economy
In God to save the like

—is given in that rime to "economy." Between Byron and Pope come
Voltaire and Rousseau and the French Revolution, and Byron the satirist
has less affinity with Pope than with Burns: the positive to which he appeals in the stanzas quoted is a generous common humanity, something
that is indifferent to forms, conventions, and classes, though in Byron's
recklessness there is something of the aristocrat. His generosity is a cynical man-of-the-world good humor, and his irreverence moves towards a
burlesque comedy that, in its high spirits, is sometimes schoolboy:[1]

"No," quoth the cherub; "George the Third is dead."
  "And who is George the Third?" replied the apostle:
"What George? what Third?" "The king of England," said
  The angel. "Well! he won't find kings to jostle
Him on his way; but does he wear his head?
  Because the last we saw here had a tustle,
And ne'er would have got into heaven's good graces,
Had he not flung his head in all our faces.

He was, if I remember, king of France;
  That head of his, which could not keep a crown
On earth, yet ventured in my face to advance
  A claim to those of martyrs—like my own:

---

[1] "However, I knew what to think of it,
    When I beheld you in your jesting way,
  Flitting and whispering round about the spit
    Where Belial, upon duty for the day,
  With Fox's lard was basting William Pitt,
    His pupil; I knew what to think, I say:
  That fellow even in hell breeds farther ills;
    I'll have him *gagg'd*—'twas one of his own bills."

> If I had had my sword, as I had once
>   When I cut ears off, I had cut him down;
> But having but my *keys,* and not my brand,
> I only knock'd his head from out his hand."

The range of Byron's variety and flexibility (which unlike Pope's observe no keeping and relate to no stylization or impersonal code—the
unity is our sense of Byron's individuality) is not yet suggested. In a satire
that gets its characteristic effects by use of the irreverent-familiar we
find this:

> He and the sombre, silent Spirit met—
>   They knew each other both for good and ill;
> Such was their power, that neither could forget
>   His former friend and future foe; but still
> There was a high, immortal, proud regret
>   In either's eye, as if 'twere less their will
> Than destiny to make the eternal years
> Their date of war, and their "champ clos" the spheres.

This meeting between Michael and Satan is in the Romantic-heroic and
might have come from one of Byron's completely solemn poems: diction
and tone contrast oddly with the familiar-speech manner of the stanzas
quoted earlier. The noble attitude is offered seriously—not for deflation,
but simply, as something we shall be impressed by. Here again, then, we
have a positive, and it is Romantic. The transition to the man-of-the-
world cynical is got in this way:

> And therefore Michael and the other wore
>   A civil aspect: though they did not kiss,
> Yet still between his Darkness and his Brightness
> There pass'd a mutual glance of great politeness.

"They are great gentlemen"—the Romantic poet is a Regency milord:
the Romantic heroes become eighteenth century aristocrats. And the
milord—gentleman and sportsman—slips easily from his Romantic-aristo-
cratic high decorum to a positive that sorts with the irreverently familiar:

> "He is what you behold him, and his doom
> Depends upon his deeds," the Angel said;
> "If you have aught to arraign in him, the tomb
> Gives licence to the humblest beggar's head
> To lift itself against the loftiest." "Some,"
>   Said Wilkes, "don't wait to see them laid in lead,

> For such a liberty—and I, for one,
> Have told them what I thought beneath the sun."
>
> "*Above* the sun repeat, then, what thou hast
>   To urge against him," said the Archangel. "Why,"
> Replied the spirit, "since old scores are past,
>   Must I turn evidence? In faith, not I.
> Besides, I beat him hollow at the last,
>   With all his Lords and Commons: in the sky
> I don't like ripping up old stories, since
> His conduct was but natural in a prince."

—"Wilkes was a gentleman and a sportsman," and his cynical man-of-the-world tolerance supplies the criteria by which George III and Southey's sycophantic extravagance are placed.

It is not for nothing, then, that the poet who ends the line of great satirists that started with Dryden belongs to the Regency, in which the eighteenth century ends. The eighteenth century element in him is essential to his success, and yet has at the same time the effect of bringing out how completely the Augustan order has disintegrated.

Byron as Improviser

by W. W. Robson

It is not from his admiration for Burns, nor even from his interest in
the Italian poets, that Byron's comic poetry derives its inspiration and
sanction; but from the use of resources in Byron himself, which he had
not previously exploited in poetry. The Byron of the letters and journals
of the world in which he was worried and was bored, and sneered and
gossiped, comes into the verse; to provide the standards by which Wordsworth or Wilberforce, George IV or the Duke of Wellington, are judged.
In the *Vision of Judgment* it is the demeanor of Wilkes, besides that of
Junius ("I loved my country, and I hated him"), that attracts Byron,
while in *Beppo* the viewpoint is that of the amused and amusing cosmopolitan Englishman, observing Venetian sexual *mores,* with their
matter-of-factness and good sense. The extension of range appears poetically as that ability to modulate, or to pass from key to key without
modulation, which constantly appears in the letters; here, for example, is
the conclusion of a letter to Moore (Venice, 19 Sept. 1818).

I wish you good-night, with a Venetian benediction, *Benedetto te, e la
terra che farà!* "May you be blessed, and the earth which you will *make!"—*
is it not pretty? You would think it prettier still, if you had heard it, as
I did two hours ago, from the lips of a Venetian girl, with large black eyes,
a face like Faustina's, and the figure of a Juno—tall and energetic as a
Pythoness, with eyes flashing, and her dark hair streaming in the moonlight
—one of those women who may be made anything. I am sure that if I put a
poniard into the hand of this one, she would plunge it where I told her—
and into *me,* if I offended her. I like this kind of animal, and am sure that I
should have preferred Medea to any woman that ever breathed. You may,
perhaps, wonder that I don't in that case . . . I could have forgiven the
dagger and the bowl,—any thing, but the deliberate desolation piled upon
me, when I stood alone upon my hearth, with my household gods shivered
around me. Do you suppose I have forgotten it? It has comparatively swal-
lowed up in me every other feeling, and I am only a spectator upon earth,

"Byron as Improviser." From *Proceedings of the British Academy,* 1957: Chatterton
Lecture, "Byron as Poet," by W. W. Robson, pp. 49-56. Copyright © 1958 by the British
Academy. Reprinted and abridged by permission of the author and the British
Academy.

till a tenfold opportunity offers. It may come yet. There are more to be blamed than   , and it is on these that my eyes are fixed unceasingly.

Here the accent of the final sentences strikes us, not as a sudden reversal of feeling, but as the disentangling of a feeling that is already a constituent of the half-humorous, half-Romantic description of the Venetian girl. A finer example is what follows an impassioned defense of Sheridan's character, as a type of the gentleman-adventurer of genius; when there emerges, in a beautiful way, the general sense of life, at once melancholy and admiring, which gives depth to it.

Were his [Sheridan's] intrigues more notorious than those of all his contemporaries? and is his memory to be blasted, and theirs respected? Don't let yourself be led away by clamour, but compare him with the coalitioner Fox, and the pensioner Burke, as man of principle, and with none in talent, for he beat them all *out* and *out*. Without means, without connexion, without character (which might be false at first, and make him mad afterwards in desperation), he beat them all, in all he ever attempted. But alas, poor human nature! Good-night, or rather, morning. It is four, and the dawn gleams over the Grand Canal, and unshadows the Rialto. I must to bed; up all night—but, as George Philpot says, "it's life, though, damme it's life!"

It is a way of life that Byron is defending here, and the reference to it is one of the positive criteria of judgment in *Don Juan*. The other, of course, is Byron's Romanticism; the Romantic self which Byron had not so much outgrown, as come to see for one acting-part among others. And the success of *Don Juan* is mainly a matter of Byron's success in effecting a positive relation between the two. The poem is a triumph of personality.

The relation between the Romantic-tragic and the sophisticated-cynical appears in a simple form in the story of Juan's father. This is the conclusion:

> It was a trying moment that which found him
> Standing alone beside his desolate hearth,
> Where all his household gods lay shiver'd round him;
> No choice was left his feelings or his pride,
> But death or Doctors' Commons—so he died.

The predominant effect is of the Byronic obsession; Byron is still mowing the aftermath of the Separation Drama. But the effect is of course qualified by the manner of its introduction ("It was a trying moment . . ."), which invites the attitude of ironic detachment; and the astringent terseness of the last couplet is reminiscent of George Crabbe, whose poetry

Byron admired. This manner of dealing with his troubles is obvious; but often, especially in the digressive passages, the effect is more complex. Consider the celebrated outburst towards the end of Canto I. Here Byron has been alluding to the adverse reception he expects to get, as a "dissenting author," from the *Edinburgh* and *Quarterly,* and quoting Horace (*Non ego hoc ferrem calida juventa Consule Planco*) adds that in his "hot youth" he "would not have brooked at all this sort of thing," "being most ready to return a blow." Now we see Byron's way of picking up a theme for extensive development; the interest of such passages is partly that we do not know *which* element will be picked up. "Hot youth," in its Horatian context, here becomes the theme, and is developed, at first with a little irony:

> But now at thirty years my hair is gray—
> (I wonder what it will be like at forty?
> I thought of a peruke the other day),
> My heart is not much greener; and in short, I
> Have squander'd my whole summer while 'twas May,
> And feel no more the spirit to retort; I
> Have spent my life, both interest and principal,
> And deem not, what I deem'd, my soul invincible.

We notice the offhand rhymes, "forty," "short, I," "retort; I." Then the irony vanishes, in a full-volumed Romanticism; as usual in *Don Juan,* the modulation is signalized by a change in the character of the rhymes, and the general sonority: the voice, though remaining a speaking voice, takes on an underlying singing tone:

> No more—no more—Oh! never more on me
> The freshness of the heart can fall like dew,
> Which out of all the lovely things we see
> Extracts emotions beautiful and new;
> Hived in our bosoms like the bag o' the bee.
> Think'st thou the honey with those objects grew?
> Alas! 'twas not in them, but in thy power
> To double even the sweetness of a flower.

It is Byron's equivalent to *Dejection: an Ode.* But the stanza just quoted is followed by a partial return of the common sense, the reasonable, the Augustan, emerging ruefully in a still predominantly Romantic context:

> No more—no more—Oh! never more, my heart,
> Canst thou be my sole world, my universe!
> Once all in all, but now a thing apart,

> Thou canst not be my blessing or my curse:
> The illusion's gone for ever, and thou art
> Insensible, I trust, but none the worse,
> And in thy stead I've got a deal of judgment,
> Though heaven knows how it ever found a lodgment.

"None the worse": the very un-sonorous rhyme of "judgment/lodgment"
gives the manner. This returning reasonableness takes on a color of light
irony:

> My days of love are over; me no more
> The charms of maid, wife, and still less of widow
> Can make the fool of which they did before—
> In short, I must not lead the life I did do;
> The credulous hope of mutual minds is o'er,
> The copious use of claret is forbid too;
> So, for a good old-gentlemanly vice,
> I think I must take up with avarice.

The Horatian regret (*nec spes animi mutua creduli*) appears as a foil to
middle-aged matter-of-factness; the stanza running out into flippancy.

The return to the general manner of the poem is effected in an interesting way. There is first a surprise turn: a blast on the trombone of *Childe
Harold:*

> Ambition was my idol, which was broken
> Before the shrines of Sorrow, and of Pleasure;

But this leads into four lines, neither ironic nor Romantic, though serious
enough:

> And the two last have left me many a token
> O'er which reflection may be made at leisure;
> Now, like Friar Bacon's brazen head, I've spoken,
> "Time is, Time was, Time's past":

and these serve as a bridge passage to the conclusion, or culmination:

> . . . a chymic treasure
> Is glittering youth, which I have spent betimes—
> My heart in passion, and my head on rhymes.

This culmination is Romantic in feeling; but the Romanticism is subtly qualified by the reversion to a completely Augustan manner, a Popean neatness:

> . . . glittering youth, which I have spent betimes—
> My heart in passion, and my head on rhymes.

The general nature of the effect is obvious without all this analysis, but analysis perhaps serves to bring out the peculiar significance, the dramatic force, of that closing couplet. The Romantic and the Augustan come together with an air of momentary reconciliation; nostalgia for lost youth, for the loss of the emotional spontaneity and power of empathy that belong to youth, is accommodated to a practical acceptance of reality; giving the effect of a resolution (*Aufhebung*) of the two contrasting attitudes on which the passage is built. This dialectic is the life of *Don Juan*.

It may be worth adding that neither the Romanticism, nor the irony, nor their coming from the same poet, is specifically Byronic. There is such a thing as Romantic irony, as in Heine or Musset. What *is* highly personal to Byron, is the temporary stabilization of conflicting emotions, in a manner which is neither Romantic nor ironical. There is no calculation, of course, in this effect, but in all the wayward progress of the verse there is an internal control which is lacking in other semi-serious poetry, W. H. Auden's for example; the poet knows what he is doing; at any given moment he knows just how serious, or how un-serious, he is.

In range and variety of emotional tone, as in other respects, *Don Juan* is the antithesis of *The Prelude*. One difficulty in reading the latter is Wordsworth's habit of moving placidly on from dull passages, or passages of fair to middling interest, to inspired passages, without break, transposition, or change of gear. In *Don Juan* Byron has solved for himself and his purposes, as Wordsworth in my opinion did not, the problem of the long poem. His solution is to come forward frankly as an improviser.

> I don't know that there may be much ability
> Shown in this sort of desultory rhyme;
> But there's a conversational facility,
> Which may round off an hour upon a time.
> Of this I'm sure at least, there's no servility
> In mine irregularity of chime,
> Which rings what's uppermost of new or hoary,
> Just as I feel the *Improvvisatore*.

One need not dwell on the dangers and temptations of the *Improvvisatore* in poetry. Perhaps his most tiresome characteristic is Byron's recurrent self-satisfaction that, without taking any pains, he is writing better poetry than his fellow poets who do. This makes him the victim of a technique, or lack of technique, which permits him not only to tolerate second-rateness but elaborate it with gusto.

> Who holds the balance of the world? Who reign
> O'er congress, whether royalist or liberal?
> Who rouse the shirtless patriots of Spain?

And in fact Byron is perpetually aware, unlike Wordsworth, or the Tennyson of *In Memoriam*, that he has a reader. Then, his sociable tone, his friendship with that reader, is founded on the tacit agreement that he too is a fellow sinner.

> They [the sailors] vow to amend their lives, and yet they don't;
> Because if drown'd they can't; if spared, they won't.

> And Malthus does the thing 'gainst which he writes.

We know what human nature is like, and have not too exalted a conception of it; since we ourselves are the examples that we know most intimately. The air of nonchalant familiarity, which finds its sanction in this fellow-feeling, is not un-Augustan; but it is nearer to Dryden than to Pope. And this is not the only way in which the Regency, as illustrated by Byron, reminds us of the Restoration. But Byron's true analogue in Restoration poetry is not Dryden but Rochester.

> Without, or with, offence to friends and foes,
> I sketch your world exactly as it goes.

"Without, *or with*" is the touch of recklessness typical of Byron; but it reminds us also of the isolated, anarchic flouting of society which we often find in Rochester, and never in Dryden. There are interesting social and political parallels, as well as personal and poetic ones, between these two rebellious patricians of different epochs; quite apart from their aristocratic anarchism and will to *épater le bourgeois,* there are likenesses between the Rochester seen by Bishop Burnet, and the Byron seen by Dr. Kennedy.

But this debonair freedom, and the ease with which Byron manages his transitions and expatiates at whatever length he pleases, and on whatever occasion, about anything which interests him—none of these vivacities convince us that the poet is always enjoying himself. He is not always letting himself go with such satisfaction as he shows in the flyting of Southey. His success in elevating drunken inconsequence to the status of art, is itself as much a product of the unhappy libertine's trying to persuade himself that he is cheerful, as of the half-earnest moralist's ambition to be serious. Even his fun is more the evidence of a gay, than of a cheerful, temperament. It is not hard to see a desperately uncomfortable man in the author of *Don Juan*; the very writing of it is part of the attempt to cheer himself up.

> And if I laugh at any mortal thing,
> 'Tis that I may not weep.
> (That make old Europe's journals squeak and gibber all),
> Who keep the world, both old and new, in pain
> Or pleasure? Who makes politics run glibber all?
> The shade of Buonaparte's noble daring?
> Jew Rothschild, and his fellow-Christian, Baring.

The nullity of the writing appropriately accompanies the sentiment of a writer in *Gringoire*. At the other extreme, there are many lapses into the histrionic-profound, from which Byron is never free in any of his work, "Between two worlds life hovers like a star" and all the rest of it; unimaginable from a poet like Leopardi, beside whom, with all his bookishness, Byron often seems an essentially uneducated spirit.

But the aplomb of the improviser, and the reader's awareness of it, are essential to the art of a poem which Hazlitt described, felicitously, as "a poem about itself."

> But Adeline was not indifferent: for
> (*Now* for a commonplace!) beneath the snow,
> As a volcano holds the lava more
> Within—*et caetera*. Shall I go on? No,
> I hate to hunt down a tired metaphor,
> So let the often-used volcano go,
> Poor thing! How frequently, by me and others,
> It hath been stirred up till its smoke quite smothers!
>
> I'll have another figure in a trice—
> What say you to a bottle of champagne?
> Frozen into a very vinous ice,
> Which leaves few drops of that immortal rain,
> Yet in the very centre, past all price,
> About a liquid glassful will remain;
> And this is stronger than the strongest grape
> Could e'er express in its expanded shape.

Byron's improvisation here, after the hit at conventional poetry, his own included, is a justification in practice of figures drawn from "Art," rather than "Nature," Pope's use of which he defended against Bowles. But the important point about it is this: the false start shows not only the slip into commonplace which he notices, but an inability which he was perhaps not conscious of, to concentrate his effects; he needs space to be a poet. This of course has bearings on the lack of a distinctive diction, noted earlier. A poet like Keats might have done something with that "volcano"; Byron could not, but he turns his incapacity into a virtue by rejecting the figure in full view of the reader.

The switches and reversals of mood are not so much the result of a critical check upon his emotion, as a flinching away from it; he hastens to a superficial kind of self-revelation, for fear of a deeper self-betrayal. Sometimes he seems actually frightened by a thought that has arisen in composition. The strange opening of Canto XIV, with the typical change between stanzas vi and vii, is a case in point; and earlier in the poem, after a moving rendering of the madness and death of Haidée, he intervenes with:

> But let me change this theme, which grows too sad,
> And lay this sheet of sorrows on the shelf;
> I don't much like describing people mad,
> For fear of seeming rather touch'd myself—

And a similar fear seems to spring up, when he has let himself go in some tender sentiment, of a kind which he will commit to verse, though rarely to prose; but will be quick to abandon, if he thinks he is being caught out, or "placed" in any single attitude. Indeed, one of his unpleasant traits of character, the caddishness that he showed in the Guiccioli episode (in his letters to friends), seems to be due, not merely to an obvious dislike of ridicule, but to this fear of being "typed," thought of as committed to any one part—especially if it is undignified: among the Christian virtues which Mr. Wilson Knight has found in Byron, indifference about one's personal dignity was not included.

Don Juan: A Thousand Colors

by Guy Steffan

Some readers and critics of *Don Juan* have complained that its conversational facility deteriorates into trivial and frivolous volubility, its
manner becoming mannerism, its ornament gaudy, its sentiment silly and
factitious. For them, *Don Juan* is not poetry at all, but contrived verse
or idle rhyming, oversimple, repetitious, full of banalities, noisy rhetoric,
and mechanical tricks. Its wit and paradox and calculated variety they
take as the stunts of an exhibitionist who never grew up, who tried too
hard to be clever and succeeded only in being smart. Probably they are
irritated most because Byron, the self-conscious man, obtrudes too conspicuously upon Byron, the self-conscious writer. They find scarcely a
restrained line, for Byron was rarely a restrained person. His under-
statements are a shouting artifice. Whatever is vulgar in the poem is so
because Byron in daily life could at times be very vulgar. All these objec-
tions can be resolved into the single charge of immaturity, and hence
into the contention that *Don Juan* lacks serious substance, complex understanding, and a sincere and valid criticism of the world.

But even if we concede some of these strictures, *Don Juan* is a great
poem of extraordinary sharpness and force. Topics, methods, manners,
and designs do recur with steady insistence. This determined but ever-
shifting recurrence springs both from Byron's temperament and from
his view of his world. His fertile, vigorous variation of a few simple
patterns of thought and technique gives him a thousand hues for his
carnival and midnight sky, but it also stabilizes his irregularity of chime
and concentrates the flashing of his satiric wit.

Byron's technique of exposing sham to mockery recurs on every other
page of *Don Juan* with the most versatile diversification, and it is always
successful when it is motivated by an earnest social purpose and sup-
ported by a consistent, penetrating, and deflating evaluation of man's
infinite devices of pretense. Byron is constantly peering into the palaces
of man's vanity, "Much in the mode of Goethe's Mephistopheles." His
mocking negation is humiliating not only because most of us are crickets

"A Thousand Colors." From *Byron's* Don Juan, Vol. I: *The Making of a Masterpiece*
(Austin, Texas: University of Texas Press; Edinburgh: Thomas Nelson & Sons, 1957)
by Truman Guy Steffan, pp. 278-296. Copyright © 1957 by the University of Texas
Press. Reprinted by permission of the author and the University of Texas Press.

jumping about aimlessly in the futile grass but also because many of us pretend to be wise or important or virtuous crickets, and because some of us are not just foolish impostors or a noisy nuisance, but voracious vermin.[1]

Byron's negative penetration persists from one end of the epic carnival to the other, piercing the frauds of modern marriage in the first canto and the zealous ritual of matchmaking in the later ones. He puts individuals and armies through the same embarrassing, bathetic tumble to demonstrate the fallacies of appearance. In Spain, the misdirected and rationalized educational ambitions of Donna Inez collapse into loud and shabby domestic scandal. In eastern Europe, some eight hundred stanzas later, personal and national ambitions, misdirected and rationalized on a vast scale, are triumphant, but the glory they gain is won at sickening price and the dream becomes a nightmare. Political aspiration and military exploit are exposed as crimes against humanity, and suffer a moral collapse when Ismail falls after thirty thousand are slaughtered and when the Pacha smokes his pipe among the ruins and Suwarrow sends his witty rhyme of victory.

Byron brings up his heavy weapons against moral paragons and imperial potentates. He uses lighter armory when he sets his sights on comic frivolity or the elegant façade of decorum. A farce is made of sham when Juanna's disguise in the seraglio falls to the foolish subterfuge of an apple and a bee, and again when the hoax of the Black Friar, a masquerade for the fashionable lust of the Duchess, is exposed by a thrust of Juan's arm. Dudù is more a pleasant partner in a harem caper than a feminine humbug, but when the Duchess, vain and voluptuous, empty-headed and professionally alluring, contrives an elaborate little sex frolic, her intrigue is gleefully unmasked to show again to the twice two thousand that "You are *not* a moral people, and you know it."

Most of the women in the carnival are divested of their cloaks of artifice, and sin "without a rag on" is sent "shivering forth." Inez, Julia, Gulbeyaz, Dudù, Catherine, the Duchess, Adeline, even Haidée and perhaps Aurora are sisters of the flesh. Only the island girl and the Catholic orphan are gently spared.[2] The flaws in the virtuous veneer of

---

[1] Mephistopheles uses the cricket or grasshopper image to disparage man's spiritual aspiration and abuse of divine reason in the "Prologue in Heaven" scene of Part I of *Faust*.

[2] Haidée is the ideal sublimation of normal and innocent passion. She does not pretend to be more than she is, nor does she wear the clothing of convention. Byron does not strip a dream of nature because it is already free of sham. We cannot guess what he would have done in future cantos with Aurora, a self-admitted variant of Haidée. Although they are not exposed in the ruthlessly comic way that the other women are, Haidée, Aurora, and even Leila are not exempt from a few good-natured smiles, a few amused strokes, for even these artless children do not thoroughly know themselves and on occasion slip into, or are naïve victims of, a venial kind of deception; e.g., see Canto II, stanzas 131, 135-36, 174; III, 13; X, 56; XV, 73; XVI, 106.

Inez show up almost too easily in her persecution of Jóse and her moral miseducation of her son, in the rumors about her old affair with Alfonso, and in the insinuations about her motive for not stopping Julia's flirtation. Julia is timid and self-reproachful, conscious of duty and propriety, but she pretends to be what she is not and tries to deceive herself and others. Her real desire and her real self become active in arbor and bedroom, seducing a boy and railing with consummate hypocrisy at her suspicious husband. She may later write a pathetic farewell letter and we may be expected to believe her grief genuine. But is there not at the end some penetrating laughter at the delicate postures of sentiment in the little ironies about the "gilt-edged paper" and "neat little crow-quill," her sunflower seal of "superfine" vermillion wax, with its motto "cut upon a white cornelian"—*"Elle vous suit partout"*?

The Sultana and the Empress deceive nobody, unless he be as fatuous as the Sultan, and Byron's main purpose is to let the public peep into the royal boudoir and gossip about the royal gigolos, to disenchant the lofty and splendid luxury of power and rank, and to lay bare its passionate sensuality that is as hard and crude as its despotism. We could expect that a sensual Byron would let concupiscence be the particular precipitate of imperious authority.

It seems clear, too, that correct and chaste Adeline was eventually to show herself a member of the same family. Recall the frozen champagne image, the ambiguous definition of her affection for Juan, her derogatory survey of the eligible girls, her disparagement of Aurora, her malicious satisfaction when Juan at first makes no headway with that gem of society, her chagrin when he does arouse Aurora's interest, her dread that her rival would "thaw to a coquette," her ostentatious display of her easy arts when she sings the Black Friar ballad, and—above all—her too gracious, too vivacious, too versatile entertainment of the guests at her husband's political open house and her too willing detraction of them after they leave. Juan wondered if Adeline were real, and any reader can be certain that if Byron had completed his epic history of the Amundevilles, he would have cut through to the real Adeline as he had done with his other less charming and less genteel frauds.

Byron's negative penetration is impartial toward the sexes, and is never sharper than when directed against that model chamberlain, that proud, superior, and pertinacious peer whose prepossessions were "like the laws of Persians / And Medes," and whose rationalized patriotism would not let him "quit his king in times of strife." Byron, as always in his best satiric types, finds the universal beneath the special, and Lord Henry becomes the eternal politician, the studious campaigner, "burrowing for boroughs," and apologetically clinging to his sinecures, which "he wished abolished, / But that with them all law would be demolished." In four cantos, every time Byron picks him up, he slices away a layer of sham. He may hate hacking into "the roots of things," when he wants to perplex us about Adeline's virtue, her interest in Juan, and her aversion to Aurora, but he never hesitates to penetrate Lord Henry's almost aseptic inadequacy as a husband, the cordial smugness of his reasons for befriending Juan, the bland banality of his confident advice to Adeline about Juan and the Duchess, and all his little pretentions as a Sabine showman. The parliamentarian of Canto XIII shrinks in Canto XVI to a breakfast babbler, mumbling about his ill-buttered muffin, asking the Duchess about her Duke and Juan about his pallor—there's tact—and willing to chat on and on about his family ghost and his honeymoon, until Adeline checks him.

Byron gives less space to his other male pawns, but he cuts as quickly into the trimmer-poet, the wonderful Sultan, Peter Pith, and two dozen or more minor masculine frauds. In the crowded character galleries— spiteful Raucocanti and the band of operatic vagabonds, the portraits of the formidable Amundeville ancestors, the long roster of guests at the Abbey, most of them proud of nothing to be proud of, pretentious in some foolery or other—here the penetrating technique is the same. The Honorable Mrs. Sleep is not the only one of the flock who looks a white lamb but is a black sheep—after shearing. And if this shearing were universal, if the truth could be told wholesale, then

> The new world would be nothing to the old,
>   If some Columbus of the moral seas
> Would show mankind their soul's Antipodes.
>
> What "Antres vast and desarts idle," then
>   Would be discover'd in the human soul!
> What Icebergs in the hearts of mighty men,
>   With Self-love in the centre as their Pole!
> What Anthropophagi in nine of ten
>   Of those who hold the kingdoms in controul!
> Were things but only call'd by their right name,
> Caesar himself would be ashamed of Fame.
>
>   XIV, 101-102

Juan suffers similar penetration. The eloquent newcomer, applauding British law and order on Shooter's Hill, and the dizzy, muddled soldier-youth at Ismail, ignorant of what the bloody excitement is all about, swearing to punish the whole Russian army if his girl friends are molested, then following his nose and blundering gloriously—these are social versions of the earlier boy on shipboard, waving farewell to his native Spain and mouthing fine words of patriotic and gallant devotion. Juan's seasickness, his guarding the rum, his rescue of the spaniel, his getting lost in battle, his foolish conversation with German-speaking General Lascy, and poor Tom's knife in his ribs on the outskirts of London are all humiliations (none of them so recognized by Juan) of fallacious and gesturing sensibility.

Juan has performed so often in the carnival that we hardly need to put him through his paces again. He appears invariably in such a crowd and clatter, or with other people or in events that are more dynamic than he is, that we may overlook the care Byron took with his performance and development. We should not underestimate the versatility of Byron's social and psychological use of his unheroic hero. Juan is the conductor, the refractor, the catalyst, the reagent of a blindly priggish education, of the frippery, inanity, and intrigue of fashion, of the depravity and despotism of monarchs and courts, of the savagery of man when panic cracks the bonds of social responsibility, and of the crimes of war.

Juan's functional service in the epic did not freeze Byron's affection for him. He was as fond of Juan as he was of any of the friends of his early manhood, though he girded at him as he did at them. Juan is a favorite because he is natural man, whose illusions and impulses are sound and normal, and because he is ideal. The mean and sordid things that happen to him are real in an ordinary physical sense, but they cannot corrupt or destroy his spirit. He is the child of the passionate doctrine that reality is the mind.

> Don Juan . . . was real or ideal,—
> For both are much the same, since what men think
> Exists when the once thinkers are less real
> Than what they thought, for mind can never sink,
> And 'gainst the body makes a strong appeal.
>   X, 20, 1-5

He participates in many of the vices and abuses of society, and although he is not often an unwilling sinner, he is never a self-tormented one, never defiled or contaminated, and never really guilty. He survives, neither saint, nor devil, nor the cynic that Johnson had already become, and even when cool in manner is still "good at heart."

Juan's vicissitudes are thus never pointless, but always controlled by one or more of several thoughtful, temperamental, and literary purposes. Some of his actions and feelings are subjected to Byron's mockery, some are instrumental in the satiric exposure of others, some represent the impulses of unspoiled and freedom-loving youth. Taken all together, Juan's adventures became a coherent set of variations on a pessimistic idea about the relationship between the individual and society. His history is the growth of natural man into social man and of naïve youth into sophisticated maturity. And everywhere his history is also the dramatic course of man at the mercy of whimsical fortune, the sport of the gods of circumstance.

In the very first canto Juan is a boy adrift on the tides of events beyond his control. Byron makes him a victim of a misguided education and of stupid, unhappy parents, and then lets him slip into seduction and a bedroom scandal. He sends him abroad into the hysteria of tempest and shipwreck, where he acts foolishly but innocently and honestly. Still drifting, literally and emotionally, he is embraced by the gentle and tonic arms of Nature's bride, only to be roughly snatched from her and transported out of the pastoral, shackled, to a slave mart, sold, dressed in feminine disguise, and led to the chamber of a sensual autocrat. Here, for the first time, he begins to take some absurd initiative in rebellion and becomes the shrill champion of natural freedom—of choice—and then is helplessly and gracefully pushed into Dudù's bed. He is suddenly swept out of the harem into the horror of Ismail, where he catches the contagion of glory madness, but kills without hatred or malice, saves the life of the little orphan, the "one good action in the midst of crimes," and is honorably shunted off to his purgatory at Petersburg, emerging after dissipation and mysterious illness, neither purified nor innocent but equipped to defend and acquit himself in the glittering, dreary void of the "microcosm on stilts," outfacing the Blues, eluding the matchmakers, doing his bit with the fox hunters, moving at ease with Lord Henry, Lady Adeline, and their horde of the bores and bored, and then falling into the ghostly sex trap of the Duchess, but not before Aurora had already begun to revive his natural goodness.

Although Juan on no single occasion is as vital or as arresting as some others who burst for a spell into the carnival sky—Inez, Julia, Lambro, Haidée, Gulbeyaz, Suwarrow, Johnson, Adeline, Henry, and even Zoe and Raucocanti—he seems often to be the polar star in the epic, where more brilliant figures and circumstances wheel round him. Or he is the one planet that gleams every morning or evening—though which?—now Venus, now Mars, one after the other, but never Jupiter. And here we see still another major achievement. Through sixteen completed cantos, the logic and variety of Juan's temperament and of his response to whimsical fortune are continuous and thorough. He is foolish and amorous with Julia, eager and melodramatic on shipboard, sweet, devoted, and sentimental with Haidée, strident and sprawling with Alfonso and Lambro's pirates, dispirited with Johnson and Raucocanti, disgruntled, sad, and defiant with Baba and Gulbeyaz, playful and chivalrous with Dudù and Leila, confused, excited, and determined at Ismail, vain and dissolute with Catherine, plastic and poised in Britain. Polar star? Planet? The aurora borealis itself!

Of all the people in the carnival, which is Byron? *Don Juan* is a scabrous song of himself. It is an epic of re-creation and reminiscence, an unquiet, lambent rhyme of his codes and antipathies, of his own tensions and contradictions. He is not a detached observer, but self-assertive, volubly confessional, actively engaged in person, talking, jesting, sighing, upbraiding, and gibing, in bedroom and on battlefield, in storm and at dinner, in cave, palace, and abbey, fuming with his passions and prejudices, disgorging bits of his reading—histories and travel books, Scott, the Bible, Shakespeare, and many others, past and contemporary—ejecting memories of his parents and his childhood, of his wife and her lawyer, of his daughter and his mother-in-law, of Newstead, Piccadilly, Venice, Ravenna, and the Albanian tour, and of a flirtation over a game of billiards. But with whom in this autobiographical epic can we identify him? He is everyone in part and no one completely. Johnson is a faithful image, but only of one piece of Byron. He is also Julia and Haidée, Lambro and Raucocanti, and of course Juan. Why? Because Byron just as often subconsciously as consciously puts *self* into his people, and because he is not only what he appears and does not appear to be, but what he says he is and what he wants to be without saying it. Do not these habits, these self-conceptions, these realities and pseudo realities explain why Haidée demands no vows, why Lambro is the soul of courtesy and ferocity, a rebel-gentleman, who finds his hearth a tomb, why Raucocanti exposes his own malice as he shreds his companions, why Juan dances so gracefully and is so fond of Leila—and so on and on for dozens of specific shadows of Byron himself? Now and again he aims the same penetrating laughter at himself and his manner of writing as he does at his people and his societies. Years before in *English Bards* when he chuckled at that miracle, the young author-sinner lecturing like a moralist, he gave us a forecast of the kind of mocking amusement that he was to find in the inward-looking writer of every canto of *Don Juan*.

Common principles control Byron's treatment of his individuals and societies. The Ecclesiastian persuasion and Pilate's jest are the theoretical beginning and end of negative penetration. Byron everywhere applies his axiom of vanity and futility, from the catalogue of forgotten heroes to the eclipse of contemporary notables in the *ubi sunt* declamation. His questioning of fame is consistent with his prevailing skepticism that makes a puzzle of the commandant's street murder and of Berkeley's philosophy and that finds mutability as the only constant law, controlling love and all other human experience.

Skepticism, denial, the stripping of tinsel are temperamental habits, a projection of Byron's own dealings with men and of his interpretation of his own life. They are also an outlet for his rebelliousness, which is aroused by any settled system because it is settled and because it is a system. Derisive doubt is the rebel's response to safe and complacent certainty. If any confident assurance in this mutable world is superior, if it is presumptuous, if it is assumed as a protective dogma, an armor of smug security, if its generalizations ignore or restrict individual differences and empirical variety, then rebellious doubt becomes all the more aggressively derisive. "Dost thou think because thou art virtuous, there shall be no more Cakes and Ale?"—"Yes, by St. Anne; and Ginger shall be hot i' the mouth too!" Byron's skepticism and negative penetration are but two forms of his rebellion.

His temperamental contrariness places him automatically in opposition to existing creeds, conventions, and institutions, first because they are rigidly self-righteous and blandly or fatuously stable and secondly because they are repressive of all nonconforming individualists. Byron was lightly and candidly amused that his opposition to dogmatic authority was partially a perverse spirit of contradiction. He was "born for opposition." But then " 'tis mostly on the weaker side." If they who now bask in power were shaken down, he might at first "deride / Their tumble," but then he would "turn the other way, / And wax an Ultra-royalist," partly because he hated "even democratic royalty," and partly because he was, after all, born for opposition. And so he wears "the motly mantle of a poet" possibly in defiance of someone who had told him "to forego it."

There is therefore more negative than positive expression of his passionate impulse for freedom. He admires Leonidas, Epaminondas, Milton, Boone, Washington, Wilberforce, and a few others, but he uses them mainly as ideal opponents of a tyranny he detests. When near the very end in Canto XVII, he favors toleration and "free discussion / Upon all points—no matter what, or whose," he is protesting the abuse of original minds. His attacks on Southey and Wordsworth as apostates; on Haidée's poet as an unscrupulous opportunist; on Wellington and Castlereagh as agents and protagonists of oppression; his handling of the contest between Juan and Gulbeyaz; his onslaught against Catherine and all ruthless warmakers; his democratic manifesto against tyranny in Canto VIII and his qualification of it in Canto IX to include an aversion to despotism by the mob; his angry indictment of England in Canto X, abhorred as an aggressive traitor of free minds everywhere and as its own enslaver; his disgust with the pressures of aristocratic convention that binds the individual in a social strait jacket; his ironic advice to time-servers— "be cautious, be / Not what you *seem*, but always what you *see*"; his lament for all brave genius—Pythagoras, Socrates, Jesus, Galileo, Locke, who have been ignored, scorned, persecuted, or silenced—all these and more are the habitual negative outbursts, not of a cool, rational concern for an abstract principle of liberty, but of a passionate and jealous devotion to personal freedom. His observation of the struggle between the impulse for liberation and the forces of bondage ranges from Johnson's psychological platitude that "most men are slaves," if only of themselves, of "their own whims and passions" to a perverse paradox about the irrational enslavement of an entire topsy-turvy world. Wilberforce, the "moral

Washington" who freed the blacks, should now shut up the whites. "Shut up the world at large, let Bedlam out; / And you will be perhaps surprised to find / All things pursue exactly the same route."

Although Byron might have worn out his fame by knocking his rhyme against the entrenched fact of convention and authority, he always recognized sensible, social, and psychological fact and had an almost academic regard for local, historical, and geographic fact. His "Muse by no means deals in fiction," for "fact's a fact—and 'tis the part / Of a true poet to escape from fiction / Whene'er he can." His scrupulous respect for his repertory of facts supports his account of the sea adventure and of the siege of Ismail. Facts are made grimaces in the shipwreck and on the battlefield, during the Russian visit, along the journey across northern Europe, on the ride through London streets, and in the dress parade of the hierarchy of English fashion. "I sketch your world exactly as it goes." Anecdotal facts, picked up in Italy and Spain, are stretched to farcical narrative in Cantos I and VI. He repeatedly injects factual, practical folk (Antonia, Zoe, Baba, Johnson, Lord Henry) into situations that puzzle more emotional and sensitive hearts. Sensible fact is the common principle when Zoe fries eggs, when Baba recommends circumcision, when Lord Henry advises Adeline not to meddle in Juan's affairs, when Johnson counsels resignation in the slave market, when he refuses to attempt escape, when he retreats in battle, when he demurs at helping the orphan lest he miss his chance for plunder, and when Antonia chides the kissing lovers ("keep your nonsense for some luckier night"), frets lest indiscretion will cost her job, wonders that Julia risks so much for a mere child, and pushes Juan into a closet.

These literary practices in narrative and characterization are natural to one who regards skepticism as the only sensible approach to unriddled wonder and to a satirist who persists in trying to crack the shell and reach a truth. Tangible, actual experience, with all its contradictions, fact recorded and verified as accurately as human limitations allow, is the solidest residue of confused and elusive existence and can also be a filter, even a corrosive acid, to be used on the illusion, deception, and pretense that contaminate, conceal, and encrust reality.

"But what's reality? Who has its clue?" Certainly not philosophy, which rejects so much that each new system reverses the myth of Saturn and eats up the one that spawned it. And the clues of religion lead but to a jest: *which* sect is more convincing than indigestion? Is it faith or sublime credulity to believe the impossible simply because it is so? "Ask a blind man, the best judge." Theoretical skepticism stumbles out of its blind alley into the bracing air of mocking contradiction: "I know nought; nothing I deny, / Admit, reject, contemn," for he "who doubts all things, nothing can deny."

There's no such thing as certainty, that's plain
  As any of Mortality's Conditions:
So little do we know what we're about in
This world, I doubt if doubt itself be doubting.

It is a pleasant voyage perhaps to float,
  Like Pyrrho, on a sea of speculation;
But what if carrying sail capsize the boat?
  Your wise men don't know much of navigation;
And swimming long in the abyss of thought
  Is apt to tire: a calm and shallow station
Well nigh the shore, where one stoops down and gathers
Some pretty shell, is best for moderate bathers.

                                        IX, 17-18

Truth cuts through "such canals of contradiction, / That she must often navigate o'er fiction," and yet fiction is a lie. Millions must be wrong and yet all may be right. God help us!

Skeptical catharsis does not purge sensible fact. On a social and psychological level, the only speculative one where Byron's irony can be positive, he juggles with materialistic common sense, but never really comes to rest with it. He praises the power of cash in politics and the world's affairs and both ironically and sanely exalts the capitalist—saint, poet, and "intellectual lord of all"—his version of Shelley's preserver and destroyer—even as he grins at his own assumption of avarice. Body is a fact, and spirit is only a hope. In the antipodes of Canto II and again in the savagery of Canto VIII, he demonstrates the dominion of body over spirit and is bitter and discouraged about it in Canto V, where Johnson's recital and counsel, the description of the slave mart, and the contemplation of the sudden death of the commandant are heavy with disillusionment. The thirty forgotten heroes at the beginning of Canto I and Cheops' pyramid, that could not preserve a pinch of his dust, De Foix's pillar, smeared with human excrement, triumphant Lucullus, commemorated only on menus, and all the lords of fame and ladies of fashion pile up on a simple text—*ubi sunt?*—and deflate spirit. Materialism and pessimism combine when Byron finds Cuvier's cyclical theory of cosmic deterioration congenial to satiric purpose, and both are drugged with the potion of sentimentality when he, unlike Haidée's trimmer-poet, praises the past in order to damn the present.

The spells of idealism that can become sentimental are as temperamental as his skeptical pessimism. On one occasion, he avers that human progress is uncertain or hopeless and that spirit cannot transcend body; on another, that mind is free and "can never sink," that "the people" will by and by be stronger, and that all men have some good in them. But he finds no reasonable basis for confident idealism and posits no prior condition or reform as prerequisite for goodness or betterment, as do Wordsworth, Coleridge, Shelley, and Keats. As we have seen, the nearest Byron comes to a prime essential for melioration is the impulse of personal liberty.

His idealism is consistently emotional. His mite of human goodness is a capricious assumption, an impulsive concession, a compensating necessity, a single grain in the silo, a warming speck in a universe of cold things. There must be one good deed among the atrocities at Ismail, and so Juan rescues Leila. The mind must delight to lose itself in Haidée, in the prolonged dream idyl of natural love, and in Aurora, even while it knows that they will be smashed, and must linger tenderly over Julia's desolate letter, over dying sons and bereaved fathers in the long boat, over Daniel Boone, and over the scarlet girl waiting with the constable for Lord Henry. So, too, Byron has to soften his most hardened souls. Lambro loves his homeland, music, the streams, and his daughter. Gulbeyaz, Suwarrow, and Johnson are given twinges of gentleness and kindly sympathy.

Discontented or wearied with the dull present, Byron consoles himself with other kinds of sentimentality that are pleasant interludes out of his past: a list of "sweet" memories in Canto I, affectionate recollections of Newstead Abbey, of Auld Lang Syne in Scotland, of friendship with Sir Walter Scott, of his former literary popularity and the old sanction of Jeffrey. Byron's evidences of mutability and his preoccupation with the fall of the mighty and the fickleness of fame also have a pedal bass of regret running through his satirical negation. Where are the orators and the dandies? "Where is the unhappy Queen, with all her woes? / And where the Daughter, whom the Isles loved well?"

Chafing under the monotony of the ordinary, his emotional idealism can also lose itself in a spectacular kind of sentimentality, occasionally hard to take today, in too many rainbows, too many sofas, pigmies, bronze doors, and gurgling marble fountains, in flamboyant decoration and excitement, in aristocratic elegance at home and abroad, in the exoticism of Oriental palaces, in sensational and outlandish adventure across a stormy Mediterranean, among the languishing Cyclades, at corrupt Petersburg and explosive Ismail.[3] Byron could justify his fondness for exotic ornament, in both the Eastern tales and in the later *Juan,* as fidelity to environmental fact. But his larded accuracy sometimes seems a literary affectation screening his personal taste, which, however, had improved

---

[3] The rescue of Leila is not the only sentimental episode here; recall some of Byron's lines about the heroic last stand of the Khan and his five sons.

by the time he got to Canto V. Often his elegant descriptive detail is the well-groomed, gaudy child of his aristocratic bias.

Byron's snobbery is a sentimental obsession, ostentatiously guarded throughout his life, acquired in youth, nurtured at Harrow and Cambridge, possibly in compensation for physical and financial liabilities, and later aggravated by his travels and by his career in the high world of lord and dandy. Not to find it in *Don Juan* would be a bigger surprise than any the poem now provides. In spite of some strong democratic utterances, the aristocratic bias is unpleasantly strong in his boasts (the ancient name of Biron), in his slur at Southey and Coleridge for marrying two milliners of Bath, his assumption that great minds (*read* "lordly souls") dominate little minds (*read* "plebs"), and most conspicuously in his epic actors. The only commoners are menials (Antonia, Zoe, Baba) or a coarse lot of cheap mercenaries (Raucocanti and his fellows). If he slaps at aristocracy *per se*, it is always at spurious rank. Yet factual common sense and the habit of negative penetration prevent complete obsession. He never overlooks whatever is shabby or disagreeable in his aristocracy. The nobles on the battlefield are inhumane snobs in their neglect and wholesale sacrifice of the common soldier. Gulbeyaz is a splendid creature but she is tyrannical, arrogant, and heartless; grand Catherine, equally heartless, is a nymphomaniac; and the poised, correct Amundevilles are hollow. The rest are thoroughbreds. Haidée, a perfect physical image, is a vision of innocent and uninhibited passion in her aristocratic pastoral. Paradoxical Lambro, the outlaw-patriot, brutal but sensitive, is a gentleman of cool patrician discipline. Johnson, cynical adventurer, recognizes a peer in Juan. His casual and disillusioned detachment, his flexible diplomacy, his calm efficiency, and his stoical sophistication are the durable, if cheerless, virtues of the aristocrat of abundant worldly experience. And even Jóse, henpecked and philandering, is a "true Hidalgo, free from every stain / Of Moor or Hebrew blood," able to trace "his source / Through the most Gothic gentlemen of Spain." [4] Suwarrow is an anomaly, the only major figure who does not quite fit the pattern, and Byron puzzles over what to make of him.

The literary manifestations of Byron's temperamental contradictions and of his basic attitudes and purposes are variety, paradox, incongruity, surprise, bathos, and irony. These are the appropriate media of a mind intent on showing things as they are, but ever doubtful that things are what they seem, and sure only that they are inconsistent, fleeting, and changeable, of a mind oscillating between fact and skepticism, between

---

[4] Byron readily laughs at the accomplishments of his gentlemen: "A better cavalier [than Jóse] ne'er mounted horse, / Or, being mounted, e'er got down again." Recall the accomplishments of the English ladies and the vacuities of many a duke, "who was—a duke."

negative penetration and futility. They are also the formal literary devices of a satirist who negates much that society assumes (and presumes) to be positive and who makes a profession of irreverence, of suddenly confronting sham with itself, and of shocking smugness out of its nap. Moreover, surprise and bathos, incongruity and irony, variety and paradox provide the sort of mental activity that can occupy and please a restless man, who, bored or irritated by the limitations of existence, is now rebellious and theatrical, now insulting and abusive, at times disillusioned, at times eagerly leaping to idealized and sentimental extremes.

To say that Byron loved paradox, incongruity, and surprise is to say that he loved wit and that versemaking for him was a play of intellect. His thousand colors coruscate most frequently in the witty language that is the satiric expression of his thought, his conception of experience, and his evaluation of particular motive and social action. Although his desultory rhyme, his conversational facility, and his easy colloquialism were natural talents and could become a fluent and wayward indulgence, they also made a rapid and pliant carrier of his wit. Colloquial speech not only carried but caused the shock of surprise and paradox, of bathetic quip and incongruous image. The burden of substance in his witty verse was poised on a verbal point that deflated smugness, folly, fraud, and authority. Colloquial speech was a suitable language for jaunty and irreverent skepticism.

Byron liked to say that he never strained hard to versify and that he rattled on as he talked, but his castanets were metrical, and he kept his ear tuned for those rhythms and sounds that were appropriate to wit. He saw and *heard* the value of subtle adjustments in the structure of a phrase and sentence, and he also heard the values, not merely of pert and wicked rhyming, but of assonance, consonance, and alliteration within a verse. Perhaps his bold and farcical rhyming has been so conspicuous that we have not listened to what he does elsewhere in a line. Yet it is an axiom of wit that the sounds of its language be as memorable as its design and its sense. I should think that more people would exclaim about the music of Byron's best wit than about the wit in some of the best music of Haydn and Mozart. When on the *Beppo* manuscript he deleted the phrase "reign of Dandies" and wrote "dynasty of Dandies," it was his ear that came to the aid of his satiric thought in shaping an epithet about those autocrats of nothing at all. The same alliance of sound and sense continued to ring out the witty harmonics of hundreds of lines in *Don Juan*.

Turn to the place where you least expect to find him an artist of musical wit, to the concluding pages of the last complete canto, where you think he might be tired or careless, and listen to the rhythms, some of them rugged and irregular, some rapid and vigorous, some firm and balanced, and many varied within a single verse. Listen again to the cadences and to the inner harmony of the vowels and consonants in a few lines taken from a small range of fourteen stanzas. Do not, of course, set your ears for *andante cantabile e grazioso,* nor for honied and "linkèd sweetness long drawn out."

> Thus on the mob all statesmen are as eager
> To prove their pride, as footmen to a beggar.
>> XVI, 76, 7-8

> But 'twas a public feast and public day,—
> Quite full, right dull, guests hot, and dishes cold,
> Great plenty, much formality, small cheer,
> And every body out of their own sphere.
>> 78, 5-8

> There were some massy members of the church,
> Takers of tithes, and makers of good matches,
> And several who sung fewer psalms than catches.
>> 80, 6-8

> I sate next that o'erwhelming son of heaven,
> The very powerful Parson, Peter Pith,
> The loudest wit I e'er was deafened with.
>> 81, 6-8

> And not a joke he cut but earned its praise
>> 82, 3

> A fat fen vicarage, and nought to think on
>> 82, 8

> No longer ready ears and short-hand pens
> Imbibed the gay bon mot, or happy hoax:
> The poor priest was reduced to common sense
>> 83, 4-6

> He had paid his neighbour's prayer with half a turbot
>> 88, 8

> And this, and his not knowing how much oats
> Had fallen last market, cost his host three votes
>> 89, 7-8

The zest for musical wit and plangent irony, the itch for variety and paradox are symptoms of a vigorous and boisterous mind. The poem must not be dull. How he dreaded dullness and worked to kill it! How he feared boredom and pranced to shake it off! If necessary he will stand on his head in the square to capture applause or rush in his clowns, freaks, and calliopes to enliven the carnival. He worries when he feels that Cantos III and IV are "damned dull" or that his subject—British society—is dry and barren. The clever cynicism, the shock of unorthodox jibes at pleasant lust, anxious matchmaking, and the unstable vinegar of marriage, at animal man and social woman, at lawyers, journalists, and generals; the quizzing of philosophy and religion, of progress and finance, of heart that is never free of the belly (without Ceres and Bacchus, "Venus will not long attack us");[5] the strenuous invective against Wellington, Castlereagh, and the warmakers; the abuse of Wordsworth and Southey, Inez and Catherine—all these may be grounded in conviction, but the gusto of their expression has an end in itself: to blast dullness out of the epic. The more earnest Byron is about what he has to say, the more energetic he becomes in the way he says it.

Hence, too, the spasms of bustle, the fracas between Juan and Alfonso and between Juan and Lambro's band, the sensational action of ocean storm and land battle, the sensational characterization of the Moslem monarchs and of those unsolved puzzles, Lambro and Suwarrow. It is likewise Byron's physical and mental energy that makes him dash through those many runs of parallel amplification and comic accumulation, all of them solidly concrete—the funny Italian and Russian names, the classical and historical allusions, the long lists of people, rapidly tagged, the catalogue of heroes, the boatload of rascals, the guest roll at the Abbey and the paintings, and the eligible girls on the marital mart.

The quick, straight parallels of contradictions in individual and group feeling and behavior are his vigorous way of bringing together the amazing variety of confused fact, of letting the diametric differences ridicule each other by their very proximity: the conduct and emotions of the hysterical crew sinking in the storm and drifting in the open boat; Julia's tortuous rationalizations and her later high-pitched harangue in the bedroom; Gulbeyaz' wild and inconsistent impulses after she has been spurned by the freedom-loving boy; all the many busy nothings of the daily London routine and the desperately tedious pastimes at the country estate of the Amundevilles.

The pages stuffed with foods, costumes, and house furnishings on the Greek island, in Constantinople, and at the Abbey use the same method to gratify his factual appetite for the decorative and the sumptuous and to burn off energy by stacking up an abundance of odd items. The two longest set descriptions in the English cantos also apply this technique for different effects. The stroll through the Abbey grounds is sentimental, nostalgic, and theatrical. The leafing of the enormous menu is satiric, sportive, and almost as tiresome as those who gormandized at Lord Henry's massive table.

All the rowdy stanzas, scattered throughout the poem, the scores of

[5] Both the idea and the phrasing provide one of Byron's echoes, a distant but persistent one. The earlier, more dramatic, and more energetic version occurs in Canto II, stanzas 69-70; the second one, over four years and seventeen hundred stanzas later, in Canto XVI, stanza 86.

clever rhymes and impudent images that are funny *per se,* the dozens of deflating ironies, large and small, the surprising stunts that turn up on almost every page are likewise the pranks of a vital talent showing what it can do, exercises of the irreverent skeptic who regards the world as a glorious blunder, and the useful blades of a satirist bent on penetrating sober fraud.

Byron's temperamental vitality, his emotional energy, and the literary methods that are their natural expression in *Don Juan*—variety, paradox, incongruity, surprise, bathos, irony, natural and calculated colloquialism, and the witty and rhetorical exploitation of sounds, rhythm, and structure of a phrase—are the main reasons why we often find the superlative merits of the poem in momentary flashes, in short phrases, in single lines, couplets, stanzas or small sections, in parallel amplification and comic accumulation, and not in large design or development. These are the streaks of lightning, the comets, and the thousand bright stars of his midnight sky. We saw these merits in the accretive process, in the focus of revision, and in the details of furbishing. We can therefore be struck as much by the manner as by the matter, and frequently only by the manner. The poet should make the manner, but sometimes in *Juan,* the manner makes the poem.[6] When his constructive voltage runs too low, when content is thin or dissipated, his wit can continue to crackle, but merely for the sake of isolated jest, and his vigorous methods then become mechanical and wearisome.

Byron is always at his best in *Don Juan* when the brilliant jets and the rapid thrusts are grouped and organized into solid and sustained impressions. His best editorial commentaries are the dozen or so more spacious and unified ones on scientific progress, on the poetical commandments, on his creed of burlesque, on misers, constancy, mutability, the mystery of death and the futility of the search for truth. His strongest narrative episodes are those that are most detailed and expanded, in the bedroom, at sea, during the siege, and with the ghost. His liveliest scenes are the big ones with Julia, Johnson, and the Sultana, and with the

[6] Many writers are erratic judges of their own work, and Byron is no exception. Recall his views about *Hints from Horace,* his translation of Pulci, and his dramas. But he knew more about what he was doing in *Juan* and how he was doing it than any one who has written about it. He knew when manner triumphed over matter. He saw that danger in his earlier poetry before he began *Beppo* ("I certainly am a devil of a mannerist, and must leave off"). Byron was so restless and so conscious of his treacherous facility that I have doubted he ever could have written his hundred cantos, though he surely would have gone past the seventeenth. But would he have completed the poem? For other reasons—the unending train of abuses of society, the inexhaustible subject— it would have been impossible to *finish* the job. Still, although his *Juan* medium came as near as any could to satisfying his demand for novelty, it seems likely that he eventually would have become so uneasy about the dominion of manner that he would have left off and possibly returned to it at intervals.

Amundevilles in town and country. The crowded galleries of the Italian opera company and the English guests, the fuller character types of Inez, Julia, Haidée, Johnson, Gulbeyaz, Adeline, and Henry, and the strange contradictions of Lambro and Suwarrow, the functional employment of Juan himself in several situations, and above all, the many stanzas on group activities and daily routines—in all of these, Byron's penetration and energy are not dispersed but concentrated into his most impressive constellations.

In *Don Juan* one particular quality, purpose, attitude, or technique always involves another, and that is why in these concluding pages, while glancing at one passage or one incident or one habit of thought, we have invariably recalled that passage in another context as a manifestation of another quality. Any one thing that Byron does in the poem is merged with everything else he does. There are multiple variants, but the patterns recur in the carnival and make it, both in content and expression, all that Byron in the chronicle and in verse said it was. And that is enough.

Don Juan

by Helen Gardner

It is a striking example of the neglect of Byron as a poet, in a century which has seen a spate of studies of Byron as a man, that when in 1944 Mr. Steffan began to hunt for the holograph manuscripts of *Don Juan,* and the fair copies which Mary Shelley made of the later cantos, there did not exist any census of Byron manuscripts. An entertaining book had even been made out of letters written to him by besotted women seeking his acquaintance; but nobody looking round for a research subject had apparently thought it worthwhile to make a study of the manuscripts of the most amusing poem ever written. Now, in the year which sees the publication of Professor Marchand's admirable biography, the result of ten years labor, Professors Steffan and Pratt of the University of Texas, after even longer labors, have produced a four-volume edition of *Don Juan,* recording below each stanza as it was finally printed all the manuscript variants, and noting which stanzas were afterthoughts, either scribbled crosswise on the original draft, or added on slips, or sent to Murray with a note for insertion.[1] We can now watch Byron at work on his masterpiece. We can see him fumbling for a beginning, or dashing at one; watch him changing his mind and crossing out, going back to recast a line to get a better rhyme, making a point sharper, or seeing a new point to be made. We can see him reading over what he had written and going off at a tangent to write additional stanzas of comment or reflection or abuse, or of pure virtuosity. We can see him going back over a line to fill it out, revising to make a satiric implication more stinging or a joke funnier. We can see how sometimes the perfect epithet, obvious once found, was only found at the last moment.

The two editors discovered early on that they had each begun work independently on the *Don Juan* manuscripts and decided to make the production of a text which would record all the manuscript variants their

"Don Juan," by Helen Gardner. From *The London Magazine,* Vol. V, No. 7 (July 958), 58-65. Copyright © 1958 by William Heinemann. Reprinted by permission of the author and William Heinemann.

[1] *Byron's* Don Juan. A Variorum Edition, edited by Truman Guy Steffan and Willis W. Pratt. In four volumes. University of Texas Press, Austin; Nelson and Sons, Edinburgh, 1957.

joint responsibility. (It is now too late to do more than lament with Dr Chapman the current misuse of the term *Variorum* for an edition o this kind. It seems to have become an established vulgarism.) This tex occupies the second and third volumes. The very difficult problem of how to reproduce Byron's scrawled and heavily corrected and interlined manu script has been solved extremely well. Any reader who will trouble to master the note on editorial practice can construct for himself what hap pened in any particular stanza, and enough pages are reproduced for u to compare Byron's drafts with the translation of them into print.

Here is an example of the kind of interest to be found in these two volumes of text and of the light they throw on Byron's habits of composi tion and on the nature of his gifts as a poet. The first stanza of the famou lyric which the renegade poet sings at Haidée's feast sounds like one o those immediate, inevitable, and rhythmically haunting openings whicl Byron excelled at creating, as noble and natural as the opening phrase of Verdi's arias. In fact it by no means came easily. Byron did not orig inally intend to write a lyric. He began with two lines for a stanza ir *ottava rima:*

> The isles of Greece—the Isles of Greece—where sung
> The Lesbian Sappho and the blind old man.

Then I suppose the rhythm of the repeated phrase—"The isles of Greece" —struck him as a lyric rhythm and he started to recast the lines anc produced

> The isles of Greece—The Isles of Greece
> Where Lesbian Sappho sung
> Where rose the arts of war and peace
> Where Delian Phoebus sprung.

This is a banal tune, with its heavy-footed second and fourth lines. He went back and with the line

> Where Sappho loved where Sappho sung

he got the lilting rhythm he wanted and expanded his fourth line to match:

> Where Delos rose, and Phoebus sprung.

He then went on, having completed his stanza with a firm couplet, to a second stanza, over which he had great difficulty. He had some trouble with his third stanza, less with his fourth, and rather more with his fifth. After this he went straight ahead, with no fumblings or false starts and with virtually no revision at all, pouring out, now he had got the tune into his head, a succession of heart-stirring stanzas, effortlessly incorporating into their music the great evocative Greek names. It was not until he came to make his fair copy that he hit upon the perfect second line for his first stanza, found his classic epithet for Sappho, and achieved the opening which seems so supremely natural, easy, and spontaneous:

> The isles of Greece, the isles of Greece!
> Where burning Sappho loved and sung. . . .

The two volumes of text are flanked by two others. The fourth is Professor Pratt's and provides a commentary, including, as well as Byron's own notes, those of Moore. The first volume is Professor Steffan's and is really a book on *Don Juan*. I do not always agree with Professor Steffan, and he has a tendency both to over-write, wrenching the language to strange effects, and to repeat himself. But his learning and enthusiasm and the fascination of his material are so great that I feel ungrateful in making any complaint. I wish this edition was not so expensive; but I doubt whether it could have been produced much more cheaply. To anyone who loves Byron and wants to come into contact with Byron writing out of the fullness of his mind it is wonderful value for the money.

In discussing Byron's revision of his poem, Professor Steffan deals first with "accretion," that is, additions which Byron made at different stages to his first drafts. This is heaviest in the first five cantos. Byron can be seen writing himself into his poem, creating its character as he went along. By far the greatest number of additional stanzas occur in the first canto of all. Sixty-six of its two hundred and twenty-two stanzas were afterthoughts, some, including Julia's pathetic letter, and the catalogue of rejected heroes (stanzas 2-5), being written as late as a month after the canto had been dispatched to Murray and sent after it to be inserted in London. After Canto V very little was added to the first drafts, only thirty-two stanzas being added in the whole of the last eleven cantos. Professor Steffan takes this as evidence of Byron's greater enthusiasm for the enterprise at the beginning; but surely the pattern for the whole poem is like the pattern for the "Isles of Greece" lyric: initial experiment, and then, the manner once found, an absolute assurance in the use of it. The amount of accretion in the first canto shows Byron discovering as he writes that his little bedroom-farce anecdote can serve him as a starting-point for reflection on anything in heaven and earth, and that the manner of *Beppo*, "a little quietly facetious upon everything," had not exhausted the potentialities of the *ottava rima* stanza in English, or given scope for all that he had to say about the world and himself. Professor Steffan discusses at length the substance of these accretions, as revealing Byron's obsessive interests, what could be relied on to spark him off.

Contrary to what one would have expected perhaps, there was very little expurgation. What there was seems to have been motivated by artistic rather than prudential reasons. One brilliant couplet was, however, sacrificed to the prudes, when the description of Inez's Sunday school (II. 10) was allowed to end rather tamely with

> The great success of Juan's education
> Spurr'd her to teach another generation.

The original conclusion was

> Their manners mending and their morals curing
> She taught them to suppress their vice and urine.

Even more interesting is the evidence the manuscripts furnish of the extent to which Byron worked on separate lines and phrases, particularly of the trouble he took to give his final couplets their punch. The impression given, and Professor Steffan from his study of the actual manuscripts confirms this, is of writing and revision often taking place together, creation and critical evaluation proceeding apace at white-hot speed. The handwriting is a scrawl, and Byron dashes at lines, sometimes beginning with a kind of written stammer, as if he had to write down something while the line or stanza was forming itself in his head. On the other hand, a great many revisions were obviously made at a later reading; some do not occur until the fair copy and some were made between fair copy and print. All the same, the overwhelming impression is of the rapidity and vehemence of Byron's intelligence, the amount of correction and improvement he made as his pen ran on. There is no suggestion of labored revision; but the amount of fundamental brain-work that lies behind the "rattling-on" of *Don Juan* is none the less impressive because it plainly took place at high speed.

It is fascinating to see Byron packing a line with extra point, as when Raucocanti's mere malicious aspersion on the professional competence of the prima donna

> And somewhat subject to a cough and cold

is turned into a sarcasm on her temperamental vanity:

> And subject, when the house is thin, to cold.

Julia's boast that she has chosen

> a Confessor so old
> That any other woman it would vex

is heightened by the substitution

> so old
> And deaf that any other it would vex.

This implies, as Professor Steffan comments, that she has no sins which she is not quite prepared to shout aloud. A hackneyed address to death as "Old Skeleton" is transformed to the vivid image "Gaunt Gourmand." An obvious antithesis becomes a line which the whole world has laughed over, as, for instance, the rather flat

> Would sometimes have changed Royalty for Beauty

gives place to the ludicrous image of

> In Royalty's Vast Arms he sighed for Beauty.

Many aspects of Byron's temperament are reflected in his revisions: his almost neurotic concern with precision of fact, his desire above all things not to be dull, his interest in psychology, his lively concern with the latest scientific and pseudo-scientific discoveries, and his delight in description, which he thought was his *forte,* but which in fact he rather overdid. The most impressive revisions to my mind are those which show Byron's critical attitude to language and the keenness of his ear for the tone and rhythm of his lines, his passion to combine the natural with the pointed, to achieve the virtues of a colloquial style without losing the beauties of the rhetorical. Sometimes he will tighten and pack a line; sometimes he will slacken its tempo and lighten it by a parenthesis. Thus the rather over-chatty line

> Have lived my Summer out ere it was May

was strengthened by the alteration to "have squandered my whole summer"; while, on the other hand, the tone of

> 'Twas Midnight—dark and sombre was the night

was lowered into

and a hint of melodrama was removed. The impression which a mere
cursory study of this edition gives of Byron's intellectual vitality and
vivacity is overwhelming. At first sight nothing would seem easier to
imitate than the manner of *Don Juan;* but the imitations and continua
tions, which began almost at once, disprove, by their extreme feebleness
the notion that Byron is only a mannerist whose tricks can be copied
by anyone who has the mind to. It is the mind of Byron which is beyond
imitation. The fullness of his experience of life, his range and ease of
reference, his curiosity about all things human, the candor and courage
with which he exposes himself as well as his world, his intellectual tough-
ness and temperamental resilience created the manner of *Don Juan* as
their appropriate vehicle. The revisions show Byron's effort to give the
maximum expressiveness to the truth of substance and force of feeling by
which his poem still chiefly lives.

Byron made many different statements at different stages in the poem's
composition about what he was trying to do in *Don Juan.* He began by
claiming that it was to be in the style of *Beppo,* "a little quietly facetious
upon everything." Later he said he was writing a "comedy of the passions," and, on another occasion, that *Don Juan* was "a satire on the
abuses of the present state of society." When asked what his plans were,
he said that he had no plan, but that he had "materials," and protested
that the very soul of such poetry was its license. But soon after this he
produced an impressive plan of a tour of Europe and a study of the
manners of society in different countries in the age of the French Revolution. He defended himself against criticism on various grounds, most
often by appealing from "this very moral age" to the standards of the
past. One position he never swerved from. He always insisted that his
poem was "true": that it gave a candid and faithful picture of human
nature. He did not claim that he was attempting to reform society, or to
unmask hypocrisy, or to scourge vice; but that he was writing a "human"
poem which told the truth about man and society.

Strong as the satiric element in *Don Juan* is, and in spite of the power
of Byron's bursts of satire, the underlying impulse of the poem is not
satiric. It began as a farce and developed into a comedy. Professor Steffan
is, I think, wrong to complain, as he does more than once, that Byron
often blunts a satiric point by concessions to his victims and that his
attack on the "abuses of the present state of society" is weakened by
shifts of feeling. He complains, for instance, that in the great war cantos
the force of Byron's attack on the waste and squalor of war is dissipated
by his admiration for Suwarrow as a "great man," and by his glowing
stanzas on the courage of the Tartar Khan and his sons. This is surely
a fine example of Byron's strength. His realistic insight into the folly,

wickedness and futility of war does not blind him to the facts of human nature. Suwarrow is not only a general who regards human beings as expendable, and thus a target for satire; he is also a man with a gift for leadership, who puts fresh spirit into disheartened troops by unorthodox means and gets what he wants out of them. Suwarrow in his shirt-sleeves drilling his men has the Monty touch. Byron's sympathy and admiration goes out to professional competence in the same way as Chaucer's does. And it is surely rather odd to complain because Suwarrow is momentarily touched by the distress of Juan's girl friends. Byron is not attempting to create a pacifist's Aunt Sally. The war is purposeless and the men who fight in it are the victims of despots, politicians, generals, and dishonest contractors. Byron knows this; but he also knows that human courage, however exploited, abused, and misguided, is fine. "Though a quarrel in the Streets is a thing to be hated," wrote Keats, "the energies displayed in it are fine." The satirist uses all the resources of his art to divert our attention from the fineness; the romantic writer ignores, and persuades us to ignore, the hatefulness of the quarrel. Satire is a major element in *Don Juan;* but so is romance. Neither is pure, and both are contained within a comic vision of man. Suwarrow is allowed his "greatness," and not merely as a concession that makes his inhumanity more shocking. That most romantic couple, Juan and Haidée, spend a good deal of their time together in eating. Juan's splendid declaration to Gulbeyaz of the freedom of the will comes from a Joseph absurdly dressed in women's clothes. His virtue immediately wobbles (like Tom Jones, he cannot bear a woman's tears) and is only saved by Baba's agitated entrance.

The great theme of *Don Juan* is the power of illusion. Byron said that the reason his mistress Teresa disapproved of it was because it was the wish of all women "to exalt the sentiment of the passions and to keep up the illusion which is their empire. Now *Don Juan* strips off this illusion and laughs at that and most other things." The root of Byron's attack on the heartless frivolity and cynicism of the ruling classes, and on the idol Legitimacy which they made the shield for their self-interest, is his skepticism. Like the child in the story of the Emperor's new clothes he continues to reiterate that the Emperor is naked. His defense of *Don Juan* as a moral poem was grounded on the salutariness of being undeceived. There are some critics who declare that *Don Juan* is neither moral nor immoral, that it is written to amuse, to shock, to horrify and startle, to make the serious absurd, and to play tricks with our feelings. But it is preposterous to call *Don Juan* an amoral work. Apart from the obvious moral passion in many passages, we are in no doubt as we read that Byron admires courage, generosity, compassion, and honesty, and that he dislikes brutality, meanness, and above all self-importance, hypocrisy, and priggery. If he does not denounce, he displays with great force the satiety which dogs, as its appropriate nemesis, the life of sensation. He offers no panaceas and does not pretend that men can be saved from themselves by love, sensual or Platonic, by politics, or by patriotism. His resolute refusal to be taken in by cant of all kinds is so far-reaching as to deserve to be called a positive devotion to truth, and *Don Juan* is the most moral of poems in this, at least, that it does not flatter what Swift, along with higher authorities, thought was man's worst vice, his pride and vanity. But, unlike many who hold a low view of human nature, Byron is not driven by it into political reaction. If men are not capable of ruling themselves, they are certainly not to be trusted to rule others. Tyrants themselves are only men, and man's weakness and folly are no arguments for depriving him of his freedom. Byron was a good hater and he hated many hateful things. Although he had no very clear notions of what he was fighting for, he was quite clear as to what he was fighting against. We get no reasoned doctrine of liberty from Byron, as we do from Milton; we get a very good idea of tyranny and its companion, sycophancy:

> But still there is unto a patriot nation
>   Which loves so well its country and its King,
> A subject of sublimest exultation—
>   Bear it, ye Muses, on your brightest wing!
> Howe'er the mighty locust, Desolation,
>   Strip your green fields, and to your harvests cling,
> Gaunt Famine never shall approach the throne—
> Though Ireland starve, great George weighs twenty stone.

(Byron first wrote "forty stone"; but hyperbole had to yield to his passion for exactness. The joke is improved by his moderation.)

Although Byron's vision of man and the world is not very flattering to our self-esteem, or very comforting to our hopes, it is not discouraging. Man may not be a very noble animal, but he has his moments of glory, and life provides pleasures and satisfactions of many kinds. Although most men are fools, by no means all are knaves. The human race has even produced a few heroes, and common men are capable of loyalty and kindness. "Chequered as is seen our human lot," it is still better to be alive than dead, better to be young than old, better to be generous than cautious, and better to be compassionate than censorious. For all its bursts of cynicism, savagery, and melancholy, there is a fundamental good humor in *Don Juan* which becomes the dominant tone when Byron finally gets his hero to England. Byron should be congenial reading today. There are many and obvious affinities between his age and ours, both exhausted by a great revolution and its aftermath of war; and no writer has been more heartily and consistently "against the Establishment." But although Byron can be bitter and astringent he is not sour. His skepticism and irreverence are echoed today; but not his high spirits, and his zest for life.

It is rather doubtful if we rise from reading *Don Juan* as wiser men. Wisdom of the highest kind Byron did not attain to, and this prevents him from ranking with the greatest poets. But if we are not wiser we are certainly not sadder from reading *Don Juan,* and there is something for us to learn from the courage and buoyancy with which Byron came to terms with a world as shabby and confused as ours.

Don Juan: "Carelessly I Sing"

by George M. Ridenour

Toward the end of Canto VIII the poet announces:

> Reader! I have kept my word,—at least so far
>   As the first Canto promised. You have now
> Had sketches of Love—Tempest—Travel—War,—
>   All very accurate, you must allow,
> And *Epic,* if plain truth should prove no bar;
>   For I have drawn much less with a long bow
> Than my forerunners. Carelessly I sing,
> But Phœbus lends me now and then a string.
>
> [VIII. 138]

It seems that he is taking particular pains at the end of the two "war cantos" to remind us of the claim his poem has been making to be epic. And the terms are such as should be familiar to us. Not only have his "sketches of Love—Tempest—Travel—War" presumably fulfilled the external thematic and episodic requirements of the epic form but, we are told, they are "All very accurate." The comment is especially justified at this point, of course, since the cantos on the Siege of Ismail follow their source (Castelnau's *Histoire de la nouvelle Russie*) with a fidelity unusual even in Byron. And there is the highly characteristic uneasiness as to the compatibility of accuracy and epic: "if plain truth should prove no bar." He accordingly reminds us that while he emphatically considers himself in the line of epic poets, he is an epic poet in the plain style: "I have drawn much less with a long bow / Than my forerunners." There is an explicit association between content and style, the truth with which the poem deals and the manner in which it deals with it. The "carelessness" of his song is connected with the truth it is to express. Hence the

chatty, conversational manner, the easy, informal tone which gains much
of its significance from an implied contrast with the grand manner of
epic—especially that manner as communicated by Milton and Pope.

But if it is accurate to say that this is an epic which is plain in manner
and veracious in content, the emphasis can be reversed. This is what
happens at the end of the stanza. The manner is simple and the matter
the simple facts, but at the same time it is epic. It claims the inspiration
of the Leader of the Muses: "Phœbus lends me now and then a string."
The stylistic problem of *Don Juan* should, then, be clear enough. The
manner must be informal and conversational ("careless"), a deliberate
scandal in terms of the traditional concepts of epic style. But while, as I
have pointed out, the primary reference of stylistic level is to intensity of
tone, the poet will be well-advised to provide a rhetorical organization
that will facilitate our acceptance of the epic pretensions of the poem. It
is, then, the more specifically rhetorical aspects of the art of *Don Juan*
with which I shall concern myself here.

Just as it is essential for the content of the poem to seem random and
rambling when in fact it is relentlessly coherent and unified, the style of
the poem itself presents a striking combination of the conversationally
offhand and the elaborately rhetorical. Now perhaps the simplest way of
giving form to a stanza of *ottava rima,* and a way highly congenial to a
lover of Pope, would be to treat the eight lines as four rhythmically independent units—as a kind of unrhymed heroic couplets. Byron sometimes
does this:

> But Juan was no casuist, nor had pondered
>   Upon the moral lessons of mankind:
> Besides, he had not seen of several hundred
>   A lady altogether to his mind.
> A little *blasé*—'tis not to be wondered
>   At, that his heart had got a tougher rind:
> And though not vainer from his past success,
> No doubt his sensibilities were less.
>
> [XII. 81]

More often, however, he will prefer a freer movement, tightening up
only in the final couplet:

> While things were in abeyance, Ribas sent
>   A courier to the Prince, and he succeeded
> In ordering matters after his own bent;
>   I cannot tell the way in which he pleaded,
> But shortly he had cause to be content.
>   In the mean time, the batteries proceeded,

> And fourscore cannon on the Danube's border
> Were briskly fired and answered in due order.
>
> [VII. 38]

The tone of this stanza is studiously unpoetic ("careless"), helping persuade us of the poet's objectivity and scrupulous regard for truth ("I cannot tell . . ."). It is only in the unbroken movement of the concluding couplet that the conscientiously prosy movement is resolved. But the couplet does more than that. In its brisk pace, vigorous rhymes, and circular movement it provides a precise rhetorical equivalent to the efficient futility of the cannonade. (It might be worth noting that the stanza does not appear to be a close translation of the source; but it is made to sound as if it were.)

But Byron has a virtuoso mastery of the elements of his octave (the very fact that it is so generally unrecognized is a kind of tribute to his unobtrusive control), and he is particularly resourceful in his use of the final couplet:

> And that still keeping up the old connection,
>   Which Time had lately rendered much more chaste,
> She took his lady also in affection,
>   And certainly this course was much the best:
> She flattered Julia with her sage protection,
>   And complimented Don Alfonso's taste;
> And if she could not (who can?) silence scandal,
> At least she left it a more slender handle.
>
> [I. 67]

The octave is arranged in couplets, with a pause or full stop at the end of every line. There are no strong internal pauses to retard the speed—he is being gossipy here—or, to look at it in another way, to relieve the monotony. This throws a great deal of weight on the final couplet (all the greater because the stanza is grammatically and rhetorically an extension of the previous one), which must provide a satisfactory resolution. And it seems to me no denigration of Byron's skill to point out that the devices used are simple (not, after all, the same thing as "easy"). They are devices of elementary manipulation of rhythm and sound-pattern:

> And if she could not (who can?) silence scandal,
> At least she left it a more slender handle.

The rhythm is broken first of all by the series of five consecutive stresses in the first line—"could not (who can?) si-." Rhythmically (as opposed to metrically) the first line ends with two strong spondees followed by two trochees (which gain force by the alliterating *s's* and the repetition of the *l's* and *n's*): "could not (who can?) silence scandal." [1] The *l* is picked up again in the second line, this time in the alliterating accented syllables of the introductory iambs. The conclusion of the second line parallels the first, ending in two dissyllables forming strong trochees. [2] The first ("slender") picks up the *s* from the conclusion of the preceding line, as well as the *n*, which occurs again in "handle." In addition, the two words share voiced dentals (*d*) between a nasal (*n*) and a liquid (*r, l*) —the point of which is to suggest how Byron builds up his couplet acoustically and rhythmically, endowing it with the substance required by its rhetorical function as the climax of fourteen lines of chit-chat. It is strong enough for its purpose and yet discreet enough not to make one conscious of the presence of rhetoric in a passage where our awareness of it would spoil the gossipy effect. For one of the most important manifestations of the *persona* is the rattle-brained chatter-box—so putting us off guard when the thrust comes ("I'm sure I mean no harm"). [3] It is among the richest sources of Byronic irony.

While criticism of Byron is well supplied with vague observations about "energy" and "force," it seems never to have been adequately appreciated that Lord Byron had a real genius for the handling of rhythm. The couplet we have just been examining is quiet and unobtrusive, and rhythmically accomplished; there is no excuse to suppose that Byron shines only in the loud passages. Both in tone and in manner he has much greater range than is usually granted (*Childe Harold* has suffered especially from the stubborn insistence on always hearing Byron shout). In neither of the next two stanzas I shall be considering is there any denunciation or beating of the breast; but both are brilliant specimens of rhythmical modulation, and both are characteristically Byronic:

[1] I should scan it:

And if she could not (who can?) silence scandal.

In terms of traditional scansion there are no "trochees" in the line. At the risk, however, of initial misunderstanding, I have in this chapter sometimes used the traditional metrical feet to describe what are not always strictly metrical units.

[2] I should scan this second line:

At least she left it a more slender handle.

Perhaps the relative intensity of "more" (felt rhythmically as the third beat of an anapest—the accent on *a* is honorific) makes it easier to feel the last two words as rhythmical units.

[3] IX. 7.

At one o'clock the wind with sudden shift
   Threw the ship right into the trough of the sea,
Which struck her aft, and made an awkward rift,
   Started the stern-post, also shattered the
Whole of her stern-frame, and ere she could lift
   Herself from out her present jeopardy,
The rudder tore away: 'twas time to sound
The pumps, and there were four feet water found.

                                      [II. 27]

No small part of the effect of this stanza is the result of Byron's close following of the fine vigorous prose of his source (it is the work of the "truthful Muse"):

Night came on worse than the day had been; and a *sudden shift of wind,* about midnight, *threw the ship into the trough of the sea, which struck her aft, tore away the rudder, started the stern-post, and shattered the whole of her stern-frame. The pumps were immediately sounded,* and in the course of a few minutes the water had increased to *four feet.*[4]

Since Byron has already informed us in the previous stanza (26) that it was night, he can omit the first part of the passage. "One o'clock" is both more definite and less obviously melodramatic than "about midnight." It also makes possible a *w* alliteration which, in context and in conjunction with the concluding alliterating sibilants ("*s*udden *sh*ift"), composes a line of effective auditory mimesis (onomatopoeia)—the whistling and the soughing of the wind. The fact that four of the five accented syllables bear the further weight of alliteration emphasizes the strictly regular beat (metrical and rhythmical stresses coincide almost exactly). This is important, because the verse of auditory is followed immediately by a verse of rhythmical mimesis: "Threw the ship right into the trough of the sea." Byron has taken the passage intact from his source, with the addition of an adverb. That the metrical irregularity of the line is intended to mimic the tossing motion is clear. The spondaic second foot (strengthened by the half-rhyme of "shift" with "ship," cutting across the line divisions, adding to the feeling of impetuosity) and the (whatever it may be metrically) anapestic rhythm of the end of the line ("-to the trough of the sea")[5] help to create as nice a specimen of neoclassical sound and sense as

---

[4] *The Works of Lord Byron, Poetry,* edited by E. H. Coleridge, Vol. VI, 88-89, n. The italics are the editor's.

[5] For purposes of scansion I should read it:

          /   x| |/ x| x / |x   x /
    Threw the ship right into the trough of the sea.

one could hope to find. The addition of the adverb may facilitate our feeling the end of the line as strongly anapestic.

The third line—while providing a welcome reassurance as to the metrical norm from which the variations of the preceding verse and (especially) the following verses derive much of their force—also contributes a mimetically valuable strong caesura, emphasized by the internal half-rhyme of "aft" and "rift." It is in the next two lines, however, that the rhythmical mimesis becomes most interesting (the first line and a half, except for the connective, is taken over unchanged from the source):

> Started the stern-post, also shattered the
> Whole of her stern-frame, and ere she could lift . . .

Rhythmically the first line is suspended between two almost-rhyming dactyls: "Started the . . . shattered the." [6] This device, with remarkable economy, gives both shape and impetus to the line. It is rushed into the next line, passing easily over the very light rhyme-word ("the"), and the whole rhythmical unit is finished off with a repetition of the two strong stresses that had concluded the first phrase ("stern-post . . . stern-frame"). The passage has an almost jazzy quality about it. And the effect is all the greater not only because of the resistance of the metrical norm (which has been impressed on us in the previous line), but also, perhaps, from the invitation to special emphasis one may discover in the piling up of sibilants. All this is very subjective, but as I feel the passage there is a kind of tension between the forces pushing the movement forward and those tending to retard it that helps make these lines a particularly effective imitation of physical thrust and resistance and final overthrow. The halting conclusion of the line ("and ere she could lift") moves us into the metrically regular sixth line (but still with a weak rhyme: "jeopardy"), and the whole movement is concluded in the inexorable "sound/found" rhyme of the couplet. The feeling of helplessness in the face of natural forces has received less effective expression than in these lines of Byron's.

But Byron's rhythmic gifts are not apparent only in passages of imitation (or better, in passages imitative of external, as opposed to internal, events) and in reworkings of source materials. The action of the second specimen is the expression of a state of mind, and so far as I know (aside from the precedent of Sir Epicure Mammon) it is entirely original. It is part of the brilliantly Augustan praise of avarice at the beginning of Canto XII. Byron is speaking of the miser:

---

[6]   Started the stern-post, also shattered the.
The final accent is merely a tribute to the metrical pattern. It is obviously very weak; and the rhythmic effect is dactylic.

He is your only poet;—Passion, pure
  And sparkling on from heap to heap, displays
Possessed, the ore, of which *mere hopes* allure
  Nations athwart the deep: the golden rays
Flash up in ingots from the mine obscure:
  On him the Diamond pours its brilliant blaze,
While the mild Emerald's beam shades down the dies
Of other stones, to soothe the miser's eyes.

                                        [XII. 8]

It is the first three lines with which we are especially concerned. And it should be clear that the same rhythmical devices are being used here as in the stanza just analyzed. The *s's* and *t's* of the earlier passage are paralleled by the *p's* and *s's* of this one. The push of the enjambment has again to contend with the opportunities for declamation presented by the alliterating words, while the movement from line three to line four is retarded by the half-rhyme of "the ore" and "allure" (there is, in fact, a rhythmical and acoustical balancing of *"Possessed,* the ore . . . *mere hopes* allure" that is reminiscent of the "Started the . . . shattered the" of the first passage). There is again, in short, the same tension between push and resistance that we have seen used to such fine effect in the earlier passage. Byron is seeking rhythmically to validate the romance with which, as I have observed, he chooses at this moment to invest the miser. For, as I read it, the passage is an element in the poem's shift in emphasis from innocence to experience, of which "avarice" is a powerful symbol.

After the vigorous rhythms of the opening lines, the octave resolves itself in five lines phrased with the most elegant formality. The formal center of the section is line 6: "On him the Diamond pours its brilliant blaze." Reading from this line in either direction, one finds a line without caesura in enjambment with two iambs—followed after a caesura by three iambs at the beginning and end of their respective lines. The phrasing is exquisitely balanced.[7] A proper reading of the lines will make it clear that the effect is not merely visual; for if the poet is carefully shifting the weight of the poem toward the pole of experience, he himself is experienced enough not to be simple-minded about it. And the most appropriate form of irony is that implicit in the fine control of both tone and rhythm manifested by this octave.

The most striking piece of internal (or psychological) mimesis would be, I suppose, the five stanzas of Haidée's dream (IV. 31-5):

---

[7] A particularly tidy Augustan specimen of this kind of phrasal symmetry is the first stanza of Pope's "Epistle to a Young Lady on Her Leaving the Town after the Coronation."

> She dreamed of being alone on the sea-shore,
>   Chained to a rock; she knew not how, but stir
> She could not from the spot, and the loud roar
>   Grew, and each wave rose roughly, threatening her;
> And o'er her upper lip they seemed to pour,
>   Until she sobbed for breath, and soon they were
> Foaming o'er her lone head, so fierce and high—
> Each broke to drown her, yet she could not die.
>
> Anon—she was released, and then she strayed
>   O'er the sharp shingles with her bleeding feet,
> And stumbled almost every step she made:
>   And something rolled before her in a sheet,
> Which she must still pursue howe'er afraid:
>   'Twas white and indistinct, nor stopped to meet
> Her glance nor grasp, for still she gazed and grasped,
> And ran, but it escaped her as she clasped.
>
> [31-2]

The breathless quality of these long sentences (each a whole octave) is well adapted to the expression of the terror of a nightmare. The smooth sequence of independent clauses loosely connected by "and" (which occurs eight times in the two octaves) suggests both the significant inconsequence of dreams in general and, in the second stanza quoted, the anxious pursuit of something that ever eludes the grasp (emphasized by the alliteration of "glance nor grasp . . . gazed and grasped") of this particular dream. The monotonous reiteration of the personal pronoun (sixteen in so many lines), on the other hand, expresses the obsession with self characteristic of the dreamer. The whole passage is restrained, economical, and thoroughly admirable.

In all the passages examined so far one is struck by the skill with which Byron manipulates such simple and conventional rhetorical devices as alliteration, assonance, consonance, internal rhyme. This is, in fact, characteristic of the poem as a whole. One is appreciative, for example, of the contempt expressed by the alliterative labials of "Power's base purveyors, who for pickings howl" (IX. 27), or in the *st's* of "modern, reigning, sterling, stupid stamp!" (XII. 12). Or of the suggestions of speed and monotony in the internal rhyme and alliteration of "waste, and haste, and glare, and gloss, and glitter" (X. 26). Or of the further extension of the same device in the pointless briskness and orderliness in the central four lines of an octave from the Siege of Ismail:

> The troops, already disembarked, pushed on
>   To take a battery on the right: the others,

Who landed lower down, their landing done,
  Had set to work as briskly as their brothers:
Being grenadiers, they mounted one by one,
  Cheerful as children climb the breasts of mothers,
O'er the entrenchment and the palisade,
Quite orderly, as if upon parade.

[VIII. 15]

Closely related to this would be certain elementary forms of sound-imi-
tation, such as we find in the following couplets:

When amatory poets sing their loves
In liquid lines mellifluously bland.
[V. 1]

Bombs, drums, guns, bastions, batteries, bayonets, bullets—
Hard words, which stick in the soft Muses' gullets.

[VII. 78]

The liquids and nasals of the first passage are obvious enough, and Byron
himself provides a gloss on the array of rhyming and alliterating vowels
and mutes in the second. This last, of course, is part of the "epic" theme,
and is closely related to the stanzas of cacophonous Russian names (VII.
14-17). There is probably an implicit reference to the common neoclassic
notion that even the commonest and most vulgar utensils took on nobility
in Greek.

Byron's trick rhymes need no comment from me, and we have already
had good specimens of his fondness for internal rhyme. His most effective
internal rhymes, it might be noted, seem usually to be half-rhymes (assonance or consonance). Think, for example, of "Thicker than *leaves* the
lives began to fall" (VIII. 9; my italics), where the consonance of the
italicized words emphasizes the likeness between leaves in autumn and
human lives in war. From which it is but a step to the actual repetition
of the same word (my italics):

Or know who *rested* there, a foe to *rest*.
[III. 1]
. . . risen from *death,* to be
Perchance the *death* of one she loved too well.
[IV. 36]
They either *missed,* or they were never *missed,*
And added greatly to the *missing* list.
[VII. 27]

In neither of the first two passages just cited is the repeated word used in quite the same sense each time, and the participle in the third passage is a rather grim pun. It is the two senses or different applications of the same word that is emphasized in such passages as the following (my italics):

> And the waves oozing through the port-hole *made*
> His berth a little damp, and him afraid.
>
> [II. 25]
>
> Some *take* a lover, some *take* drams or prayers,
> Some *mind* their household, others dissipation.
>
> [II. 201]
>
> The loud tempests *raise*
> The waters, and repentance for past sinning.
>
> [V. 6]

The zeugmas in the first and third passages dramatize with admirable economy that relationship between physical cause and psychological (or spiritual) effect which is a principal motif of the poem. The same verb that indicates the objective event serves also for the subjective effect. Besides the obvious connection with the theme of the relationship between the Fall and the law of gravity, it displays another aspect of the poet's elaborately clinical objectivity in dealing with moral situations.

The second passage is interesting for its bland pairing of such apparently unlike things as lovers, drams, and prayers; or of housekeeping and dissipation. In other words, it is a form of juxtaposition, seen in its pure form in such lists as the following:

> A priest, a shark, an alderman, or pike.
>
> [II. 157]
>
> After long travel, Ennui, Love, or Slaughter.
>
> [II. 180]
>
> They all were heroes, conquerors, and cuckolds.
>
> [II. 206]
>
> Dwarfs, dancing girls, black eunuchs, and a poet.
>
> [III. 78]

Apart from the general function of giving shape to the material, and the specific function each of these smaller devices may serve in their different contexts, they may also be of interest for their generally Augustan quality. All are staples of Augustan satire, and it was from reading the Augustans that Byron learned how to handle them. They constitute another link between Byron and the tradition of Pope.

There is little point in merely listing examples of Byron's word-play, but one might be permitted a mild protest against the condescension with which it seems often to be dismissed. The examples already cited might suggest that Byron usually knew what he was doing. And perhaps one or two not uncharacteristic specimens may profitably be invoked. First of all, consider the lines dedicated to

> That monstrous hieroglyphic—that long spout
> Of blood and water—*leaden* Castlereagh!
> [IX. 50; my italics]

These verses are part of a larger passage dealing with the familiar theme of the connection between literature and society. Here it is specifically verbal obscurity and social violence (war). After converting Castlereagh into a sphinx ("That monstrous hieroglyphic") and then into a "monstrous" combination of leviathan and drainpipe (the "spout" image is defined by the images on *both* sides of it), he concludes economically with the single attribute of "leaden"—referring at once to the *quality* of his oratory (dull, obscure, "heavy"), the *effect* of his oratory (bullets, war, death), and the *personal characteristics* that produced such oratory (his leaden stupidity; cf. VIII. 10).

The second passage is from the conclusion of the famous *ubi sunt* stanzas in Canto XI:

> But *"carpe diem,"* Juan, *"carpe, carpe!"*
> To-morrow sees another race as gay
> And transient, and devoured by the same harpy.
> [XI. 86]

I call attention to the use of the word "race" in the second line. It is useful that we first think of race in terms of a race to be run, with the suggestion of excitement and bustle and competition (and no place to go). It is only when we come to the third line that we find the primary reference to be to the human race. But since the human race is seen as engaged in a race against time, the confusion is a valuable one. This, however, is not the only element of word-play in these lines. Byron is joining the large number of poets who have produced variants of the *carpe diem* theme. And he has his own contribution. *Carpe diem,* he says, make the most of the day, before you too are devoured by the monster death (or time). And death is a harpy for more reasons than that it makes possible a clever rhyme. When we recall that it was the Harpies who snatched the food away from King Phineus (the word "harpy" is related to *harpazô,* "to seize or snatch") and that *carpe diem* means literally "Seize (or snatch) the day" (*carpo* and *harpazô* are, in fact, cognates), the point of the etymological pun becomes clear. Snatch the day, then, before death snatches you. Or, even better, thinking of the harpy as time: Snatch time before time snatches you. In any case the point is clear and the device potent.

Both of the passages provide more material for analysis than what I have called vaguely "word-play." Both, for example, are highly metaphoric, and both are specimens of the bright, showy, self-consciously clever sort of metaphor called conceit—a kind of image of obvious utility to a poem in which, as we have seen, the speaker's brightness and sophistication are of thematic importance.

We have glanced at some of the more valuable conceits in *Don Juan* in the course of the previous chapters. One recalls, for example, the meteorological and physiological conceits concluding Canto II ("The heart is like the sky, etc."; 214-15), or the "frozen champagne" conceit of Canto XIII (37-8). The best known, I suppose, is the "Microcosm on stilts" passage from Canto XII (56). But these only begin to suggest the range and variety of Byron's conceits. We are given both the extended and many-faceted comparison between the coming of Suwarrow to the Russian army and a "grand illumination" in London (VII. 44-6) and two lines of compressed social history (referring to the portraits at Norman Abbey):

> Steel Barons, molten the next generation
> To silken rows of gay and gartered Earls.
> [XIII. 68]

There is the brilliant conceit of war and disease developed from a hint in the source (VIII. 12)[8] and the conceit of "cities, that boil over with their scum," developed from the "dead metaphor" of a city street in "ferment" (XI. 8).

But for brilliance, originality, and thematic relevance the following ranks second only to the "frozen champagne" stanzas:

> Suppose him in a handsome uniform—
>   A scarlet coat, black facings, a long plume,
> Waving, like sails new shivered in a storm,
>   Over a cocked hat in a crowded room,
> And brilliant breeches, bright as a Cairn Gorme,
>   Of yellow casimire we may presume,
> White stockings drawn uncurdled as new milk
> O'er limbs whose symmetry set off the silk;

---

[8] *Poetry*, ed. Coleridge, Vol. VI, 334, n. 2.

Suppose him sword by side, and hat in hand,
  Made up by Youth, Fame, and an army tailor—
That great enchanter, at whose rod's command
  Beauty springs forth, and Nature's self turns paler,
Seeing how Art can make her work more grand
  (When she don't pin men's limbs in like a gaoler),—
Behold him placed as if upon a pillar! He
Seems Love turned a Lieutenant of Artillery!

His bandage slipped down into a cravat—
  His wings subdued to epaulettes—his quiver
Shrunk to a scabbard, with his arrows at
  His side as a small sword, but sharp as ever—
His brow converted into a cocked hat—
  But still so like, that Psyche were more clever
Than some wives (who make blunders no less stupid),
If she had not mistaken him for Cupid.

                                         [IX. 43-5]

Coming as it does at the very beginning of Juan's adventure with Catherine the Great, this passage occupies a particularly crucial position in the development of the action. For, as Steffan has observed, the affair with Catherine is for Juan an initiation in a sense in which none of his previous affairs had been.[9] In spite of everything, Byron manages to make us accept the idea of Juan's "innocence" (in the special sense of the word used in this essay). But after his excursions in Petersburg this is no longer possible. But then, it is no longer the effect Byron wants to produce. Catherine is, in the first place, an "older woman." She is described, I have suggested, in terms of a kind of travesty of the "stern sweetness" paradox. She is an empress, an embodiment of absolute secular power (a tyrant). She is lustful and she is given to waging war. She possesses great wealth. She is, in fact, like Lambro, an almost definitive expression of "experience"—*from one point of view*. When Juan enters her arms, he is entering an entirely new phase of existence. The attitude is, of course, a double one, but at least with regard to Catherine herself the judgment is predominantly adverse. It is only with Adeline (so very different and so very like) and (in still another way) Aurora that the weight shifts distinctly toward the other pole. But at no time is Byron unaware of what is involved, as these three splendid octaves make clear.

[9] Don Juan: *A Variorum Edition*, ed. T. G. Steffan and W. W. Pratt, Austin, Texas, 1957; I. 284. It is worth noticing that this is the point in the poem where Juan comes in contact with the little Turkish orphan, Leila. As Rupert Palmer has called to my attention, the little girl now serves to replace Juan as the embodiment of what I have been calling "innocence." In so doing she can serve as a means of gauging the extent of Juan's departure from this state.

This is, as I see it, one of those passages that occur from time to time in which a number of central issues dealt with throughout the poem are brought together and given a firmer and more authoritative statement than is possible in the more diffuse, discursive mode of the poem as a whole. They are of greatest value, perhaps, in the sharper definition of relationships which they make possible. The importance of such centers of meaning in so long and so deliberately casual a poem is obvious.[10] This is especially the case when we recall that Byron (like Spenser in the Bowre of Blisse) normally works by building up and tearing down his values, relating them by juxtaposition and by means of plot, *persona,* and structural metaphor. It is only at certain points (such as the passage just quoted) that we have the kind of irony we have been instructed to admire. But these centers merely affirm what is implicit throughout.

Here, then, on the threshold of Juan's definitive initiation into the world of experience, we are given a passage that not only reminds us of much of what is involved in this initiation, but, much more important, looks beyond the affair with Catherine to kinds of value that can emerge only later (that is, in the English cantos). We have here a particularly effective rehearsal of the art-nature motif presented by the description of the hero as a military Eros: "Love turned a Lieutenant of Artillery." Even this particularly repellent manifestation of the world of experience is at least susceptible of aesthetic exploitation—by a good tailor, say, or a poet. The conceit itself is a remarkably resonant one, with its reminiscence of the blind god who arouses irrational passions, often maliciously, through the wounds made by his arrows (Juan has changed roles from I. 88; he is now the wounder rather than the wounded). The effect is achieved, it will be noted, by combining the two cupids, the mischievous little god with the bow and arrows and the beautiful youth of the Cupid and Psyche legend.

With the discussion of this group of three stanzas we have moved beyond the smaller elements with which we have been for the most part concerned to the larger structural units. Now the centrifugal pressure in a poem like *Don Juan* is clearly enormous. And just as one may feel that a tension between push and resistance is one of the most exciting qualities of Byron's handling of rhythm, much of the peculiar effect of the poem as a whole is a function of the interaction of forces pushing us onward and forces compelling us to linger. There are all kinds of interesting possibilities. An element (e.g. a digression) that may be retarding with reference to a larger unit (e.g. a particular episode) will have an opposite effect with regard to smaller retarding elements within itself. Byron is ingenious in devising ways of inducing the reader not to move through

---

[10] Byron's use of this device is one of the most interesting stylistic analogies between *Don Juan* and *Childe Harold.*

the poem too quickly. Rhythm, rhyme, formal rhetorical patterning, as
we have seen, all have a part to play in the creation of this singularly
fruitful tension between octave and the conversational flow.

But if Byron shows admirable inventiveness in investing his octaves
with sufficient interest to keep them from getting lost in the conversational rush, he is perhaps not uniformly successful in his control of the
rush itself. While there is no lack of substance in *Don Juan,* there is sometimes lack of direction. Some of this, of course, is good, in that it serves
to make us pause and wonder about the function of any one particular
element. But sometimes it is merely clumsy.

Byron was not unaware of the problem. Indeed, one of the most effective ways of dealing with it is one he inherited from his Italian models—
to disarm us by calling attention to the difficulty. The device has the
further advantage, from one point of view, of dramatizing the difference
in style and technique between *Don Juan* and the "other epics":

> I feel this tediousness will never do—
> 'Tis being *too* epic.
>
> [III. 111]

Another useful method of sharpening the direction of the stanzas is displayed in the extended conceit examined above. It is the simple rhetorical
device of repeating the (usually) first phrase of (usually) successive octaves
(here "Suppose him," "Suppose him"):

> It was upon a day, a summer's day . . .
> 'Twas on a summer's day—the sixth of June . . .
> 'Twas on the sixth of June . . .
>
> [I. 102, 103, 104]
>
> So Juan stood . . .
> Don Juan stood . .
>
> [II. 13, 14]
>
> So Juan wept . .
> And Juan wept . . .
>
> [II. 16, 17]
>
> Oh, thou eternal Homer!
> Oh, thou eternal Homer!
>
> [VII. 79, 80]
>
> He was a bachelor . . .
> But Juan was a bachelor . . .
>
> [XI. 46, 47]

But no amount of merely rhetorical organization, after all, or even of accomplished manipulation of individual image and individual unit of meaning can confer real structural (as opposed to merely thematic) unity on a poem. They themselves derive their significance from their participation in the ruling structural principles. The greater part of this study has been concerned with analysis of three of these: the metaphor of the fall, the use of the *persona,* and the idea of epic satire. The development of these three patterns may be thought of as constituting the proper plot of *Don Juan.* It is in terms of them that Juan's personal development from his boy-love of Julia through the testing on the sea, the edenic relationship with Haidée, the more sophisticated transitional adventures in Constantinople, the morally compromising experiences at Ismail and Moscow, and the urbane doings in London and Norman Abbey (that is, the movement from innocence to experience) is dramatized, defined, made humanly relevant. For if the poem is unified, it is not static. The same points are made again and again, presented in (and tested by) different contexts, elaborated and sophisticated. Along with the exposition and elaboration of motif we have not merely the movement of the narrative plot, but also that much more central plot movement which may most clearly be conceived in terms of the altering relationship between speaker and protagonist. And all these plots and devices lead to and are constantly involved in the delicate expression of a highly individual attitude—that is, the *tone* of *Don Juan.*

Byron in the 'Twenties

by Edmund Wilson

I. The New Byron Letters

I cannot accept the opinion of Mr. Maurice Hewlett and others who
have asserted that the new collection of Byron letters, *Lord Byron's Correspondence* (a supplement to the six volumes of *Letters and Journals*
published at the beginning of the century) only supply more conclusive
evidence that Byron was a "blackguard" and a "cad." This is to simplify
the matter too much. It is to assume that when Byron writes "Maid of
Athens, ere we part, Give oh give me back my heart!" in one breath and
in the next tells Hobhouse that "the old woman, Theresa's mother, was
mad enough to imagine I was going to marry the girl, but I have better
amusement," and when he sneers at his wife in his private correspondence,
not long after having written, "even though unforgiving, never 'Gainst
thee shall my heart rebel," he is sincere in his cynicism but not in his
warmth of emotion. It is to assume that one cannot take a personal relation with cynicism and seriousness at the same time—that Childe Harold
and Manfred did not represent realities of Byron's experience as well as
Don Juan. The truth is that Byron was a man of picturesque and violent
moods, who reacted to life with extraordinary vividness, but without
discipline or order. He never knew where he stood nor what he really
wanted. He was a force of enormous energy, running amuck through a
world in which he could not find peace. His compromises with civilized
society were doomed to disaster from the beginning, though in them he
was surely sincere in seeking tranquillity or discipline. To say, as Mr.
Hewlett does, that he cold-bloodedly seduced Lady Frances Webster seems
to me to melodramatize the situation. Even if Lady Frances had not been
all of a flutter from the moment Byron came into the house and in a
mood of violent reaction against the clumsy and stupid husband who had
boasted that she was as passionless "as Jesus Christ," these letters seem

amply to prove that Byron believed himself in love with her and was ready at any moment to drop everything and run away with her.

The fact that he was an old hand at lovemaking and was amused by the humors of the situation and dramatized the whole affair in almost daily bulletins to Lady Melbourne does not prove him to have been much more of a popinjay than the average imaginative person. In a similar fashion, it is certainly true that he was honestly seeking happiness in his marriage; he wanted, he said, some one to "govern" him—which was unquestionably what he needed. The trouble was that Annabella Milbanke was a quite unsuitable wife for Byron. He had qualms at the last moment and was ready to give the whole thing up; but Lady Melbourne, who had been "governing" him lately and in whose judgment he seems to have trusted absolutely, had arranged the marriage herself and urged it upon him as a panacea. The relationship was impossible from the start. It is clear that Byron behaved abominably, but, then, he was by nature and fortune a spoiled and refractory child, while poor little Miss Milbanke was a correct jeune fille, charmless and unsophisticated, who went in for mathematics and was a little priggish about it. With the best intentions on both sides, the situation could hardly have turned out differently. "Disease or not," says Lady Byron, speaking of Byron's supposed madness, "all my recollections and reflections tend to convince me that the irritability is inseparably connected with me in a greater degree than with any other object, that my presence has been uniformly oppressive to him from the hour we married—if not before, and in his best moods he has always wished to be away from me . . . had we continued together, he *would* have gone mad."

It is, therefore, a great pity that Byron was ever persuaded to marry Miss Milbanke. He had already a sharp sense of his unfitness to play a role in English society. When Miss Milbanke finally came to accept him, he had been fully prepared to go back to the East; *there* were fighting and adventure—gaiety, color and sun; *there* was no boring politics or business; women were not taken seriously; *there* he would be able to find something like the kind of life he understood. His genius has its happiest expression in his letters to Hobhouse from the Continent and in the harlequinade of *Beppo* and *Don Juan*.

For Byron's gift was for living rather than for literature. He had neither the intensity nor the fineness to fuse, for perdurable brilliants, the shifting moods of the soul. Don Juan, after all, was always more real than Childe Harold. The windy storms of passion that were blown off in *Childe Harold* and the tragedies were never the most solid realities of that deeply sensuous life. If he had only not tried to live in England, if the women only hadn't set their hearts on him, what an amiable figure he might have been! There is nothing more exhilarating in literature than Byron's first trip to Greece—his duels and skirmishings with bandits, his heroic swimming of the Hellespont, his reception by Vely Pasha and his delight at the Pasha's present of "a very pretty horse," his defense of the Temple of Athena against the depredations of Lord Elgin and his row with the authorities at Constantinople because they would not allow him, as a Peer of the Realm, to take first place in a Turkish official reception. To read Byron is to watch a panorama of the Europe of the early nineteenth century—the morrow of the French Revolution and of the victory of Napoleon seen through the eyes of a sophisticated man who is as much alive to how people are feeling and to what sort of struggles they are waging as to how they are drinking and making love. How amusing he makes Milan and Geneva and Venice!—that Venice of which Stendhal wrote that it constituted "a distinct world, of which the gloomy society of the rest of Europe can form no conception; care is there a subject of mockery." Here as yet was neither Burbank with his Baedeker nor Bleistein with his cigar, but balconies to which one looked up to encounter romantic black eyes peeping out from behind long blinds; covered gondolas gliding at night through narrow canals of wavering water; the dancing, the delirious wines and the masqued flirtations of the Carnival; the revolutionary young countess Guiccioli with her aged and complacent husband and her English *cavalier servente*, the scandalous witty Lord Byron.

Yet this record, as we follow it further, produces an effect of depression that at last becomes almost unbearable. For one thing, life had played poor Byron not the least annoying of its tricks: by the time he had acquired enough judgment not to make any further disastrous mistakes and to be sure in what manner of life his hope for happiness lay, he had already hurt others and himself so grievously in the process of learning that both his peaceful pursuits and his pleasures were forever impaired by the wounds. Among the motley baggage of his soul, there was a sort of Calvinistic conscience (supposed to have been implanted by his early education in Edinburgh) which gnawed its nails and gnashed its teeth amid the very laughter of Venice. "It must be admitted," says Stendhal, writing of Byron at this period, "that during nearly a third of the time we passed in the poet's society he appeared to us like one laboring under an access of folly, often approaching to madness. . . . One evening, among others, the conversation turned upon a handsome Milanese female who had eagerly desired to venture her person in single combat with a lover by whom she had been abandoned; the discussion afterward changed to the story of a prince who in cold blood had murdered his mistress for an act of infidelity. Byron was instantly silent, endeavored to restrain his feelings, but, unequal to the effort, soon afterward indignantly quitted the box."

Then, Byron had by this time another remorse to stave off by cham-

pagne. Jane Claremont, a connection of the Shelleys and a romantic
foolish young girl, mad to give herself to a poet, had laid violent siege to
Byron and had finally nagged him into gratifying her. They had parted
in Switzerland, Byron refusing implacably ever to see her again, and
when Jane with the Shelleys had returned to England, she bore Byron
a daughter. The new documents published here in elucidation of this
affair take glamor from both Byron and Shelley. They reveal the dismal
underside of that stimulating lyric revolt. One is chilled to find the price
these poets paid—and that other people paid—not only in pain and
grief, but in sordidness and raw distress. How much good life was plowed
under in the triumph of that noble defiance! And how messy the triumph
itself appears when looked at in the process of its making.

Well, art has its origin in the need to pretend that human life is
something other than it is, and, in a sense, by pretending this, it succeeds
to some extent in transforming it. What we see when we turn back our
eyes to the age of Shelley and Byron is not the ignominy of mute broken
hearts, of hurriedly muffled-up births, but a blaze of divine white light
and the smoky torches of rebellion. And yet, poor Jane Claremont, to
have set her heart on a love affair with a poet! Poor Annabella Milbanke,
to have been so naïve and misguided as to marry an inspired rake! Poor
Shelley and poor Byron, to have carried in their hearts the consciousness
of such guilt as no wine could for long disguise, no songs could forever
relieve. Poor male and female human beings, who, understanding life
in different fashions and unfitted to live together, yet cannot leave each
other alone! For a moment, as we read these letters, the very splendors
of *Childe Harold* and *Prometheus* seem dwindled and insubstantial, like
witch-fires above a bog.

July 2, 1922

II. Byron and His Biographers

The Political Career of Lord Byron by Dora Neill Raymond is an interesting, though not very penetrating, book, written from the point of
view of the conventional admiring biographer. For Miss Raymond, all of
Byron's political lampoons and parliamentary speeches, as well as his
revolutionary activities in Italy and Greece, are the results of wise and
well-considered opinions. Byron's motives are invariably generous, dis-
interested, and straightforward; and the question of his complex and
unsteady character does not arise at all. In discussing Byron's hatred of
the radicals, to take a single example, Miss Raymond describes the squib
that he wrote about Hobhouse's relations with them as "a rollicking and
somewhat sarcastic ballad"—whereas it will perhaps seem more likely to
a reader of the ballad in question and of the poet's letters dealing with
this period that he had merely given vent to his own irritation at the

aimlessness of his life in Italy and his envy of his friend's achievement
at home by an outburst less rollicking and sarcastic than jeering and ill
natured. Furthermore, it seems clear that Byron's hatred of oppression
and the readiness of his sympathy with the unfortunate were somehow
bound up with what would be nowadays called a sort of "inferiority
complex." But it never occurs to Miss Raymond to question either the
soundness of Byron's character or the exaltedness of his position, so she
quite fails to understand either his personal or his social situation.

Mr. Harold Nicolson, on the other hand, in *Byron: The Last Journey*
understands these matters only too well. Mr. Nicolson is a pupil of the
school of Strachey, and he has picked up the whole technique of em-
phasizing the idiosyncrasies and the personal imperfections that, ignored
by the contemporary public, fix the shape of spectacular public careers.
This enables him, if not to rival the consummate successes of the Master,
at least to write such a passage as the following, which comes nearer to
arriving at the truth about Byron than a biography in Miss Raymond's
vein can do: "It must be realized that the life of Byron is not, as has
often been imagined, a series of wasted opportunities; rather is it a
catalogue of false positions. His brain was male, his character was
feminine. He had genius, but it was misunderstood and misdirected; he
had beauty, but it was branded by deformity; he had rank, but no position; fortune, but it came too late; fame, but it blazed for him too early.
From his childhood the foreground of his life had been out of focus with
the background; throughout his career this error of focus marred the
sincerity, the completeness and even the meaning of the whole."

Yet this formula of Strachey's has its penalties as well as its dazzling re-
wards. One of these is the use or the excessive use of irony where irony
is not really in order. The irony of Strachey himself always serves to con-
vey some criticism: as Mr. Clive Bell has said, Strachey's attitude toward
the Victorian Age implies a judgment derived from a study of the history
of society. We do not find Lytton Strachey writing about Madame du
Deffand or Racine in the same vein as about Florence Nightingale,
Cardinal Manning or Dr. Arnold. Even in *Eminent Victorians,* where he
is most cruel, perhaps most unfair, all his efforts are directed toward
compelling us to accept a certain definite point of view. But his followers
are always in danger of taking over the mocking tone without understanding this point of view. The worst offender in this regard is perhaps
Mr. Philip Guedalla. The biographical writing of Mr. Guedalla is full of
details and inflections that have an invidious mocking sound but which,
when one comes to examine them, seem to lack any real significance.
And Mr. Nicolson, in writing of Byron, is not entirely free from this
vice. " 'Our visit was a long one,' records Lady Blessington. It was. They
sat in the large, cool room," etc. Now, what is there ridiculous about the
fact that this visit to Byron was rather long? Why does Mr. Nicolson

write "It was" in such a sly knowing way? For no other reason on earth than that he has caught the tone from Lytton Strachey. There is certainly some place for irony in a biography of a figure like Byron, whose romantic reputation has been swollen by so much nonsense; but, except in his preface, Mr. Nicolson has surely leaned a little too far over backward in his endeavor to avoid the legend. For the legend, after all, was a reality as much as Byron's effeminate voice, which Mr. Nicolson is so unwilling to have us forget.

Here is a typical passage: "That in this sudden ferment of unexpected adulation Byron should have been manoeuvred into adopting the postures which were expected of him was perhaps inevitable. . . . [The provoking specter of Childe Harold] thrust upon him the exacting function of being a very dangerous and enterprising man. His slightest civility was interpreted as a seduction; his chance encounters became assignations. They persisted, all of them, in taking him at his word. For a man who, although kindly and sentimental, was only adequately sexed, all this became extremely exhausting." But, after all, it was Byron himself who had created Childe Harold and his postures. He had certainly more than half believed in them, and he succeeded in making others believe in them, and they thus became actual values, which Mr. Nicolson should have brought on the stage. "Kindly and sentimental" is a quite inadequate description of Byron in his relations with women: on the contrary, he seems always to have been ready to flare up, if only momentarily, into a fever of eager devotion, and in even the most unpromising of his love affairs, to have been able to work up at least a mood or two of something like passionate conviction. Even from the half-humorous bulletins that he sent off to Lady Melbourne, it is plain that he pursued his mistresses with an energy and an anxiety considerably more than "kindly and sentimental." Mr. Nicolson, in writing about Byron with Childe Harold left out, has illustrated the un-humanistic point of view to which Stracheyism is likely to lead. If a biographer be too wary of taking the figures of history and the heroes of literature at their own valuation and that of their contemporaries, he is likely to miss the point altogether. Every age has its complacent failures of intelligence, and we have learned in our own time to laugh at the "reasonable" point of view that was fashionable in the eighteenth century and the moral point of view of the nineteenth, but it looks as if this new sort of ironic belittlement were likely to become characteristic of our own. What should be most interesting at any time is to find out to what actuality of human ideals and adventures a creation like Childe Harold corresponded.

For the rest, Miss Raymond's book is a readable and useful one, and Mr. Nicolson's a vivid and amusing one, which has a great deal more of his own in it than his preceding biography of Tennyson, in which one found him paraphrasing, as if for a literary exercise, the whole last page of Strachey's *Queen Victoria*. Confining itself, as Mr. Nicolson's book does, to the last year of Byron's life, it cannot be expected to supply a satisfactory full-length portrait of Byron. Mr. Nicolson presupposes on the part of the reader a knowledge of most of what has gone before and concentrates on Byron's last year, of which he makes an absorbing narrative. Mr. Nicolson has unpublished documents and a firsthand knowledge of Greece, and both these books are of the picture-filling-in sort particularly valuable in connection with Byron. For Byron, in literature, presents a peculiar case: he was not a great literary artist, and it is only by familiarizing ourselves with his life as well as with his work that we come to appreciate his merits and understand why it was possible for Arnold to speak, as he did, in one breath, of "Goethe's sage mind and Byron's force." What we come to do justice to then—and both Miss Raymond's and Mr. Nicolson's books help us to do justice—is the knowledge of Europe and the world, the consciousness of the stage upon which he was playing, that make Byron so remarkable among nineteenth century Englishmen; the generous ideas and impulses which counterbalance his faults and his errors; and the inexhaustible capacity for experience that is so satisfactory today in its contrast with the limitations of the typical literary man who agreeably diverts the hours of a safe and regular life by turning out novels or poems.

June, 1925

The Poet and His Vulture

by *Gilbert Highet*

We know the faces of most poets only as stereotypes: the frail, earnest features of John Keats, Tennyson's dark beard and brooding eyes, the suave, enigmatic mask of Shakespeare. But there is one dramatic figure which, as we think of it, lives and moves. It stamped its appearance on the memory of a whole generation, and even set the style for young men's faces and young men's clothes and young men's manners. It still lives. It is Lord Byron.

Mention the name: at once the man appears. Slender; handsome, nobly, arrogantly handsome even in an age of fine-looking men; bold and unconventional, with collar open on a strong white neck; dark curling hair; intense gray eyes with dark lashes. And then the figure moves, and we see that it is lame. Byron could ride a spirited horse, he could swim for hours in rough seas, he could even box if he did not have to move about much, but he could not walk normally, because one or both of his feet were deformed. This (he said) was due to his mother's behavior while he was being born; he could never forgive her; it worried him all his life, and he overcompensated for it. His lameness adds a touch of penetrating grief to our picture of him. Melancholy seems to surround Byron. No; something deeper: a gloom almost Satanic. Men and women were actually afraid of him. He created new characters, who lived in darker worlds: Manfred, the wizard of the high Alps, knowing more of spirits than of mankind and oppressed with a nameless guilt; savage Turkish pashas; daring rebels; lonely pirates whose names are

linked with one virtue, and a thousand crimes.

Byron wrote one splendid poem in which he addressed the Titan Prometheus—crucified on a remote mountain by an unjust god—as a fellow sufferer. And his life ended in bitter frustration. He died not as he would have chosen, on the battlefield, but of fever in a small Greek town, foreseeing no success for the struggling of liberation which he was endeavoring to keep alive, and leaving his finest, most ambitious poem forever incomplete. A somber destiny. Before he had worn his laurels long, their leaves were blackened.

When you first read Byron's poems, you are struck by their unrelenting pessimism. It is not hysterical, or revolutionary, nor is it the pessimism of the isolated intellectual. It sounds like the considered verdict of an educated, experienced, reflective man who has the gift of poetry. Here is a brief meditation on the heaped ruins of Rome, in a vision that evokes the pessimistic historian of a later century, Oswald Spengler.

> Cypress and ivy, weed and wallflower grown
> Matted and massed together—hillocks heaped
> On what were chambers—arch crushed, column strown
> In fragments—choked up vaults, and frescos steeped
> In subterranean damps, where the owl peeped,
> Deeming it midnight:—Temples—Baths—or Halls?
> Pronounce who can: for all that Learning reaped
> From her research hath been, that these are walls—
> Behold the Imperial Mount! 'tis thus the Mighty falls.
>
> There is the moral of all human tales;
> 'Tis but the same rehearsal of the past,
> First Freedom, and then Glory—when that fails,
> Wealth—Vice—Corruption,—Barbarism at last;
> And History, with all her volumes vast,
> Hath but *one* page.

That is the tone of most of Byron's poems. That is the tone which caught the ear of so many other young poets, and molded the minds of Heine, Lamartine, De Musset, Leopardi, Pushkin; yes, and Berlioz: lonely pessimism; heroic disillusionment; Promethean endurance; Titanic scorn. That is the dark vision that appears when we hear the name of Byron: proud face, lame foot, tragic gaze, tormented heart.

But look through his poems again; or, better still, open his letters and his diaries. At once a new Byron appears. Roars of laughter strike th' astonished ear. A constant flow of epigrams, personal jokes, and nonsense rhymes gushes out. Byron turns out to be extremely good company, a loyal and cheerful friend, and a young man full of animal spirits, who would write a funny letter as readily as he would box five rounds with a visitor. That was the age of wits and eccentrics, when a reputation could be made by a brilliant talker. It was the age of Sydney Smith—who said that Daniel Webster was like a steam engine in trousers, and declared it required a surgical operation to get a joke into a Scotchman's head. Byron was brought up in Aberdeenshire, far in the northeast of Scotland, and that is where his strong character and his love of solitude were formed; but when he went to school at Harrow and then on to Cambridge, he was thrown into a rough but cheerful society, in which a man needed both wits and guts to make his mark. Byron made his mark.

Occasionally he hated it: society, and success, and his mother, and his wife, and the whole thing. But quite often he enjoyed it. When he did, out poured his gaiety and his fun. His letters are full of jollity. It must have been a cheerful fellow who described a stag party as "all hiccup and happiness." In his letters he kept improvising satirical poems like this:

> The world is a bundle of hay,
> Mankind are the asses who pull,
> Each tugs it a different way,—
> And the greatest of all is John Bull!

And in conversation he was equally amusing. Lady Blessington wrote down some of the epigrams he threw out to her:

After a season in London, one doubts one's own identity. I have not quite made up my mind that women have souls. No man dislikes being lectured by a woman, provided she be not his wife, sister, mother, or mistress.

Really, Byron seldom became bitter unless when he spoke of the British climate, his own reputation, or his female relatives. It was a little naughty of him to describe his honeymoon as the treacle-moon (or we should say the "molasses-moon"). There is a very funny letter, too, in which he talks about the poem that brought him fame, *Childe Harold:*

I was half mad during the time of its composition, between metaphysics, mountains, lakes, love unextinguishable, thoughts unutterable, and the nightmare of my own delinquencies. I should, many a good day, have blown my brains out, but for the recollection that it would have given pleasure to my mother-in-law; and, even *then,* if I could have been certain to haunt her . . .

Yet Byron's humor goes deeper than that; it runs all through his work. His first poems were lyrical, and sentimental. When they were badly reviewed, he published a sharp, vigorous, and very funny satire called *English Bards and Scotch Reviewers.* (He still thought of himself, at that time, as an Englishman; he was cured later.) Thenceforward, although he was best known for his gloomy works, he kept producing poems of laughter also. Probably he is the last of the great satiric poets writing in English. The favorite of most readers who know Byron's satires is his *Vision of Judgment,* which pokes irresistible fun at the Poet Laureate's conception of George III's arrival at the pearly gates and his triumphal entry into heaven. And his final work, *Don Juan,* was a cross between epic, romance, and satire, in the manner of the gayest and most irreverent of Italian poets, Ariosto. It is full of good things. It specializes in one difficult but amusing art, which could be practiced only by a genuine humorist: comic multiple rhymes. Here is Byron's epitaph on Keats, whose death was partly brought on by bitter reviews of his poetry:

> John Keats, who was killed off by one critique
> Just as he really promised something great,
> If not intelligible, without Greek
> Contrived to talk about the gods of late
> Much as they might have been supposed to speak.
> Poor fellow! His was an untoward fate;
>   'Tis strange the mind, that very fiery particle,
>   Should let itself be snuffed out by an article.

From the same poem, here is a magnificent description of London, huge, fogbound as so often, and crowned by St. Paul's Cathedral. This is worth putting beside Wordsworth's sonnet on London:

> A mighty mass of brick and smoke, and shipping,
>   Dirty and dusky, but as wide as eye
> Could reach, with here and there a sail just skipping
>   In sight, then lost amidst the forestry
> Of masts; a wilderness of steeples peeping
>   On tiptoe through their sea-coal canopy;
>   A huge, dun Cupola, like a foolscap crown
>   On a fool's head—and there is London Town!

In fact, the whole of *Don Juan* gives us a better impression of Byron's real character than any other of his poems. The tragedies and romances are pervasively somber. The satires are uproariously scornful. This poem contains love affairs, battles, shipwrecks, splendid descriptions of scenery, scornful vignettes of society, the love of travel, and fits of hearty laughter: all these, we know, were parts of Byron's life. Small but important details of his personality come out of it, usually illuminated by flashes of wit. There is recurrent anxiety about money, once pointed by an allusion to Machiavelli:

Alas! how deeply painful is all payment!
Take lives—take wives—take aught except men's purses:
As Machiavel shows those in purple raiment,
Such is the shortest way to general curses.
They hate a murderer much less than a claimant
On that sweet ore which everybody nurses.
Kill a man's family, and he may brook it,
But keep your hands out of his breeches pocket.

There is some very acute observation of the psychology of women: for
instance, this description of the Englishwoman, with a cold manner and
hot heart. Byron looks for a suitable image, and then cries:

What say you to a bottle of champagne?
Frozen into a very vinous ice,
Which leaves few drops of that immortal rain,
Yet in the very centre, past all price,
About a liquid glassful will remain;
And this is stronger than the strongest grape
Could e'er express in its expanded shape:

'Tis the whole spirit brought to a quintessence;
And thus the chilliest aspects may concentre
A hidden nectar under a cold presence . . .
And your cold people are beyond all price,
When once you've broken their confounded ice.

Besides this, there are several hangovers, and quite a lot of liver trouble;
listen:

I think, with Alexander, that the act
Of eating, with another act or two,
Makes us feel our mortality in fact
Redoubled; when a roast, and a ragout,
And fish, and soup, by some side dishes backed,
Can give us either pain or pleasure, who
Would pride himself on intellects, whose use
Depends so much upon the gastric juice?

Now, reading Byron's life and letters, and thinking over that last
stanza, I believe I can suggest one reason for the extraordinary variations in his outlook and his personality. It is this. He was not naturally
a slender, elegant, athletic, grave young man at all. Naturally, he was a
plump, pleasant, pot-bellied person, and he spent tremendous, almost un-

remitting efforts on keeping down his natural fat. He was about fiv
feet eight. When he was nineteen years old, he weighed 202 pounds. B
cause of his lameness and his difficulty in taking normal exercise, th
corpulence would soon have become quite irremovable. Byron had
strong will. He resolved to get it off, and keep it off. He did so by painfu
exercises and the most Spartan regime of dieting, which may well hav
wrecked his liver. He took exercise wearing seven waistcoats and a heav
topcoat; then he took hot baths; he ate hardly anything. By the time h
was twenty, he had got down to 147 pounds. Only once or twice through
out the rest of his life did he rise above that. But it meant that he wa
constantly hungry. He would sometimes fast for forty-eight hours. I
1816 he lived on a diet of one slice of thin bread for breakfast, a dinne
of vegetables, and green tea and soda water in between. To keep dow
his hunger, he chewed tobacco and mastic gum; sometimes he too
laudanum. He was starving.

The Anglo-Irish critic Cyril Connolly says that inside every fat ma
there is a thin man, screaming to be let out. The reverse is sometime
true, I think, and it was true for Byron. He was a thin man, and insid
him there was a fat man roaring to be set free. Or, to put it in scientifi
terms, Byron was by nature what Sheldon calls a viscerotonic, plump
and jovial. He converted himself, by a terrible effort, into a muscular
balanced somatotonic with strong touches of the nervous, gloomy cere
brotonic. All three Byrons played their parts in his life and his poetry
The thin cerebrotonic conceived the grim otherworldly tragedy of *Man
fred;* the tough athlete swam the Dardanelles, and wrote of pirates an
duels and the storming of cities; the invisible fat man poured out the
jokes and satires at which we still laugh. We can see now why Byron
chose to compare himself to Prometheus, for that unhappy giant not only
was crucified, but had a vulture tearing eternally at his flesh. Byron had
several vultures with their beaks buried deep in his vitals; but the one
which he felt most constantly, if not most painfully, was that haggard
eyed, sharp-clawed, tireless monster, a starvation diet.

Byron

by Bertrand Russell

The nineteenth century, in comparison with the present age, appears rational, progressive, and satisfied; yet the opposite qualities of our time were possessed by many of the most remarkable men during the epoch of liberal optimism. When we consider men, not as artists or discoverers, not as sympathetic or antipathetic to our own tastes, but as forces, as causes of change in the social structure, in judgments of value, or in intellectual outlook, we find that the course of events in recent times has necessitated much readjustment in our estimates, making some men less important than they had seemed, and others more so. Among those whose importance is greater than it seemed, Byron deserves a high place. On the Continent, such a view would not appear surprising, but in the English-speaking world it may be thought strange. It was on the Continent that Byron was influential, and it is not in England that his spiritual progeny is to be sought. To most of us, his verse seems often poor and his sentiment often tawdry, but abroad his way of feeling and his outlook on life were transmitted and developed and transmuted until they became so widespread as to be factors in great events.

The aristocratic rebel, of whom Byron was in his day the exemplar, is a very different type from the leader of a peasant or proletarian revolt. Those who are hungry have no need of an elaborate philosophy to stimulate or excuse discontent, and anything of the kind appears to them merely an amusement of the idle rich. They want what others have, not some intangible and metaphysical good. Though they may preach Christian love, as the medieval communist rebels did, their real reasons for doing so are very simple: that the lack of it in the rich and powerful causes the sufferings of the poor, and that the presence of it among comrades in revolt is thought essential to success. But experience of the struggle leads to a despair of the power of love, leaving naked hate as the driving force. A rebel of this type, if, like Marx, he invents a philosophy, invents one solely designed to demonstrate the ultimate victory of

"Byron." From *A History of Western Philosophy* (New York: Simon and Schuster; London: George Allen & Unwin) by Bertrand Russell, pp. 774-780. Copyright 1945 by Bertrand Russell. Reprinted by permission of the author, Simon and Schuster, and George Allen & Unwin.

his party, not one concerned with values. His values remain primitive: the good is enough to eat, and the rest is talk. No hungry man is likely to think otherwise.

The aristocratic rebel, since he has enough to eat, must have other causes of discontent. I do not include among rebels the mere leaders of factions temporarily out of power; I include only men whose philosophy requires some greater change than their own personal success. It may be that love of power is the underground source of their discontent, but in their conscious thought there is criticism of the government of the world, which, when it goes deep enough, takes the form of Titanic cosmic self-assertion or, in those who retain some superstition, of Satanism. Both are to be found in Byron. Both, largely through men whom he influenced, became common in large sections of society which could hardly be deemed aristocratic. The aristocratic philosophy of rebellion, growing, developing, and changing as it approached maturity, has inspired a long series of revolutionary movements, from the Carbonari after the fall of Napoleon to Hitler's *coup* in 1933; and at each stage it has inspired a corresponding manner of thought and feeling among intellectuals and artists.

It is obvious that an aristocrat does not become a rebel unless his temperament and circumstances are in some way peculiar. Byron's circumstances were very peculiar. His earliest recollections were of his parents' quarrels; his mother was a woman whom he feared for her cruelty and despised for her vulgarity; his nurse combined wickedness with the strictest Calvinist theology; his lameness filled him with shame, and prevented him from being one of the herd at school. At ten years old, after living in poverty, he suddenly found himself a Lord and the owner of Newstead. His great-uncle the "wicked Lord," from whom he inherited, had killed a man in a duel thirty-three years ago, and been ostracized by his neighbors ever since. The Byrons had been a lawless family, and the Gordons, his mother's ancestors, even more so. After the squalor of a back street in Aberdeen, the boy naturally rejoiced in his title and his Abbey, and was willing to take on the character of his ancestors in gratitude for their lands. And if, in recent years, their bellicosity had led them into trouble, he learnt that in former centuries it had brought them renown. One of his earliest poems, "On Leaving Newstead Abbey," relates his emotions at this time, which are of admiration for his ancestors who fought in the Crusades, at Crecy, and at Marston Moor. He ends with the pious resolve:

> Like you will he live, or like you will he perish:
> When decay'd, may he mingle his dust with your own.

This is not the mood of a rebel, but it suggests "Childe" Harold, the modern peer who imitates medieval barons. As an undergraduate, when for the first time he had an income of his own, he wrote that he felt as independent as "a German Prince who coins his own cash, or a Cherokee Chief who coins no cash at all, but enjoys what is more precious, Liberty. I speak in raptures of that Goddess because my amiable Mama was so despotic." He wrote, in later life, much noble verse in praise of freedom, but it must be understood that the freedom he praised was that of a German Prince or a Cherokee Chief, not the inferior sort that might conceivably be enjoyed by ordinary mortals.

In spite of his lineage and his title, his aristocratic relations fought shy of him, and he was made to feel himself socially not of their society. His mother was intensely disliked, and he was looked on with suspicion. He knew that she was vulgar, and darkly feared a similar defect in himself. Hence arose that peculiar blend of snobbery and rebellion that characterized him. If he could not be a gentleman in the modern style, he would be a bold baron in the style of his crusading ancestors, or perhaps in the more ferocious but even more romantic style of the Ghibelline chiefs, cursed of God and Man as they trampled their way to splendid downfall. Medieval romances and histories were his etiquette books. He sinned like the Hohenstaufen, and like the crusaders he died fighting the Moslem.

His shyness and sense of friendlessness made him look for comfort in love affairs, but as he was unconsciously seeking a mother rather than a mistress, all disappointed him except Augusta. Calvinism, which he never shook off—to Shelley, in 1816, he described himself as "Methodist, Calvinist, Augustinian"—made him feel that his manner of life was wicked; but wickedness, he told himself, was a hereditary curse in his blood, an evil fate to which he was predestined by the Almighty. If that were indeed the case, since he *must* be remarkable, he would be remarkable as a sinner, and would dare transgressions beyond the courage of the fashionable libertines whom he wished to despise. He loved Augusta genuinely because she was of his blood—of the Ishmaelite race of the Byrons—and also, more simply, because she had an elder sister's kindly care for his daily welfare. But this was not all that she had to offer him. Through her simplicity and her obliging good nature, she became the means of providing him with the most delicious self-congratulatory remorse. He could feel himself the equal of the greatest sinners—the peer of Manfred, of Cain, almost of Satan himself. The Calvinist, the aristocrat, and the rebel were all equally satisfied; and so was the romantic lover, whose heart was broken by the loss of the only earthly being still capable of rousing in it the gentler emotions of pity and love.

Byron, though he felt himself the equal of Satan, never quite ventured to put himself in the place of God. This next step in the growth of pride was taken by Nietzsche, who says: "If there were Gods, how could I endure it to be not God! *Therefore* there are no Gods." Observe the suppressed premise of this reasoning: "Whatever humbles my pride is to be judged false." Nietzsche, like Byron, and even to a greater degree, had a pious upbringing, but having a better intellect, he found a better escape than Satanism. He remained, however, very sympathetic to Byron. He says:

> "The tragedy is that we cannot believe the dogmas of religion and metaphysics if we have the strict methods of truth in heart and head, but on the other hand, we have become through the development of humanity so tenderly sensitively suffering that we need the highest kind of means of salvation and consolation: whence arises the danger that man may bleed to death through the truth that he recognizes. Byron expresses this in immortal lines:
>
>> Sorrow is knowledge: they who know the most
>> Must mourn the deepest o'er the fatal truth,
>> The Tree of Knowledge is not that of Life."

Sometimes, though rarely, Byron approaches more nearly to Nietzsche's point of view. But in general Byron's ethical theory, as opposed to his practice, remains strictly conventional.

The great man, to Nietzsche, is godlike; to Byron, usually, a Titan at war with himself. Sometimes, however, he portrays a sage not unlike Zarathustra—the Corsair, in his dealings with his followers,

> Still sways their souls with that commanding art
> That dazzles, leads, yet chills the vulgar heart.

And this same hero "hated man too much to feel remorse." A footnote assures us that the Corsair is true to human nature, since similar traits were exhibited by Genseric, King of the Vandals, by Ezzelino the Ghibelline tyrant, and by a certain Louisiana pirate.

Byron was not obliged to confine himself to the Levant and the Middle Ages in his search for heroes, since it was not difficult to invest Napoleon with a romantic mantle. The influence of Napoleon on the imagination of nineteenth century Europe was very profound; he inspired Clausewitz, Stendhal, Heine, the thought of Fichte and Nietzsche, and the acts of Italian patriots. His ghost stalks through the age, the only force which is strong enough to stand up against industrialism and commerce, pouring scorn on pacifism and shop-keeping. Tolstoy's *War and Peace* is an attempt to exorcize the ghost, but a vain one, for the specter has never been more powerful than at the present day.

During the Hundred Days, Byron proclaimed his wish for Napoleon's victory, and when he heard of Waterloo he said, "I'm damned sorry for it." Only once, for a moment, did he turn against his hero: in 1814, when (so he thought) suicide would have been more seemly than abdication. At this moment, he sought consolation in the virtue of Washington, but the return from Elba made this effort no longer necessary. In France, when Byron died, "It was remarked in many newspapers that the two greatest men of the century, Napoleon and Byron, had disappeared almost at the same time." [1] Carlyle, who, at the time, considered Byron "the noblest spirit in Europe," and felt as if he had "lost a brother," came afterwards to prefer Goethe, but still coupled Byron with Napoleon:

"For your nobler minds, the publishing of some such Work of Art, in one or the other dialect, becomes almost a necessity. For what is it properly but an altercation with the Devil, before you begin honestly Fighting him? Your Byron publishes his *Sorrows of Lord George,* in verse and in prose, and copiously otherwise: your Bonaparte presents his *Sorrows of Napoleon* Opera, in an all too-stupendous style; with music of cannon-volleys, and murder-shrieks of a world; his stage-lights are the fires of Conflagration; his rhyme and recitative are the tramp of embanded Hosts and the sound of falling Cities." [2]

It is true that, three chapters further on, he gives the emphatic command: "Close thy *Byron*; open thy *Goethe*." But Byron was in his blood, whereas Goethe remained an aspiration.

To Carlyle, Goethe and Byron were antitheses; to Alfred de Musset, they were accomplices in the wicked work of instilling the poison of melancholy into the cheerful Gallic soul. Most young Frenchmen of that age knew Goethe, it seems, only through *The Sorrows of Werther,* and not at all as the Olympian. Musset blamed Byron for not being consoled by the Adriatic and Countess Guiccioli—wrongly, for after he knew her he wrote no more *Manfreds.* But *Don Juan* was as little read in France as Goethe's more cheerful poetry. In spite of Musset, most French poets, ever since, have found Byronic unhappiness the best material for their verses.

To Musset, it was only after Napoleon that Byron and Goethe were the greatest geniuses of the century. Born in 1810, Musset was one of the generation whom he describes as *"conçus entre deux batailles"* in a lyrical description of the glories and disasters of the Empire. In Germany, feeling about Napoleon was more divided. There were those who, like Heine, saw him as the mighty missionary of liberalism, the destroyer of serfdom, the enemy of legitimacy, the man who made hereditary princelings tremble; there were others who saw him as Antichrist, the would-be destroyer of the noble German nation, the immoralist who had proved once for all that Teutonic virtue can only be preserved by un-

---

[1] Maurois, *Life of Byron.*
[2] *Sartor Resartus,* Book II, chap. **vi**.

quenchable hatred of France. Bismarck effected a synthesis: Napoleon remained Antichrist, but an Antichrist to be imitated, not merely to be abhorred. Nietzsche, who accepted the compromise, remarked with ghoulish joy that the classical age of war is coming, and that we owe this boon, not to the French Revolution, but to Napoleon. And in this way nationalism, Satanism, and hero worship, the legacy of Byron, became part of the complex soul of Germany.

Byron is not gentle, but violent like a thunderstorm. What he says of Rousseau is applicable to himself. Rousseau was, he says

> He who threw
> Enchantment over passion, and from woe
> Wrung overwhelming eloquence . . .
>   yet he knew
> How to make madness beautiful, and cast
> O'er erring deeds and thoughts, a heavenly hue.

But there is a profound difference between the two men. Rousseau is pathetic, Byron is fierce; Rousseau's timidity is obvious, Byron's is concealed; Rousseau admires virtue provided it is simple, while Byron admires sin provided it is elemental. The difference, though it is only that between two stages in the revolt of unsocial instincts, is important, and shows the direction in which the movement is developing.

Byron's romanticism, it must be confessed, was only half sincere. At times, he would say that Pope's poetry was better than his own, but this judgment, also, was probably only what he thought in certain moods. The world insisted on simplifying him, and omitting the element of pose in his cosmic despair and professed contempt for mankind. Like many other prominent men, he was more important as a myth than as he really was. As a myth, his importance, especially on the Continent, was enormous.

The Search for Identity

by John Wain

Slowly, the literary biographies of the English nineteenth century are being steamrollered by those of the American twentieth. Dowden's two bulky volumes on Shelley were nudged aside, some years ago, by Newman Ivy White's even bulkier two; and now it is the turn of Tom Moore's three volumes on Byron to be replaced by Professor Marchand's.[1] Actually, the surprising thing is how much still remains of the obsolete ones; White discovered and/or incorporated much detail that had come to light since Dowden wrote, and yet it remains true that there is no important facet of Shelley's character that can't be found in Dowden, if you read him carefully enough. It is the same witih Moore; his biography was a scissors-and-paste job (its full title is *Letters and Journals of Lord Byron, with Notices of his Life*), and there is hardly any individual flavor, hardly any unifying presence of the biographer himself, in its pages. But for the person who simply wants "a good read," without caring too much whether the information he is getting is the last word in completeness, Moore is likely to survive.

The question for a reviewer, however, is nothing so cosy. What (he must ask) does the Marchand biography add to our understanding of Byron's character? The answer is plain: not a great deal. Its usefulness is that it marshals everything into one book (albeit a tripartite and ruinously expensive book) and so makes for convenience. Anyone who has attentively read the huge compilation of eye-witness accounts of Byron, edited by Mr. E. J. Lovell, Jr., under the title *His Very Self and Voice*, and followed that up with his letters, and followed those in turn with his poems (which, we might remind ourselves, constitute the reason why we are interested in him at all)—such a reader, if he exists, could safely assume that he understands Byron, or has the means of understanding

"Byron: The Search for Identity." From *Essays on Literature and Ideas* (London and Toronto: Macmillan & Co. Ltd., 1963) by John Wain. Copyright © 1963 by Macmillan & Co. Ltd. Reprinted by permission of the author, Macmillan & Co. Ltd., William Heinemann, and Curtis Brown Ltd. Published first by *The London Magazine*, Vol. V, No. 7 (July 1958), 44-57.

[1] *Byron* by Leslie A. Marchand.

him, as well as Professor Marchand does. The one really big fact which, if I am not mistaken, sees the light for the first time in Professor Marchand's book comes near the beginning of the first volume, and concerns Mary Gray. This Scots lass, a pious Calvinist, had charge of Byron in early boyhood, succeeding her equally pious sister Agnes, and the niche into which the pair of them have always been fitted is "early Bible training." They it was who instilled that knowledge of the Old Testament which came out in *Hebrew Melodies,* and also inoculated him with what the *Encyclopaedia Britannica* pithily calls "too much Calvinism for faith or unfaith in Christianity." We can now add one more fact about Mary Gray: namely, that (to use the words of a memorandum written by Byron's friend Hobhouse) she "used to come to bed to him and play tricks with his person." Byron was nine years old at this time, and Hobhouse did not hesitate to trace a direct link between this nursely *divertissement* and the poet's own statement, "My passions were developed very early—so early, that few would believe me, if I were to state the period, and the facts which accompanied it." We may go further and trace two more links: one to Byron's lifelong distaste for the Pharisaisms of church-going people, the other to his repulsive treatment of women—repulsive not merely because of his promiscuity, but because of the give-and-take-away pattern his feelings seem to have most easily fallen into. Byron would display himself before a woman until he provoked her to make the first move; then, when it was all over, he would pass harsh judgment on her for having thrown herself at him.

But there, I think, the influence of Mary Gray ends, or becomes inextricably blended with more general influences. The real root of Byron's impossible treatment of women was his failure to establish his own true identity. The friendships Byron seems to have kept longest were male ones of the hearty, pistol-shooting, all-boys-together type, in which he could wear an easily assumed mask which did not drop off every time his inner feelings underwent a change. In the more seismographic and intimate relationships offered by women—and, for that matter, by the various youths with whom he had homosexual entanglements—this was impossible to sustain.

I want now to suggest—and I know there is nothing very original about the suggestion—that it was not possible for Byron to have a fully successful relationship with his poetic imagination, either, and for the same reasons.

Byron was a poet who worked through, by means of, self-consciousness. That is to say, he projected an image of himself and then let the image do the writing. Composition, to him, was a dramatic performance: the poet, having called an audience together, walked on to the stage and delivered an oration. The subject matter of this oration scarcely mattered.

Its real purpose, from first to last, was to present the character of the poet.

Naturally this character was to some extent a false one. It was assumed, edited, deliberately posed. What man could ever present his real personality, with all its doubts, its inward hesitations, ambiguities, and contradictions, in such a way as to make *dramatic* sense of it? In Byron's time, and for half a century before, a number of authors made it their life's work to present the inner working of their minds with complete frankness. The most celebrated of these attempts was Rousseau's; it is a brave effort, and yet the figure held up for our inspection in the *Confessions* doesn't give much impression of spontaneity. It seems in many ways as posed, as consciously staged, as the Byron-figure. Stendhal likened Byron to Rousseau: to that acute and disenchanted man, neither seemed very genuine. Boswell came nearer to complete self-revelation, especially in the records he had no intention of publishing. For my money, the best of these attempts to lift the lid off a man's mind is Wordsworth's: the quickest way to make oneself realize the true greatness of *The Prelude* is to approach it after a diet of these lesser predecessors.

To return to Byron: he had no idea of attempting this kind of self-dissection. He put as much energy into covering up those sides of his character that wouldn't fit into the pattern, as he did into revealing the ones that would. Fundamentally, Byron lacked the confidence to disclose, even to himself, the basic mechanisms of his mind. He was mystified by life, and more than a trifle repelled by it: and, like many neurotics, he had no means of facing it except by fitting himself out with a character that was partly assumed. Partly, but not wholly, since no one can maintain, for more than a few minutes at a time, a character which bears no relation at all to his real one. The two characters Byron assumed during his brief life were both built up from recognizably genuine elements within his character, but they were both simplifications. They existed by virtue of suppression, rather than fabrication.

And this, of course, was the rock on which he split as a poet. He created, in turn, two over-simplified characters to write his poetry for him. He could not write it himself because he did not, in the deeper sense, have a self. His attitudinizing was a short cut to arriving at a sense of his own tangible existence. As long as he had a mold into which his emotional lava could pour, he could escape the torturing contradictions that beset him, and he seems to have discovered this very early. Professor Marchand's pages provide abundant illustration. A notable one (which, incidentally, is taken from Moore) concerns a party at which the schoolboy Byron lapsed into bashfulness in the presence of some vivacious girls.

"The first time I was introduced to him," Elizabeth Pigot recalled, "was at a party at his mother's, when he was so shy that she was forced to send for him three times before she could persuade him to come into the drawing-room, to play with the young people at a round game. He was then a fat, bashful boy, with his hair combed straight over his forehead, and extremely like a miniature picture that his mother had painted by M. de Chambruland. The next morning Mrs. Byron brought him to call at our house, when he still continued shy and formal in his manner. The conversation turned upon Cheltenham where we had been staying . . . and I mentioned that I had seen the character of Gabriel Lackbrain very well performed. His mother getting up to go, he accompanied her, making a formal bow, and I, in allusion to the play, said 'Goodby, Gaby.' His countenance lighted up, his handsome mouth displayed a broad grin, all his shyness vanished, never to return, and, upon his mother's saying, 'Come, Byron, are you ready?'—no, she might go by herself, he would stay and talk a little longer."

In other words, she had provided him with a role into which, however fleetingly, he could throw himself. Obviously he would not wish to be cast as "Gaby" for long—but it was enough to get started.

Most people are agreed that Byron failed to become the great poet that he potentially was: I do not see how else we can account for this failure than by relating it to the deeper and more intimate failure to discover his own true identity. It takes courage, after all, to abandon one's neatly carved *persona* and surrender to the contradictory richness of life itself. A little too much defensiveness in one's make-up, and it is impossible. We all know the kind of author who adopts a set of outward characteristics that make it easy to assimilate him to the characters he imagines; everything he writes has the effect of strengthening this central *persona*, until the books themselves become mere adjuncts to a personal legend. And what happens? His work becomes more and more rigidly patterned, more and more dry and predictable. The imaginative life simply cannot be contained in this way.

Not that Byron fell a victim to this kind of desiccation and repetitiveness. He was too vital, too impetuously inventive, for that to be much of a danger. In any case, he died so young that the onrush of new material kept his pen busy and produced an impression of inexhaustible fertility. This impression, I believe, was illusory. Another ten years and Byron would have been forced to come to terms with this central imaginative and emotional hiatus. The result, I imagine—though of course one is frankly guessing here—would have been a crisis which would either have silenced him altogether or set him up as a new, and very much greater, poet.

As it is, we are left with an *œuvre* which breaks into two halves. The conventional division, which seems perfectly adequate, is that the "romantic" Byron holds the stage until 1816, in which year the accumulated scandals of the poet's private life drove him from England, never to return; then, after a few months in which his romantic poetry sings its swan-song, the "satiric" Byron takes over. This classification will serve well enough, provided we notice two things. First, that the two Byrons are not different characters, but different arrangements of the same character. Insistence on the division can only encourage the pointless diversion of finding veins of satire in the romantic poems, veins of romance in the satiric. *Hours of Idleness,* the first published volume, shows clearly enough that the young Byron was fully capable of developing in either direction; there is one poem, *To a Lady Who Presented to the Author a Lock of Hair,* which Professor Marchand singles out as "amazingly" like the later satiric work, but I don't see what is amazing about it. This leads us to the second noteworthy point: that Byron, in choosing to adopt first one vein and then the other, allowed circumstances to lead him: his choice was not made from literary motives, but simply imposed by the events of his life and the pressures of his *milieu.* When he made his first appearance, it was in the entirely conventional romantic guise of the day. Except for his greater energy, there is nothing in his earlier work that cannot be paralleled in Scott, Moore, or James Beatty—except, indeed, for the handful of couplet satires which he wrote to an Augustan formula.

It was the same story with the switch to the satiric *persona.* The romantic mask had to be put aside, and Byron acted as soon as he perceived this. He did not lead; he followed. It became impossible for him to embody, in his own person, the "Byronic hero" (Mark I), because that hero was a figure of mystery—wronged, perhaps, by the world, and with a nameless sin or two stacked away in the cupboard, but mainly an unknown quantity. And when the extraordinary deluge of moral righteousness suddenly swamped Byron, the mystery was swept away. (I know, of course, that technically speaking there is still a mystery—that it is still possible to argue over whether Byron's wife left him because he was committing incest with Augusta Leigh, as Harriet Beecher Stowe claimed in 1869, or because he was compelling her to "enact the Ganymede," as Professor Wilson Knight insists. But this kind of concrete puzzle is not at all the kind of "mystery" demanded by the Byronic hero.) Once the earlier pose had become impossible, there was nothing for it but to accept the later one. Overnight, Byron became irreverent, caustic, savagely fleering, the well-appointed unmasker of hypocrisy, the anti-cant man.

Before going on to discuss the merits of the poetry written by either of these two fantasy-figures, there are one or two considerations that must detain us a little longer. The first is an obvious one: how very Scotch all this is! Every Scot—and this is a fact that can be checked by ordinary day-to-day observation—has the gift of projecting a *persona* which simplifies his real character and allows it to make a more dramatic impact.

Whether or not it is true that every Irishman is a stage Irishman, every Scotsman is certainly a stage Scotsman. If we look back over the half-century before Byron was born, there can be no doubt as to who is the best poet there; it is Burns; and Burns has a gift of self-dramatization as strongly marked as Byron's. The typical poem by Burns is a speech in character, and the character is always an important part of the poetry. When he writes a tender love poem, or an earthy piece of shrewd humorous comment on life, the character he is using is one of the conventional projections of himself. When he writes a satire such as "Holy Willie's Prayer," the mouthpiece-figure is presented in vividly economical fashion. (How the nineteenth century English could ever have admired Browning's "dramatic" pieces so much, when "Holy Willie's Prayer" was available for comparison, must remain enigmatic.) Burns also had the trick of writing in compartments; almost as strongly as Byron, he split his poetry down the middle, with satiric and sophisticated pieces on one side, "spontaneous" lyrics on the other. He even pinpointed this by issuing two volumes in successive years, the Kilmarnock edition of 1786 and the Edinburgh edition of 1787, in which the weighting is radically different.

The example of Burns, then, should make Byron's life and work seem less difficult to comprehend; particularly as they both asserted, with a sincerity there is no reason to doubt, that poetry was to them a direct and uncomplicated reaction to life. The poet finds himself in a situation, the situation throws up an emotion, and the emotion throws up a poem. Everyone knows Burns's statement, in the autobiographical letter to Dr. Moore, of how he first discovered within himself the impulse to song. "Thus with me began love and poetry." Byron might have used the same words. So, it is true, might any adolescent versifier; but these two excellent poets never broke away from the pattern, and never felt the need to break away.

A poetry directly geared to the events of one's life, and expressed through *personae* which are themselves simplifications of one's own character: that is the formula. If Byron had to adopt more challenging attitudes than those of Burns, and discard the first more dramatically in favor of the second, that in turn is due to his more complicated position. The one was a crofter's son who became an exciseman; the other, the child of a shabby-genteel mother and a raffish father, nurtured in an Edinburgh side street and suddenly flung into the life of an English *milord*.

The "romantic" Byron and the "satiric," then, seem to me too nearly the same poet to make it worth distinguishing between them. They both have the same gifts—energy, sweep, pace, scope. And in each case the deficiencies are related to this central timidity.

Let us take a quotation which shows Byron at his best—and there is no need to be afraid of using a hackneyed one. The "Dying Gladiator" set piece, from *Childe Harold,* is probably the one passage which has been oftenest quoted.

> I see before me the Gladiator lie:
> He leans upon his hand—his manly brow
> Consents to death, but conquers agony,
> And his droop'd head sinks gradually low—
> And through his side the last drops, ebbing slow
> From the red gash, fall heavy, one by one.
> Like the first of a thunder-shower: and now
> The arena swims around him—he is gone.
> Ere ceased the inhuman shout which hail'd the wretch who won.
>
> He heard it, but he heeded not—his eyes
> Were with his heart, and that was far away:
> He reck'd not of the life he lost nor prize,
> But where his rude hut by the Danube lay.
> *There* were his young barbarians all at play,
> *There* was their Dacian mother—he, their sire,
> Butcher'd to make a Roman holiday—
> All this rush'd with his blood—Shall he expire
> And unavenged?—Arise! ye Goths, and glut your ire!

A quotation of only two stanzas is, strictly speaking, too short to do justice to a long narrative poem; still, given that we are reasonably familiar with the whole, we can make some use even of these few lines. We can find, even here, the chief characteristics of Byron's poetry. Probably the first thing that meets the eye is the energy with which he sets about a conventional subject. Walking pensively among the ruins of Rome (the very phrase, *The Ruins of Rome,* is the title of a popular eighteenth century romantic poem), the poet thinks of the tumultuous scenes once witnessed by the now silent and deserted arena. A dying gladiator!—what could be more conventional? And yet, after all, gladiators *did* fight and die there, and it is reasonable that somebody should write poetry about the fact. If Byron had not existed, there would be a huge gap right down the middle of English romanticism. So we have the gladiator dying; and what does he think about? *His wife and children.* Yes, Byron actually dares one of the enormous platitudes that no modern writer would touch with a barge pole.

The people watching the gladiatorial contest are "inhuman," and this is linked with a certain tit-for-tat moralizing, never far away in Byron (his "shocking" side, as no one has ever failed to note, is merely the obverse of this). It is all very fine for the inhuman spectators to shout with glee, but we know something that they don't: Rome is going to fall, and what is more it is these same Goths who will push it over, *so there.* This mechanical (and not very accurate) moral-drawing from history is an eighteenth century taste, and the other major poets of Byron's day have hardly a trace of it. Here as elsewhere, he is less up-to-date than they are.

The conventionality, the energy, the conviction, the willingness to play on easily aroused responses in his audience—all these are obvious marks of Byron's poetry. His technical characteristics, too, are easy to recognize. The verse is impetuous but lumpy. For all its energy and rapidity, it moves in a stumbling way. Byron makes no attempt to capture those long wave-like rhythms which best justify the use of the Spenserian stanza; instead, he provides excellent single lines—strong, pithy, and quotable to an extent hardly to be matched except in Dryden—and links them with more or less inert passages. Rhymes are a bit of a nuisance, too: "He reck'd not of the life he lost nor prize," is very poor, but it has to stay because "prize" must go at the end of a line; something must rhyme with "eyes" in the magnificent opening lines of the stanza.

Similarly,

> *There* was their Dacian mother—he, their sire,
> Butcher'd to make a Roman holiday,

is a very typical piece of Byron; the introductory line, which exists for the sake of the one it leads to, is clumsy and stilted; Byron has to italicize *There* in the hope of getting the reader to stress it enough to set it apart from the two-fold repetition of "their" immediately afterwards. "Dacian" is a pure fill-in; having said that the man's hut was by the Danube, there is no need to go on and particularize—neither do we really need to be told that the gladiator was the "sire" of his children. All the line is doing is to carry us over ten syllables so that we can be there in time to receive the big punch from the second line—which, as usual with Byron, is one that no reader, having once met it, ever forgets.

Again, in the first of these two stanzas, there are numb and mechanical passages; the comparison between the last drops of blood from the gladiator's mortal wound with the first drops of a thundershower is not particularly illuminating; but the fact is that, having given us a line as magnificent as

> Consents to death, but conquers agony,

Byron can fill the rest of the stanza with anything he chooses—we're with him, whatever he does.

In fact that line, when one comes to think about it, is one of the very few lines of English verse that one cannot imagine any critic, of any period, failing to rate high. Sidney would have liked it; so would Dryden, so would Johnson; so, one presumes, would Mr. Eliot, despite his some-what harsh verdict that Byron is at his best when being sardonic, banter-ing, not "poetic." This line is "poetic"; we can say of it that it unmis-takably represents the poetic use of language, and what is more it is entirely nonironic; but it is poetic in the manner of the unselfconscious Dryden, rather than the superpoetical nineteenth century.

If we turn to Byron's later satiric work, much the same qualities will be apparent; there is no need to go over the ground twice. Obviously, it was opportune for him to adopt the stance of a searingly honest man, impatient with cant from whatever source it came. For one thing, it fitted the facts. After fondling Byron for a season or two, "England" (i.e. London society) had cast him out with exaggerated protestations of horror; and in this, there were undeniable elements of cant. London in 1816 was not renowned for its strict morality; the Victorian age had not yet set in. Professor Marchand has made it plain that Byron was a shade paranoiac about the extent of his persecution: it was not so universal or so virulent as he thought; still, he *did* think so, and that is the im-portant fact. He was in a mood to hate hypocrisy because he had been hurt, and the people who had hurt him had acted hypocritically.

Secondly, the Europe to which he turned his face was the Europe of the Congress of Vienna. The spectacle that met his eyes was one of pompous coalitions and committees sitting with the idea of restoring the pre-Napoleonic *status quo*. As Elizabeth Barrett Browning put it,

And kings crept out again to feel the sun.

Internationally, it was a time of windy protestations, of crocodile tears, of all the detestable humbug of professional politicians. For the six years that remained of his life, Byron stalked through this landscape, pushing over the lath-and-plaster buildings, withering the paper foliage, puncturing the gasbags, in the biggest one-man debunking spree the world has ever seen. Sober historians have gone on record as saying that Byron, single-handed, had a demonstrable influence in neutralizing the effect of the Congress of Vienna. He was certainly—to take one example —the imaginative inspiration of the Russian "Decembrist" rising, in 1825, the first revolt against the Tsars; one of its leaders, the poet Ryleyev, went to the scaffold with a volume of Byron's poems in his hand.

We need not doubt the sincerity of all this. To assume such a *persona* was within Byron's power, and he made full use of the opportunity. Like many people of his demonstrative type, he was more at ease before a large audience than a small one. He could act a part in public, but individuals often dried him up. In the same way, he was more generous and considerate to underdogs—children, servants, anyone who was not in a position to challenge him in any way—than to social and intellectual equals. One recalls that letter of Claire Clairmont's, written in 1818, in which she contrasted his gentle bearing towards dependants with his cold and suspicious reception of people "on a par" with him.

The psychology of the thing is quite plain. Byron found it easier to identify emotionally with the underdog because, deep down, he had cast himself in the same rôle. A childhood spent in genteel poverty, suddenly cut across by the entirely unexpected reversion of the title, had left him with a basic uncertainty as to which world he really belonged in. The scandal and ostracism of 1816 resolved that doubt. There had always been a tinsel artificiality about the welcome he had received from the *beau monde,* and now they had revealed themselves in their true colors. The very haste with which he concluded this, and took himself off, is symptomatic of a kind of relief at having his dilemma settled for him. Henceforth, his most consistent public face was that of the champion of the oppressed, the stripper away of the pretences with which greed and tyranny cover themselves. Already, in 1812, he had delivered his great speech in the House of Lords, resisting the bill which would make machine-wrecking a capital offence; already he had written his fiercely compassionate "Song for the Luddites." But after the *débâcle* of 1816, his tone became less exalted, more cynical and vitriolic. He developed a vein of satire which, while it derives directly from the great couplet satirists of the Augustan age, is a mirror image rather than a straight copy. Where their assumption is the classical one—"I, the satirist, am a better man than you"—his is "You, the righteous one, are no better than I am." The Augustan satirist knocks his opponent down from above; Byron lies in the mud, like a crocodile, and pulls his victim down from below. All his most direct statements, after 1816, are made in terms of irony, even burlesque. Thus, in 1820, after he had become finally identified with the cause of European liberty, he summed up his attitude in the idiom of the music hall.

> When a man has no freedom to fight at home,
> Let him combat for that of his neighbours.
> Let him think of the glories of Greece and of Rome,
> And get knocked on the head for his labours.

Once again, in this phase of his creative life, Byron's technical expedients were of the simplest. The Italian burlesque epic attracted him, as also did that previous attempt to reproduce its tone in English, that of J. H. Frere in his two poems, *Whistlecraft* and *Monks and Giants.*[2] His

[2] In strict fact, the first attempt to acclimatize the Italian burlesque epic in English was in a poem Byron had not read, William Tennant's *Anster Fair* (1812).

power of rapid assimilation was always remarkable; within a few months
he had mastered the *genre,* and the new tone was fully developed.

> "England! with all thy faults I love thee still,"
>   I said at Calais, and have not forgot it;
> I like to speak and lucubrate my fill;
>   I like the government (but that is not it);
> I like the freedom of the press and quill;
>   I like the Habeas Corpus (when we've got it);
> I like a parliamentary debate,
> Particularly when 'tis not too late.
>
> I like the taxes, when they're not too many;
>   I like a seacoal fire, when not too dear;
> I like a beef-steak, too, as well as any;
>   Have no objection to a pot of beer;
> I like the weather, when it is not rainy,
>   That is, I like two months of every year.
> And so God save the Regent, Church, and King!
> Which means that I like all and every thing.
>
> Our standing army, and disbanded seamen,
>   Poor's rate, Reform, my own, the nation's debt,
> Our little riots just to show we are free men,
>   Our trifling bankruptcies in the Gazette,
> Our cloudy climate, and our chilly women,
>   All these I can forgive, and those forget,
> And greatly venerate our recent glories,
> And wish they were not owing to the Tories.

That is from *Beppo*. It is worth quoting a fragment to show how completely Byron was at ease with the new manner before he began the
composition of *Don Juan*.

Of *Don Juan* itself there is no need to say much. With its quick
changes of scene, proliferation of incident, frequent ribaldry, patches of
picturesque description and continuous festal *panache,* it must be one
of the very few long narrative poems that can still attract readers in an
age like ours, when the long narrative poem is the deadest of all forms.
It is more to our present purpose to note the profound moral seriousness
which looks out now and then, especially in the descriptions of war,
which Byron was inclined to regard as a murderous confidence trick
played on the common man by his rulers.

> There the still varying pangs, which multiply
>   Until their very number makes men hard

By the infinities of agony,
    Which meet the gaze, whate'er it may regard—
The groan, the roll in dust, the all-white eye
    Turn'd back within its socket—these reward
Your rank and file by thousands, while the rest
May win perhaps a riband at the breast!

Yet I love glory:—glory's a great thing—
    Think what it is to be in your old age
Maintain'd at the expense of your good king:
    A moderate pension shakes full many a sage.
And heroes are but made for bards to sing,
    Which is still better; thus in verse to wage
Your wars eternally, besides enjoying
Half-pay for life, make mankind worth destroying.

His address to the Duke of Wellington has a deadliness which suggests that Byron had, at last, found something other than himself to be serious about:

You are the best of cut-throats':—do not start;
    The phrase is Shakespeare's, and not misapplied:—
War's a brain-spattering, windpipe-slitting art,
    Unless her cause by right be sanctified.
If you have acted *once* a generous part,
    The world, not the world's masters, will decide,
And I shall be delighted to learn who,
Save you and yours, have gain'd by Waterloo?

I am no flatterer—you've supp'd full of flattery:
    They say you like it too—'tis no great wonder.
He whose whole life has been assault and battery,
    At last may get a little tired of thunder;
And swallowing eulogy much more than satire, he
    May like being praised for every lucky blunder,
Call'd "Saviour of the Nations"—not yet saved,
And "Europe's Liberator"—still enslaved.

I've done. Now go and dine from off the plate
    Presented by the Prince of the Brazils.
And send the sentinel before your gate
    A slice or two from your luxurious meals:
He fought, but has not fed so well of late.
    Some hunger, too, they say the people feels:—

> There is no doubt that you deserve your ration,
> But pray give back a little to the nation.

And so this second *persona* satisfied him for a time, releasing a vein of satire and fantasy which he had still not exhausted when he died. What he would have done when driven, finally, to relate the two, no one can know.

Byron's early death thus interrupts a story which was just approaching its denouement. Reading the lives of other romantic poets who died young, from Keats to Hart Crane, one is conscious chiefly of the pathos of that premature silence: with Byron, I, at any rate, feel a sense of annoyance, of baffled disappointment, when I get to that final scene—Missolonghi, the fever-ridden swamp, the deathbed surrounded by scared and weeping servants, the thunderstorm which burst in the moment that life departed. I feel cheated. I want to know what Byron would have *done*—as a man, and, with that quick spontaneity of his, as a poet immediately afterwards—when time finally drove him into a corner and brought him face to face with the riddle of his own character. He would have done something, we know that; he was a man of action, and self-knowledge is the most decisive form of action; once Byron realized that, he would have made some decisive move. But what move, not even Professor Marchand can tell us.

Byron is very much of his time, in fact it is difficult to imagine him living in any other. He sums up so perfectly the crossroads at which European and English culture then stood. He seems fully typical in his unwillingness to go down either of the two available roads to the complete neglect of the other. If he has the color, sweep, and *brio* of romanticism, he also has the ironical appraising eye of the Augustan, together with the Augustan gift of writing a line whose content is "obvious" and which nevertheless strikes one with utterly disarming freshness ("Consents to death, but conquers agony"). One is tempted to say that he was ideally fortunate to live when he did.

I believe, however, that this would be a mistake. Every considerable artist (leaving aside the very greatest, who give the unmistakable impression of having the energy to triumph over any circumstances), strikes one as fortunate in this way. Dryden, for example, seems to us just as fortunate to have lived at the moment when classicism was closing in, as Byron does to have lived at the moment when it was opening out. He has an Elizabethan richness and fullness which we feel would have been dried out of him if he had lived fifty years later. In fact, of course, it is merely that Dryden was a good enough poet to pick up the materials nearest to hand and use them with such assurance that his work seems to have been created by its idiom, and to have cost its author nothing.

Whereas, in fact, it was the work which created the idiom, and the cost to the author was no less than a lifetime's devotion.

In the same way, Byron, whose working life overlaps with those of Peacock and Jane Austen as well as Shelley, Keats, and Wordsworth, gives the impression of having been placed by chance in the very position where his full range of gifts could be employed. But one does not, in such a case, speak of chance. One speaks only, and with such perceptiveness as one can muster, of the gifts.

Chronology of Important Dates

<table>
<tr><td>1788</td><td>22 January: birth of George Gordon Byron, later 6th Lord.</td></tr>
<tr><td>1792</td><td>17 May: birth of Anne Isabella Milbanke (later Lady Byron).</td></tr>
<tr><td>1798</td><td>Succeeds to the barony 19 May.</td></tr>
<tr><td>1801</td><td>Enters Harrow.</td></tr>
<tr><td>1805</td><td>Enters Trinity College, Cambridge.</td></tr>
<tr><td>1806</td><td>Fugitive Pieces.</td></tr>
<tr><td>1807</td><td>Hours of Idleness; derided by The Edinburgh Review.</td></tr>
<tr><td>1809</td><td>Takes seat in House of Lords. English Bards and Scotch Reviewers. Leaves with Hobhouse to tour the Near East; away more than a year.</td></tr>
<tr><td>1812</td><td>Childe Harold, Cantos I and II: "I awoke one morning and found myself famous."</td></tr>
<tr><td>1814</td><td>The Corsair: sells 14,000 copies in one day. Lara.</td></tr>
<tr><td>1815</td><td>Marries Miss Milbanke, 2 January. Augusta Ada born 10 December.</td></tr>
<tr><td>1816</td><td>Lady Byron leaves matrimonial home, 15 January. Childe Harold, Canto III. 8 April, snubbed at Lady Jersey's party; two weeks later leaves England never to return.</td></tr>
<tr><td>1817</td><td>Manfred, The Lament of Tasso. 12 January, birth of Allegra.</td></tr>
<tr><td>1818</td><td>Beppo in ottava rima. Childe Harold, Canto IV. Late in year becomes accepted lover of Teresa Guiccioli in Ravenna.</td></tr>
<tr><td>1819</td><td>Don Juan, Cantos I and II.</td></tr>
<tr><td>1820</td><td>Removes to Pisa.</td></tr>
<tr><td>1821</td><td>Marino Faliero, Sardanapalus, Don Juan, Cantos III-V.</td></tr>
<tr><td>1822</td><td>The Vision of Judgment in The Liberal, No. 1, 15 October. Removes to Genoa.</td></tr>
<tr><td>1823</td><td>Don Juan, Cantos VI-VIII, IX-XI, XII-XIV; The Island; Werner. Receives a message from the "Greek Committee."</td></tr>
<tr><td>1824</td><td>Don Juan, Cantos XV and XVI; The Deformed Transformed. 5 January reaches Missolonghi. Dies 19 April.</td></tr>
</table>

Notes on the Editor and Authors

PAUL WEST, editor of this anthology, has taught at the Memorial University of Newfoundland and at Pennsylvania State University. He was a Guggenheim Fellow in 1962. His books include *Byron and the Spoiler's Art, The Modern Novel* and a novel, *A Quality of Mercy.*

BERNARD BLACKSTONE, formerly Byron Professor of English at the University of Athens, has also taught in Cuba, Turkey and South America. He is best known for *English Blake, Virginia Woolf,* and *The Consecrated Urn.* He is now at the University of Libya.

HELEN GARDNER, Reader in Renaissance English Literature at Oxford, is the author of *The Art of T. S. Eliot* and *The Business of Criticism.* She has also edited an anthology of the Metaphysical Poets.

GILBERT HIGHET is Anthon Professor of Latin Language and Literature at Columbia University. His books include *The Classical Tradition, Juvenal the Satirist* and *Poets in a Landscape.*

G. WILSON KNIGHT, formerly Chancellors' Professor of English at Trinity College, Toronto, has written six books on Shakespeare and two on Byron (*Lord Byron: Christian Virtues* and *Lord Byron's Marriage*). He is Emeritus Professor of English Literature at Leeds.

F. R. LEAVIS, the principal editor of *Scrutiny,* is Fellow of Downing College, Cambridge. His most significant works are *Revaluation, New Bearings in English Poetry,* and *The Great Tradition.*

MARIO PRAZ, Professor of English at the University of Rome, is the author of *The Hero in Eclipse in Victorian Fiction* and *La fortuna di Byron in Inghilterra.* He has taught at the universities of Liverpool and Manchester.

GEORGE M. RIDENOUR teaches at Yale. He was a Fulbright Fellow in Vienna, 1952-1953, and has published *The Style of* Don Juan, as well as various essays on nineteenth century literature.

W. W. ROBSON is a Fellow of Lincoln College, Oxford, has broadcast frequently on the BBC Third Programme, and has been an advisory editor of *Essays in Criticism.*

BERTRAND RUSSELL is the eminent British philosopher. His devoting a chapter to Byron in a history of philosophy still troubles purists.

GUY STEFFAN teaches at the University of Texas, which published the Variorum Edition of *Don Juan,* edited by Steffan and W. W. Pratt.

JOHN WAIN formerly taught at Reading University and is now a free-lance writer. Some of his other essays have been collected in *Preliminary Essays* and *Essays on Literature and Ideas.*

EDMUND WILSON's many publications include *Axel's Castle, The Triple Thinkers, The Wound and the Bow,* and *The Shock of Recognition.*

Selected Bibliography

The least hectic of the lives are: Peter Quennell, *Byron: the Years of Fame*, 1935, and *Byron in Italy*, 1941 (both of them vividly written); Leslie A. Marchand, *Byron: a Biography*, 3 vols., 1958 (less vivid, much fuller). Primarily biographical are: John Drinkwater, *The Pilgrim of Eternity*, 1925; Charles du Bos, *Byron et le besoin de la fatalité*, 1929 (tr. E. C. Mayne, 1932, full of original ideas); Robert Escarpit, *Lord Byron: un tempérament littéraire*, 2 vols., 1958 (stimulating but a bit earnest); G. Wilson Knight, *Lord Byron: Christian Virtues*, 1952; E. M. Butler, *Byron and Goethe*, 1951. Doris Langley Moore's *The Late Lord Byron*, 1961, investigates the fabrication of the posthumous legend. Two interesting short studies are Peter Quennell's "The Mighty Dead" in *The Sign of the Fish*, 1960, and the same author's preface to *Byronic Thoughts*, 1960.

Anyone with more than a passing interest in critical approaches should consult Arthur Symons's essay on Byron in *The Romantic Movement in English Poetry*, 1909; also Sir Herbert Read's pamphlet, *Byron*, 1951 (Writers and their Work, 10) and G. Wilson Knight's lecture, *Byron's Dramatic Prose*, 1953 (done with relish and enthusiasm). Andrew Rutherford's *Byron: a Critical Study*, 1961, documents and summarises the poems rather than giving a personal response to them; very thin on the plays. E. F. Boyd's *Byron's Don Juan: A Critical Study*, 1945, is best on Byron's reading and the provenance of his ideas. Also worth a look are S. C. Chew's careful study, *The Dramas of Lord Byron*, 1915, and W. A. Briscoe (ed.) *Byron the Poet*, 1924. R. W. Chambers's English Association Lecture, *Ruskin (and Others) on Byron*, 1925, is of historical interest, as is Sir Harold Nicolson's Presidential Address to the same Association, *The Poetry of Byron*, 1943, while H. J. C. Grierson's chapter on Byron in *The Background of English Literature*, 1915, deals mostly with Byron's relation to the society of his time. A stimulating, mostly biographical piece is Jacques Barzun's "Byron and the Byronic in History" in *The Energies of Art* (New York, 1956).

Articles in periodicals abound. Among the best short pieces are Patricia M. Ball, "Byronic Reorientation," *The Twentieth Century*, October 1960; G. S. Fraser, "Passion's Ironist," *New Statesman*, 12 November, 1960; and John Bayley's "Byron and the Byron-Makers" in *The Spectator*, 14 July, 1961. Others are "The Token-Web, the Sea-Sodom and Canto I of *Don Juan*" by Guy Steffan in University of Texas *Studies in English*, XXVI, 108-168 (1947), Marius Bewley's "The Colloquial Mode of Byron," *Scrutiny*, XVI, 1949; Ronald Bottrall's "Byron and the Colloquial Tradition in English Poetry," *The Criterion*, XVIII, 1938-9; George M. Ridenour's "Byron: Criticism and Fact," in *The Yale Review*, Winter 1962 (pp. 321-324); and Paul West, "Byron's Writing Habits," *The Keats-Shelley Memorial Bulletin*, XI, 1960. W. H. Auden's review in *The New Yorker*, 26 April, 1958 of Leslie A. Marchand's biography contains some penetrating comments on *Don Juan*.

TWENTIETH CENTURY VIEWS

Forthcoming Titles